Barcelona Prose

Barcelona Prose

Efim Etkind

Translated by Helen Reeve
with Joyse Man
and Julia Trubikhina (poetic texts)

BOSTON
2022

Library of Congress Control Number: 2021953169

ISBN 9781644697900 (hardback)
ISBN 9781644697917 (paperback)
ISBN 9781644697924 (ebook PDF)
ISBN 9781644697931 (epub)

Copyright © 2001, Efim Etkind estate
Copyright © 2022, Academic Studies Press, English translation
All rights reserved.

Collected and prepared for publication by Svetlana Elnitsky and Masha Etkind
Book design by Tatiana Vernikov
Cover design by Ivan Grave

Published by Cherry Orchard Books, an imprint of Academic Studies Press
1577 Beacon Street
Brookline, MA 02446, USA
press@academicstudiespress.com
www.academicstudiespress.com

Contents

In Lieu of a Foreword	1
He Outsmarted Us	14
Full Repair!	20
The Marquis de Lapunaise	24
The Russian Intelligentsia: Two Generations	29
Looking through the Walls	40
The Double	50
Ferenc, Count Batthyány	59
Ebensee	70
"On the Sly"	84
How We Lived	94
"The Blond Hidden in a Bottle"	97
Triumph of Spirit	105
Up the Down Staircase	118
It Turned out Okay	127
About the Axe	134
Last Meeting	137
Pavel Antokolsky: Generation of the Blind	158
Cousin	169
"The Other"	176
The Cowardice of a Brave Man	191
Two Jewish Fates: Reading the Diaries of Victor Klemperer	199
"Youth in a Military Blouse" of My Contemporary	227
Afterword: A Knight of Culture by *David M. Bethea*	234
Index of Names	246
Photographs: Family, Friends, Colleagues	141

The English edition of *Barcelona Prose* was prepared for publication by Masha Etkind and Svetlana Elnitsky.

We take this opportunity to express our gratitude to the late Helen Reeve for her friendship and selfless devotion to the author of *Barcelona Prose* and to Russian culture in general.

In Lieu of a Foreword: The Law of the Conservation of Intellectual Energy

My generation, contemporaries of the October Revolution, grew up, studied, and matured in an atmosphere that we would now call suffocating. Looking back at the 1930s and the 1950s from the standpoint of 1997, we can clearly see what exactly limited our movements, what it was that our contemporaries could not attain, and what they would have attained under a different regime.

In January 1997, three extraordinary historians died one after the other: Mikhail Borisovich Rabinovich, Mikhail Yakovlevich Geller, and David Petrovich Pritzker. Rabinovich lived almost until he was ninety, Geller was close to seventy, and Pritzker was almost eighty. All three were Jews. In each case, this was in itself an impediment to a scholarly career. Rabinovich endured the most. He spent many years in Stalin's prison camps, fought in the war, starved, and lost his classmates one by one—some of them turned out to be "enemies of the people," others died in the fighting, still others perished during the Leningrad Blockade. Mikhail Borisovich himself lived on for some twenty-five years in relative security, but he published little. His state of well-being was mostly attributable to his wife, Elena Grigorievna Levenfish, the daughter of the renowned chess grandmaster (champion of the USSR) Grigory Yakovlevich Levenfish. Thanks to her father's past fame, she was able to become the director of Penates, a memorial museum in the village of Repino, formerly called Kuokkala. Rabinovich made his name as the author of a superb dictionary of Greek and Roman mythology, compiled in collaboration with another classicist, M. N. Botvinnik. Shortly before his death, he saw the publication of his book *Memoirs of a Long Life*, which was published by European House, a new Petersburg publisher. It had decided on an honorable undertaking: the publication of an entire series of memoirs of Leningrad/Petersburg scholars. Rabinovich's book is written in his characteristic manner, kind and deftly humorous, but it is painfully difficult to read. One feels horror, shame, despair, and disgust in turn . . . How many educated, talented, and promising historians perished in the torture chambers, camps, and prisons? And how many were killed by the Germans as hapless volunteer corps, unarmed and untrained, thrown into the path of Nazi tanks? How many more were killed after miraculously surviving the war and several waves of terror? No records of these were preserved. They had to earn their living as best they could, working any job they managed to get despite the deadly "fifth line."* Rabinovich's memoirs are a precious documentation of their era. They testify to the calm and systematic manner in which the history of our country was destroyed.

The second of our three historians, Mikhail Yakovlevich Geller, also served a long term in prison, then in the camps. In certain respects, he was fortunate. He left for Poland in time and from there to France, where he became a professor at the Sorbonne. Later, upon his retirement from academia, he became a commentator for the Parisian émigré paper *Russian Thought*, where week after week, year after year, he published analyses of Russian affairs. Together with another émigré historian, Aleksandr Moiseyevich Nekrich (who died several years ago in the United States), he published the fascinating *Utopia in Power*, which has been translated into many languages. He also published a number of historical works: *Cogs in the Wheel*, *The World of Concentration Camps and Soviet Literature*, and *Andrey Platonov in Search of Happiness* . . . Geller was able to communicate a great deal to his readers during his lifetime, a possibility that he had thanks to French democracy. Russia, however, did everything in its power

---

* This refers to the fifth line in Soviet passports indicating nationality, with reference to ethnic origin (where, for example, the word "Jewish" would appear).—Trans.

to silence and stifle him. He was a splendid public intellectual and a serious scholar, but did not know Russia well, nor could he. He was convinced that there were only executioners and victims in our country. He had no desire whatsoever to listen to how the Russian intelligentsia existed between these two categories, struggling for survival. By the way, this delusion was widespread among émigrés, particularly in the circle surrounding Vladimir Maximov and his journal *Kontinent*. Yet we did have a great culture, a subject to which I will return.

The third historian was David Petrovich Pritzker. He was not imprisoned, not poisoned, not tortured. For many years a member of the Communist Party, he chaired the international workers' movement in the Higher Party School, housed in the Tauride Palace in Leningrad. Like many of his (and my) fellow students, he had been sent to Spain as a translator in his youth, where he fought in the ranks of the international brigades. This experience was to define his interests for the remainder of his life. In the early 1960s, he published a well-written volume titled *The Feat of the Spanish Revolution* and wrote quite a few articles dealing with that period. He, better than anyone, knew the truth about the violent retribution that Stalin had visited upon the Trotskyites and the anarchists. But he was forced to keep silent, remembering the fate that had met many Russian veterans of the Spanish Civil War, precisely because they knew something that was not supposed to be known. During the war with Germany, he worked in the intelligence headquarters on the Karelian front, where his reports were highly regarded for their sophisticated analysis. How was he listed? Simply, it would seem, as a translator. Others received awards and promotions; he never rose above the rank of captain.

David Pritzker was a man who was destined for the diplomatic service: He possessed a broad intellect and a rare memory for names, dates, and faces, and he knew several languages, including French, German, Spanish, and English. He was strikingly eloquent (but not extravagant) with words and had an irresistible charm. Observing Molotov and Vyshinksy, who were a shame to my country (and this after Chicherin, after Litvinov!), I often thought about how honorably, beautifully, successfully, and masterfully David Pritzker *could* have presented it. And Pritzker had hoped for a diplomatic career; he had been among the students of yet another brilliant man, one who never realized his potential as a diplomat, Yevgeny Tarle. But he was Pritzker, and in a country under real socialism, the best that he could do was to serve in the Higher Party School. Is it not amazing that our Talleyrands were in charge of the international workers' movement? No, it is quite natural, if one recalls that our Napoleons were chess grandmasters.

How mighty Russia is! For many decades, the ruling oligarchy did everything in its power to keep talented people from achieving their potential. I have spoken of three historians. Not one of them accomplished all he wished to, all that would have brought glory on him and his school. I will make mention of a few more people who were close to me. Eleazar Krever and David Frankfurt were my fellow students in the Leningrad University Department of Philology. Both were unusually talented scholars of Romance languages, especially French literature, and both had also spent time in Spain. At the beginning of the war, they were thrown into the path of Hitler's advancing army, equipped with not so much as a rifle. They perished, victims of the Soviet leadership's flagrant incompetence, as did Alexei Diakonov, who was killed while serving in the volunteer corps when he was barely in his twenties. (Fortunately, during the second year of the war, much was actually determined by the nonparty political intelligentsia who had been mobilized to join the army.) Were it not for the interference of party secretaries, newly minted generals, and political commissars, we would have won the war without having to sacrifice many millions of lives. How mighty Russia is! She has managed to endure despite the attempts of the ruling oligarchy to drain her of blood and of the intelligentsia. Let us imagine what our country would have been like if they had not killed us, imprisoned us, or left us to rot in the White Sea Canal. If, for example, Vladimir Yakovlevich Propp had not taught German in the Leningrad State University Department of Philology (they had him teach grammar!)

but, rather, the morphology of the folktale. If Maxim Isaakovich Gillelson had not been stuck working in the camps, but had conducted a seminar on "Arzamas" and the Russian epigram. If Julian Grigorievich Oksman had not worked as a bath attendant in one of the Magadan camps, but had lectured on Belinsky, Herzen, and Gogol. If Grigory Alexandrovich Gukovsky had not died at forty-eight in a prison of the Ministry of Internal Affairs while under investigation in a case fabricated by provocateurs and if his best student, Ilya Zakharovich Serman, had not been put in a camp but had continued to research eighteenth-century Russia in the archives of Leningrad and Moscow . . . They brought the study of the humanities to a halt. In Stalin's last years, they hounded the last of the intelligentsia out of academia, and then, under Brezhnev, they sent those who had escaped harm into exile—to the US, to Israel, to Europe. Thank God Yuri Mikhailovich Lotman survived, saved by Estonia. And there, in Tartu, he defended the honor of our philology.

And so—executioners and victims. Truly, society was divided into one or the other. Regarding the intelligentsia, the tactics of the ruling oligarchy were, in essence, to annihilate some while dragging the rest into the camp of the "annihilators." All those who had not yet been imprisoned or expelled were forced to vote for the execution of their brethren. Alas, the majority did just that: they voted, they signed newspaper petitions to execute, exile, and expel. And yet, between the executioners and their victims, there remained a vast stratum, enormous and powerful, a stratum that could not be removed. Is this not why the intelligentsia was called just that, a "stratum"?

In Soviet times, whole fields of study were subject to censure and condemnation, including genetics, cybernetics, pedology, eugenics, idealist philosophy, non-Stalinist linguistics, comparative literary and linguistic studies, and psychoanalysis. Also forbidden were pessimism, "formal experimentation" in poetry, painting, and theater, any hint of the avantgarde or the absurd. In music, any deviation from the classical form was declared a suspicious imitation of the decaying West. In literature, censorship deleted any mention of God, the Church, the next world, or mystical phenomena. In historical works, anything that contradicted the official line—captured in manuals such as *A Brief History of the All-Union Communist Party*, *History of the Civil War*, and *History of the Great Patriotic War*—was eradicated.

Russian culture learned to get around these bans. I recall that the editor Minna Isayevna Dikman once retitled a poem condemned by the censor for pessimism and decadence as "Re-reading Hemingway," whereupon the work quietly slipped through the barriers. Anna Akhmatova's poem commemorating Pasternak's death in 1960 was dated back to 1957, which in itself proved sufficient. In general, these bans engendered an interesting art form: the evasive maneuver. At one point, Pushkin addressed the censor with derision:

> At all you throw a slant uncertain glance,
> Suspecting them of poison—that's your stance . . .
> . . . And what's to fear? Believe me: those who dare
> flout law, the government, and mores, care
> No whit what punishments you have in view:
> Of course you'd censure them, if only you knew
> Just who they were. Eluding Lethe's "cure,"
>   their writings thrive without your signature.

As we can see, the art of the evasive maneuver was known long ago, and in 1822, samizdat already existed. But this art reached its height during the period of Soviet censorship. There is no doubt that its master practitioner was Nikolai Zabolotsky. In 1936, he wrote:

> When Iron August stood in hunting boots
> And held a game-filled platter, everywhere
> The fields became a stage for bloody shoots,
>   with feathered bodies flashing through the air.

Here, he was likely speaking not only about the month of August and hunting but also about the emperor Augustus. And "Iron Augustus" (in boots, no less), should bring to mind "Iron Felix"* and Stalin. All this was barely perceptible. At any rate, it was not blatantly criminal. Joseph Brodsky liked to say that censorship engenders metaphors. Oppression can be useful. In this case, the curtailment of direct expression led to the refinement of indirect forms of speech.

The regime strangled poets. The majority of them were doomed to remain silent or to create only within the narrow confines of what was permitted. And yet, the regime was interested in publishing foreign classics, which created the illusion of a vibrant cultural life. Poets became translators to an extent unknown in the history of world literature. Schiller and Goethe, Rilke and Baudelaire, Mallarmé and Petőfi had also translated somewhat. However, they had limited themselves to what they needed for their own work. Rilke, for instance translated only one Lermontov poem: "I Walk Out onto the Road Alone." This translation is brilliant; it alone can convey the essence of Lermontov's lyric poetry to the German reader. Of the medieval French poet Louise Labé, Rilke translated only a few poems.

But Pasternak translated Goethe's *Faust*—both parts—all of the major plays of Shakespeare, Schiller, and Kleist, the poems of Verlaine, Petőfi, Słowacki, Leśmian, Goethe, and a multitude of other poets in different languages and from different periods. All of Pasternak's contemporaries were poet-translators, even those who considered translation a harmful occupation and a waste of intellectual energy. Anna Akhmatova left us examples of Egyptian and Korean poetry; works by Hugo, Leopardi, and Polish poets; Zabolotsky translated all of the Georgian Romantics, not to mention Rustaveli and "The Lay of Igor's Campaign." Marshak translated Shakespeare's sonnets, Burns's songs, and Heine's lyric poetry. And then there was Leonid Martynov, David Samoilov, and Boris Slutsky, and Ilya Ehrenburg, and Maria Petrovykh, and Marina Tsvetaeva. The last, having just returned to the Soviet Union, created astounding translations of

---

*   "Iron Felix" refers to Felix Dzerzhinsky, founder of the GPU (predecessor of the KGB).—Ed.

Baudelaire ("Le Voyage"), Lorca, and German folk songs. Where else do you see this? French poets of the twentieth century, such as Saint-John Perse, René Char, Michaux, Prévert, Éluard, and Pierre Emmanuel sometimes amused themselves with translation. The Americans, English, and Swedes did as well. As for us, we created an enormous body of translated poetry that has become an important part of our culture in the twentieth century.

I have confined myself to mentioning well-known poets who *also* became translators. There were among them poets who for years were known *only* by their translations. As for their own poems and plays, they kept those in their desks. Semyon Lipkin, Arseny Tarkovsky, Arkady Shteinberg, Georgy Shengeli . . . They subsequently did become celebrated for their original works, but there was also an enormous, independent translation school, a school for the professional translation of poetry, that raised this art form to unprecedented heights. (Incidentally, Russia had produced incomparable masters early on, such as Vasily Zhukovsky, Vasily Kurochkin, Nikolai Kholodkovsky, Valery Bryusov, and Vyacheslav Ivanov). The older ones among them were Mikhail Lozinsky and Benedikt Livshits. The golden era of poetic translation was made famous by Wilhelm Levick, Lev Ginzburg, Konstantin Bogatyrev, Ovadi Savich, Maurice Wachsmacher, Lev Penkovsky—these were the Muscovites. But during the same period, working tirelessly and productively in Leningrad were Tatyana Gnedich, Elga Linetskaya, Mikhail Donskoy, Yury Korneyev, Vladimir Shor, Sergei Petrov, Ivan Likhachev, Elizaveta Polonskaya, Tamara Silman, Mikhail Diakonov, Alexei Shadrin, and Alexander Engelke (here I am naming only the deceased masters). In the West, the era of Stalinism and the post-Stalinist period of "real socialism" are written about as a time of barbarism, of stasis in the development of Russian culture. Non-Russians know nothing about this translation school and the singular renaissance it represents. It is for them not particularly interesting. And we ourselves often forget what fantastic cultural wealth we produced in our recent past. Let me briefly mention just a few of these poetic achievements: *The Song of the Nibelungs* and *The Song of Roland* (Yu. Korneyev); Byron's *Don Juan* (T. Gnedich);

Boileau's *L'Art Poétique* (E. Linetskaya); Kipling's poems (E. Polonskaya); Racine's tragedies (M. Donskoy); Baudelaire's lyrics (Ariadna Efron and Pavel Antokolsky); Eastern epics (S. Lipkin); *Carmina Burana* and German poetry from the period of the Thirty Years' War (Lev Ginsburg); Heine's *Germany: A Winter's Tale* (Yury Tynyanov and Wilhelm Levik); Rustaveli's *The Knight in a Panther's Skin* (two versions by Zabolotsky, one of them for children); *The Divine Comedy* (Mikhail Lozinsky); and so many others. In the field of translation, Russia has no rivals anywhere in the world.

Why did such an unprecedented cultural phenomenon arise? There was a Russian song in our day with the line: "This song cannot be stifled or killed." And it was not simply that you could earn a good income from translations, which allowed you to live and feed your family. It was that by translating poems, a poet could express himself, his view of the world and of nature, freedom, the written word, love, heaven, art, matter, and spirit. Pavel Antokolsky translated Auguste Barbier and stayed quite close to the original. Yet how much of Antokolsky's own passions, madness, and craving for spiritual independence and freedom from the party's tutelage is contained in his Russian Barbier! Lev Ginzburg's *Carmina Burana* was sung to guitar accompaniment by Soviet students: "The university was a pinnacle of knowledge, the flowering of thought. But now, by the will of fate, it has become a puppet show." Does this resemble the original? It does. But here, you catch Ginzburg's own voice and the echoes of his time.

With culture, this seems to be the way things stand. If you dam it up in one place, thoughts, talents, and words will force their way through another. The incredible development of chess in the USSR can be explained not only by the many chess clubs in our Pioneer Palaces or that chess was encouraged by party and state authorities as a safe intellectual exercise. In postrevolutionary France, a number of brilliant military leaders emerged simultaneously. Napoleon Bonaparte was one of them, and along with him were Hoche, Moreau, and others. In Soviet times, Hoche, Moreau, and even Bonaparte himself would all have become chess players. Had he lived in Stalin's time, perhaps even Lenin would have played chess instead of getting involved in politics. Among our chess players, there are many Jews. Is this because the Jewish mind is genetically inclined to working out openings and endgames? For a long time, Jews were not allowed to work in diplomacy, advance in the army, or study theoretical physics. Should we be surprised that boys from Jewish families threw themselves into chess and became masters?

Intellectual energy concentrated itself in areas where it could find the fullest application. Among the most important were the performing arts. Original creativity was subject to relentless control. It cost a composer dearly to show independence in his search for a new direction, as *Pravda* would set him straight: "Muddle instead of Music!"* No one hindered violinists, pianists, or singers—on the contrary, the authorities valued top prizes won at international competitions. Competition winners were awarded medals and apartments. Gilels, Oistrakh, and Goldstein were encouraged by the party despite their "unfortunate-sounding" surnames. They facilitated the myth that Soviet socialism was a sort of promised land for culture. Both chess masters and violinists, by occupying the highest positions, effectively enabled the propaganda of Soviet superiority: "Even in the realm of ballet, we dominate the entire planet!"** Sports served the same purpose, with winners celebrated as model Soviet citizens—heroes of the regime. In encouraging them, no expense was spared. I repeat, however, that the high level of musical virtuosity, as in chess and translation, was the result not only of monetary encouragement but also of the possibility that these endeavors offered for self-expression, mental and spiritual.

Marina Tsvetaeva was delighted by Soviet children's poetry. As she correctly noted, nowhere could you find poems as brilliant as Marshak's

---

* Such was the title of the *Pravda* article on Shostakovich's opera *Lady Macbeth of the Mtsensk District*. The article was published anonymously but widely attributed to Stalin himself.—Ed.

** This line is the refrain of a popular non-official Soviet song written in 1964 by Yuri Vizbor.—Ed.

Kids in a Cage. And what amazingly brilliant and inventive children's verses were penned by Daniil Kharms! This same Kharms was the author of absurdist prose and magnificent poems, yet he could also publish counting rhymes for children, jokes, and humorous sayings, such as: "Ivan Toporyshkin went on a hunt. With him the poodle went, jumping over the fence . . ." Our children's poetry was also a special form of sublimation. Nikolay Oleynikov published the children's journals *Hedgehog* and *Siskin* as a substitute for reaching out to the intended audience for his brilliant humorous pieces: "Fried fish, crucian carp my dear, the smile you had just yesterday, did it disappear?" Agniya Barto and Sergei Mikhalkov came later. They were able to progress unhindered along the paths laid down by Marshak and the OBERIU.* Nevertheless, the genesis of our brilliant children's poetry is tied to those whose voices were stifled in other areas of literature.

The law of the conservation of intellectual energy manifested itself wherever it was for some reason not suppressed. This explains the development of our "Pushkinistics." Pushkin was celebrated like a champion athlete or the winner of an international competition, and Pushkin studies became an approved area of philology. This may have been accidental in one sense, although the celebration of Pushkin was an instance of the *Führerprinzip*, without which Soviet ideology would have been unimaginable. The *Führerprinzip* mandated the canonization of Stanislavsky in theater, Pavlov in physiology, Gorky in prose, Mayakovsky in poetry, Repin in painting—and in linguistics, first Marr and then Stalin. None of these "leaders" was truly suited to such a role. But it was more important for the regime to have a single leader in every field than to have the character of any individual leader fit his task. In all honesty, was Mayakovsky fit to be a lawmaker in poetry? Mayakovsky, the rebel who was capable of saying to Pushkin when he was drunk,

---

* OBERIU was an avant-garde art collective.—Trans.

"It's nice to be with you—I'm glad you're at my table. The Muze sure could winkle it out of you. What is it your Olga used to say? . . . No, not Olga! It's from Onegin's letter to Tatiana."

A hooligan, an iconoclast, and yet, he is The One, the chief, the local "leader." And here was Pushkin, not at all suited to be the precursor of socialist realism, yet anointed the "leader" of that movement. Thanks to this aberration, we were enriched by the works of such brilliant scholars as B. V. Tomashevsky, V. M. Zhirmunsky, Y. G. Oksman, G. A. Gukovsky, V. V. Vinogradov, S. M. Bondi, D. D. Blagoi, and Y. N. Tynyanov, followed later by N. Y. Eidelman, Y. M. Lotman, and others.

Was there anything comparable in Hitler's Germany? No. In the first place, German totalitarianism did not exist for long, twelve years in all, and, moreover, grueling wars consumed almost all of those years. But even if there had been no war, twelve years would have been too short for the process of which I am speaking. It had barely started by 1929 in Russia, although in that very year the Soviet regime celebrated its twelfth anniversary. Second, the intelligentsia could not have existed under the Nazi regime, not even superficially or by disguising itself. From its very inception, the ideology of Nazism was overtly cannibalistic, calling openly for the annihilation of racially unacceptable groups: the Jews, the Roma, and the Slavs. It repudiated all signs of democracy. It celebrated a Germanic imperial social order. It was not attracted by any achievements in world culture; considerations of prestige were irrelevant here. It was different in the Soviet Union: there was an acceptable façade. Humanism was preached, as were internationalism and respect for the civilizations of smaller ethnic groups and for literature in all languages. Behind this façade were the torture chambers. Many people did not know this, and those who did often pretended to accept the phraseology of propaganda on faith. A few honestly thought that by some miracle the propaganda might be transformed into reality.

∙ ∙ ∙

One of the most important tasks of Russian culture today is not to forget the victories won in past struggles. Certainly, these victories were won with great difficulty, but they were won. We must not lose what we worked so hard to build over many decades.

He Outsmarted Us

There were some strange men in the apartment, playing an odd game. They were sticking pieces of paper onto tables, easy chairs, and sideboards. Eight-year-old Fima ran after them and watched them coat paper squares with his glue using his brush and then sticking the squares onto the most visible spots. What for? Mama sat in the kitchen with her hands tightly clasped, and she had one answer to Fima's questions: "Later." Father and his younger brother, Uncle Monya, were not home—they had gone to Kirtselovo, to the factory. They returned the next day, glanced briefly at the labels, and went into the office. By then, Fima had begun to understand something. Mama said,

"This furniture isn't ours anymore. They've inventoried it. They'll be taking it away soon."

Fima was surprised by the verb "to inventory." He knew it from Puskhin's verses:

> Onegin, then? Apt inquisition!
> My friends I must for patience sue.
> His ways, their daily repetition,
> I'll inventory these for you.

Or from other lines, ones that Fima particularly liked:

> His garb I'd gladly inventory
> For scholars, with no need to ask.
> Of course I'd gain no special glory—
> To give accounting is my task.

And the word had cropped up in conversations at home. But what did the furniture have to do with it? His father had spoken dejectedly of the Kirtselovo factory, which was, as it turned out, "up to its ears in debt." Fima did finally guess the secret behind the paper squares. The details he discovered later. Here, in short, is the essence of the matter.

Several years earlier, Father had rented a half-destroyed building in the village of Kirtselovo, near Pavlovsk. There, with difficulty, he got the rusted machinery into working order. A company came into being that bore the lengthy name "Kirtselovo Paper Mill, under lease to G. I. Etkind." This was the letterhead displayed on the official stationery. Mama and the three boys occasionally stayed there, in Kirtselovo, in a small wooden house near the factory. Fima liked being there. The most interesting thing for him was the delivery, by cart, of the waste paper used to produce wrapping paper. This was dumped in a shed, and Fima would rush in to rummage through the hastily bound bales of newspapers, journals, folders of papers, and the main attraction: books. All sorts of books! Of the foreign ones, Fima, who could easily read French and German, fished out collections of poems, adventure novels, and illustrated children's books. Among the translated works, he came upon Renan's *La Vie de Jésus*. He read this to the end without stopping, and much later, he learned that this book had been purged from some library because of the "religiousness" of its title.

Rummaging through the discarded books gave the boy a happiness that would have diminished considerably if he had understood that the content of such discarded items represented his country's cruelty. The books were all from confiscated private collections—their owners had disappeared into the basements of the Cheka or had emigrated or died without heirs. There was another source: the intelligentsia was being squeezed. The previous owners of spacious professors' apartments now had to accommodate their families in a single room. It was obvious that they had to get rid of their books.

In the early 1920s, they were used as fuel in iron stoves, which for some reason were called *bourgeoiki*. Later, books began to be sold, most often by weight. In bookstores along Liteyny Avenue, there were signs saying, "We buy books by weight." For Fima, however, the sad situation of those days became the foundation of his education. Decades passed. He acquired not only a patronymic but also a pension. Yet some of the books that had been salvaged from the rubbish remained on his shelves.

The factory made regular products. The reams of gray-brown paper that emerged from its refurbished machinery served all of Leningrad. Everyone was satisfied: the workers (eight in number) received a salary; the supervisors (there were three) managed their simple tasks; Father and Uncle Monya worked tirelessly—they felt triumphant. After all, when they had rented the dilapidated premises at Kirtselovo, acquaintances, even friends, had laughed at them. "What do you want that wreck for? You won't get any profit out of it." But now, those same acquaintances were wrapping their purchases in Kirtselovo paper.

Then suddenly, thunder came out of a clear blue sky: the authorities levied a tax on the factory that was so high it would have been impossible to pay it off even after ten years. The party had decided to end the NEP, and the best way to stifle business was taxation. Father still had some hopes. His logic was reasonable: paper would still be needed, and the company was viable and profitable. Was it really in the interests of the Soviet authorities to close the factory? But the party had decided to do away with the NEP, and logic was beside the point. The class enemy, who had rooted himself in Kirtselovo, had to be dealt with, once and for all. It was at this point that the agents of the financial inspector arrived at 24 Zagorodny and inventoried the furniture for the nonpayment of taxes.

The following Sunday, strangers crowded into the apartment. Having paid the prices marked on the paper squares, they made off with chests of drawers, beds, and armchairs. That night, Mother and Father slept on the floor. Fima did too. Children's mattresses remained only for his younger brothers: Sania was four, Marik two. They ate off of the lid of a trunk and sat on books. The children thought it was funny; the adults were gloomily silent. A week later, new furniture was brought in, and life went back to normal—but not for long. Soon, it all repeated itself. The same strange men came and stuck paper squares on cupboards and armchairs. The following Sunday, crowds of buyers again appeared. The apartment was subjected to such scouring incursions three or perhaps even four times. Mother and Father, who had reacted dramatically to the initial devastation, grew accustomed to what Father jokingly termed "the hostilities of the finance inspector." Moreover, several items that were especially precious to Mother and Father kept reappearing. Nikolai Pavlovich Sapgir, the husband of Mother's sister, bought the book cases and the desk three times, carried them off, and brought them back the next day. But it was hard work to joke with the Soviet authorities: they were carrying out an attack against Father and observing all the rules of engagement. At their instigation, the workers of Kirtselovo announced a strike. As their representative declared in the newspapers, they no longer wished to endure exploitation and wanted to be saved from the NEP leaches. In the municipal court, a case was brought against a certain businessman that went something like this: he hadn't paid his taxes and had enriched himself "on the backs of the proletariat."

One morning, Father went out and took Fima with him. They boarded a streetcar and went to the Petrograd side.

"We'll try renting an apartment," he said.

They arrived on Pesochnaya Street and went up to the second floor of a plain three-story house. The door to the apartment was wide open, and it wasn't an apartment at all but a large empty room. The windows overlooking the courtyard had been broken. Through them, you could see a heap of scrap iron. There were gaping, muddy holes in the floor. There was no ceiling—a beam hung overhead.

"Do you like it?" Father asked. Fima took the question for a joke. "This spot here will be your room," he said, pointing to the last window on the left.

What did they want with a barn like that? Fima couldn't understand it. Father laughed it off.

About three months later, the family moved to Pesochnaya. The move itself was easy: There was no furniture, since it had again been inventoried and sold off the day before. The books, pots, suitcases of clothes—it all fit into two carts. The barracks on Pesochnaya had a different look now: what had been a hall was now divided by partitions into several rooms, and Fima actually did get the one that Father had promised. A shelf for books had been built into the wall. A small table under one of the windows could be raised or lowered. Fima surveyed the other rooms. A sideboard loomed in the dining room, forming part of the partition. In his parents' bedroom, the bed folded up into the wall. It was lowered at night by pressing a lever. In the study, Fima recognized the bookcases so dear to Father. They were there and not there at the same time. Small mahogany doors with bronze ornaments were used to cover gaps in the partition. In this entire strange apartment, the only things that could move were a few simple chairs in the dining room and stools in the kitchen.

Several weeks passed peacefully. The family was adjusting to this new life. Then, *they* reappeared—the same men who had stuck up the paper squares at 24 Zagorodny. Puzzled, they walked from one room to another and lingered in the study, at the mahogany doors, in the dining room, at the sideboard, in Fima's room, and at the built-in bookcase. Then, they went into the kitchen. Mama offered them tea. They sat on the stools and broke into loud laughter.

"He's outsmarted us," said one of them, glancing around. The kitchen cupboards had also been built into the wall. "Outsmarted us," he repeated, laughing.

Later, Fima understood what he had wanted to say: "That cunning Jew!"

Epilogue

The family lived for many years in this apartment with the built-in furniture, from 1928 to 1942, when Father died of starvation during the blockade and Mama, with the youngest son and Uncle Monya, were evacuated to the city of Molotov, formerly and currently known as Perm'.

What became of the Kirtselovo factory? This deserves a brief description, as it may be of public interest.

Nearly half a century later, with the threat of exile hanging over me (I didn't as yet know where to, to the east or to the west), I suggested to my wife that we visit places from my childhood. It was not very far by car. I found Kirtselovo easily, and the factory too. It still produced the same wrapping paper—the brown reels emerged from the machinery as before. Next to the factory, there stood a new, ordinary-looking building that housed the factory administration: accounting, sales, personnel . . . an entire building, dozens of staff members! I recalled that back then, in the 1920s, aside from my father and his brother, the factory was run by the two Katzes, senior and junior, an eighty-year-old man, and his sixty-year-old son. There was also the energetic Volovich, who dealt with the accounting. That was all. And it was enough for our administration.

My father was ruined by exorbitant taxes. And our country was ruined by countless parasites who pretended to do useful work.

Full Repair!

I was returning from school and, after reaching the second floor, I started to unlock the door. On the step by the entrance to the apartment sat an old man with a bushy, gray beard.

"Move over, please," I said.

He responded softly, "Fima..."

It was my father.

The last time he had been arrested had been some five months earlier. At the time, in 1930, the procedure was as follows: two men in civilian clothes would appear, accompanied by the janitor, and present their warrant. Then, after Mama gathered together a bundle with soap and a toothbrush, they would lead Father away. They would not engage in conversation, conduct a search, or look around. This was repeated several times. We did not despair. A month or two later, Father would return, and our life would begin anew. As I recall, the official pretext for this was tax delinquency. The Kirtselovo enterprise had been seized by the government long ago, and Father had already joined the staff of some failing cooperative or other, where he earned a meager salary. But they continued to demand extraordinary amounts in taxes, which had been designed to put the factory in a stranglehold. Such was the fate of the erstwhile NEP men. Arrests became a part of everyday life. Father and his friends lived in constant expectation of being detained. After several weeks of being in a common cell, they would return home, only to wait for the next time. Six or seven years later, this was to change completely; then, they would take you away forever. Relatives would receive notice that the standard sentence had been given: "Ten years with no right of correspondence." Much later, we were to learn what this meant: the detainee had already been shot. The early 1930s were relatively temperate. The terror regime was only slowly acquiring power. "Well, they've arrested him, but he'll come home." People grew accustomed even to this absurdity. As it turns out, one can get used to anything.

This time, however, the arrest lasted longer. Months went by, but Father still wasn't there. We knew that he was in Kresty Prison, and we knew his cell number (I believe we had been told by a neighbor who had been released). Occasionally, Mama and I would stroll by the prison walls. In one of the windows, a white rag would appear, and we would want to believe that it was Father waving his handkerchief. Once, I managed to climb to the roof of the opposite building and wave back from there. I had no way of knowing whether it was him waving back or not. Months passed, and still there was no news of Father. As to what had happened to him, we learned of all that later.

That was the year when the country experienced "gold fever." The Cheka, when they arrested the "formers," demanded gold and diamonds. Former NEP men were held in horrifying conditions, threatened with worse, and were promised a freedom that could be bought—together with the hope of a quiet future—for money. As Father described it, hordes of prisoners were driven into a small room where, because of the crowding, all you could do was stand, and where there was an oppressive heat, made worse by a constantly revolving spotlight that blinded you, or to put it more accurately, burned your eyes out. This occurred day after day, week after week. Prisoners lost their minds and were ready to give their tormentors not only the diamonds that they for the most part did not possess but the shirts off their backs. The Cheka had no use for the shirts; they were implementing the government's plan for currency regulation.

One morning, detainees from many cells were assembled in a large hall. An NKVD boss stood before them explaining, for the nth time, that the Soviet government was building socialism while surrounded by enemies, that the imperialists of the whole world were dreaming only of vanquishing the Soviet Union, the sole hope of progressive humanity, and that gold was essential for defending the country. "We know that every one of you has something hidden away for a rainy day. You must understand: if you do not turn your currency over to us, that rainy day will come for you very soon."

Thereafter, four men were led out of the assembly hall, my father among them. In a hoarse voice, one functionary read out the decision of the tribunal: For the malicious concealment of assets belonging to the Soviet government, so and so is subject to the most stringent measure for the defense of socialism: execution by shooting, and the confiscation of all property. The sentence is irrevocable and will be carried out without delay.

The men were led past their stunned fellow prisoners and locked in a van waiting in the courtyard. Turning to the old man sitting next to him on the floor, Father said his parting words in Yiddish. The convoy guard silenced them; talking was forbidden. Where was the van headed? It was impossible to guess. Nothing could be made out through the one narrow crack. And what did it matter? Wasn't it all the same where they would bury you? Suddenly, Father was blinded by a bright light and jolted to attention by a severe pain. The first thought that came to his mind was: I've been shot. Could it be that they have missed? Then: is this death?

He came around with difficulty and saw that he was on a sidewalk. For a long moment, he understood nothing. Then, he realized that they had thrown him at full speed from the van, which was already out of sight. The expectation of certain death had been replaced by—as he later recounted—the sensation of awakening from a nightmare. He looked around him and only then realized that he was on Pesochnaya Street. They had flung him from the prison van onto the doorstep of his own home. He walked through the main door, went up two flights of stairs, and rang his own doorbell. No one was home—or was the bell not working? He knocked on the door. Then, he sat down on the step by the door. He sat there for a long time, wondering if anyone would come. Maybe the family had been sent away? The Cheka had brought him here—they probably knew that someone would open the door. He sat by the entrance to the apartment and thought:

So, it was all make believe? They announced the tribunal's sentence merely to instill fear into the prisoners and force them to capitulate. He was alive, and soon, he might even see his loved ones. He dozed off, and through his dream, he heard, "Move over, please!" And then he realized that his own son did not recognize him.

That evening, Father told Mama and me, in a whisper, about his misadventures. My little brothers had gone to bed, but I was already twelve. Everything that I had heard seemed even more horrifying than Gogol's *Terrible Vengeance*. Was it possible to live with that? I don't recall how I handled that revulsion against the world. It's likely that I don't recall because, when you are young, other feelings can crowd out horror if you try to rid yourself of it with all your might.

In the morning, Father told me to go out with him. He was headed for the barbershop on the corner of Kirovsky Avenue and Pesochnaya Street: a well-known master barber worked there.

Father took a seat and said, "I want something completely new!"

I have always remembered those words. Within an hour, he was beardless. He started to look like himself again and cheered up a bit. But he was never the same again. It seems one cannot live through the expectation of unavoidable death and remain the same. Later, I would sometimes remember how my father changed, as I pondered the human and the artistic fate of Dostoevsky.

The Marquis de Lapunaise

Having concluded the day's lecture on French Classicism, Professor Mokulsky opened a note and read it aloud: "Could you tell us what prose Marquis de Lapunaise wrote?" He coughed and observed, "In so far as I am aware, Lapunaise left no prose." We needed no more than that. The answer had satisfied us. Both Eleazar Krever and I were happy. Marquis de Lapunaise had been granted the right to exist. Professor Mokulsky had gotten himself caught in a trap . . . A month before this incident, I had gone to another professor, Grigory Alexandrovich Gukovsky, a specialist in eighteenth-century Russian literature, and reported to him that I had found a curious manuscript by an unknown poet, a contemporary of Derzhavin's, in the archives. I read out to him the beginning of an epic poem:

> I sing thee, Bullfinch, rainbow feathered,
> Thy doleful lamentations, oh, poor captive tethered.
> Lo, on a perch art thou so haughtily uprayséd,
> As mournful tears flow down thy blackened face.

Gukovsky, who had been standing, took a seat and murmured in his characteristically deep voice, "Go on, read more!"

I continued:

> Thy tail and wings are raven's plumage dark
> Thy belly red like Caliph Uthman's blood
> Which on the tyrant's prized Koran was shed,
> As he was slaughtered by the fiendish Shia's hand.

"Fine, enough!" Grigory Aleksandrovich exclaimed and with total seriousness added, "It would all be good, but you've made seven mistakes in your eighteenth-century Russian." He pointed out to me two or three of these. I cringed with embarrassment. We laughed a bit and parted. And yet, I did once manage to squeeze from him half an admission: yes, it seemed that he had come across the name of the Futurist poet Velimir Ukrob, but he could not recall where or in what connection. I was elated: Ukrob was one of my favorite writers (his name was invented as an analogue to Pasternak's).* Ukrob's verses, composed by Kréver and myself in a five-minute competition, were a hit with our graduate students:

> Invaded by the sunray's amber
> the room fell silent like a sliced-off cord,
> like Psametichus's bedchamber
> Invaded by a drunken horde.
>
> It parted earth, it parted oceans,
> It penetrated the darkest thought.
> Drunken glasses, brimming potions
> Made us the disenchanted lot.
>
> Comb kazoos in ether rumble
> A vortex swept beneath the lee.
> Still two plus two makes four, we mumble,
> Our rules are simple as can be.
> As simple as an ass's ego,
> As any elemental curse,
> As the azure crystal of a goblet,
> As the whitened page of our blank verse . . .

Everything that I relate here took place sixty years ago, but I still remember this poetic hocus pocus. And I am not alone! Recently I asked several acquaintances to send me "homemade verses" that they could recall. One of these, the philologist Garik Levinton, sent me, among other things,

---

*   In Russian, *pasternak* means parsnip and *ukrop* means dill.—Trans.

two stanzas of this very poem. He had learned it from his father, Akhill Levinton, a senior colleague of mine at LIHPL.* How the memory of this rhyming nonsense endures!

And so, Gukovsky did take the bait with Ukrob, or maybe he pretended to, being a lover of hoaxes himself.

As to Stefan Stefanovich Mokulsky, he fell for our provocative note, so there was nothing he could do but to believe in Lapunaise. It's strange that he paid no attention to the parody of the surname, which in French means *bug*. But then, if names like La Fontaine (spring), La Bruyere (grove), Lafayette, and La Rochefoucauld are possible, why not Lapunaise? Mokulsky was lazy, we knew that very well. He would not start digging through encyclopedias! His laziness was especially apparent in the way he delivered his lectures. Two or three years before our time, his course had been taken down by a stenographer and typed up. He would bring each installment to class in his briefcase and, getting up to the lectern, he would read it out loud. In all fairness, it must be said that he read expressively. The students listened without taking notes—all the stenographic transcripts were available in the department library. We made shameless use of them, calling them *mokulatura* (from the last name Mokulsky).** Apparently, the professor knew this and was not offended. Stefan Stefanovich, a specialist in Molière's dramaturgy, possessed a Gallic sense of humor.

Soon after the note incident, Mokulsky led a seminar in which each student had to present a prospectus for a paper. I titled mine "The Poetic Dramaturgy of Marquis de Lapunaise." No one paid any attention to the outlandishness of the subject other than, naturally, Kréver, the co-author of the note and Lapunaise's co-creator. The two of us together wrote the prospectus, which I presented at the seminar on the appointed day.

* Leningrad Institute of History, Philosophy, and Linguistics; in Russian, *LIFLI*.—Trans.

** A pun on the professor's name and *makulatura*, meaning "pulp" or "wastepaper."—Trans.

Marquis de Lapunaise had apparently led a turbulent life. We took his biography partly from Dumas's novels and partly from the lives of Rochefort and Cyrano de Bergerac. A lot of it we made up. He was mad about dueling, forgave no insults, even from the husbands of the women whom he had lured into adultery. He traveled a great deal and often visited England, where he became acquainted with Shakespeare's theater (the first and surely the only one to do so during that century). He penned several successful tragedies, among them *Agrippina*, a work I analyzed using copious citations from its splendid poetic monologues.

After the presentation, as a matter of course, came a general discussion. I had hoped that Kréver would set the tone of this discussion, but I was mistaken: my co-author was lying under the seminar table with a handkerchief wadded up in his mouth, choking with laughter. It wasn't easy for me to keep a straight face and a scholarly appearance while listening to the reactions of the seminar participants who valued my discoveries highly, especially the analogies with Shakespeare's plays. It was suggested that the prospectus be printed up in the university's *Scholarly Notes*. Professor Mokulsky brought the discussion to a close, concurring with the generally positive assessment of the prospectus and supporting the suggestion to publish it, with the stipulation that the section dealing with Shakespeare be expanded. As was customary, I then took questions, and, at the conclusion of my presentation, I read out an epitaph: the inscribed verses that adorned the tomb of Marquis de Lapunaise in the Père Lachaise Cemetery.

> Passant, arrête-toi, et que ton âme s'apaise,
> Car ici git le grand marquis de Lapunaise.
> Tu n'as pas entendu en parler? Et pourtant
> Il était bien connu et aimé de son temps
> Il était écrivain, duelliste, poète,
> Son âme était élevée et son esprit honnête...

(Passerby, stop, as Mighty Lord we praise / for here lies the great Marquis de Lapunaise. / You've never heard of him? Still, his ways / Were known by all and loved in olden days/ He was a writer, poet, expert duelist. / A noble spirit, ever dear and missed . . .)

Falling silent for a moment and kicking Lelya Kréver, who was laughing under the table, I continued:

> Incline-toi devant sa tombe! Désormais,
> Apprends, mon cher passant, qu'il n'existait jamais!

(If before this grave you bow your head / Know: he who never lived cannot be dead.)

The seminar participants had not been prepared for such a turn of events. Some thought they had misheard (the epitaph had been in French, after all). Others began to laugh, at first uneasily and cautiously. Stefan Stefanovich Mokulsky did not decide immediately how to react. To his great credit, I can report that he did begin to laugh. And I continued reading the epitaph:

> O Jupiter, sur nous ne lance pas ton ire!
> Nous l'avons inventé pour te faire sourire,
> Pour te faire plaisir nous avons fait ces vers.
> Pardonne à tes esclaves E. Etkind, E. Krévert.

(Spare us your wrath, O Jupiter—we swear / We invented him just to make you smile, / and be entertained by us for a while. / Pardon your slaves, Etkind and Krevert.)

Krévert at last crawled out from under the table and, removing his handkerchief gag, collapsed with laughter once more. Then, everyone began laughing again, most of all Stefan Stefanovich. Once he was able to speak, he announced, "I knew it from the very beginning, but I didn't want to spoil the fun." Whether or not that was true, I would not care to judge.

Later on, our paths would cross. We had a cordial relationship, but I understood that he had not forgotten our 1937 subterfuge and had not entirely forgiven me.

Yes, that was in 1937, and we, not realizing what was happening, we laughed.

The Russian Intelligentsia: Two Generations

A Knight

When I first came to the Writer's House and met Alexander Alexandrovich Smirnov, he was not much more than fifty years old, but to me at thirteen, he seemed like a patriarch. Smirnov headed the French translation studio. At long tables in the Gothic-style rooms sat ladies who took down his every word. The ladies all looked alike to me at first; it was only later that I began to distinguish among them. And it was later still when I realized what good fortune had befallen me. Among Smirnov's colleagues and students were the talented critic and essayist Tamara Yurievna Khmelnitskaya; the brilliant translator of French poetry Elga Lvovna Feldman (Linetskaya), who in the 1960s and 1970s trained an entire generation of poet-translators; and Dora Grigorievna Livshitz, the author of numerous solid translations of French prose.

Every participant in the studio would translate a story by Maupassant, after which everyone would critique the different versions—in a spirit that was both kind and exacting. The Maupassant was published, and Villiers de l'Isle-Adam replaced him as the studio's focus. Smirnov had the last word in the discussions. To this day, I can still recall his thoughts on the finer points in meaning and the stylistic difference of Russian words as compared to the French. All that he wrote about Shakespeare and Molière, Mérimée and artistic translation pales in comparison to the brilliance of those improvisations. In each of his analyses, one sensed the presence of an experienced master, a "weigher" of words and sounds, and at the same time a highly erudite literary historian, an expert on France, England, Ireland, and Spain, and a connoisseur of the Renaissance and the Romantic era.

Many years later, I had to lead a similar studio for translations of German prose. I was always aware that it was ridiculous for us to compare ourselves to the older generation. We did not even have one-tenth of the cultural knowledge that A. A. Smirnov retained with amazing natural grace. I am not thinking of erudition or talent but culture. And what is that? I will try to discuss the concept in concrete rather than abstract terms.

A. A. Smirnov knew several languages: French, English, German, and Spanish. He knew these so well that he was able to understand not only new literature but also ancient poetry, whose meaning was difficult to grasp. The ancient languages that he had mastered in his student days (Latin, Celtic, and Old English) served as the foundation for his linguistic insights. All of this allowed him to speak of Petrarca, Marlowe, Cervantes, *The Song of Roland*, Molière, and Stendhal. In Smirnov's memory, linguistic expertise was integrated with his understanding of the civilizations that each of these languages represented. He knew them from books, of course, but not only from books. He had lived for extended periods in France, Spain, and Italy. He had absorbed their customs, religious idiosyncrasies, and the peculiarities of their national characteristics. He had familiarized himself with various brands of wine and cognac. Smirnov himself did not translate a great deal. He was a superb editor, a classical practitioner of the editorial art form. An editor is distinct from a translator in the same way that a conductor is distinct from the orchestra. He himself does not play the violin or the cello, strike the tympani, or beat the drum. Yet without him, the players would lose that harmonic unity which is indispensable in the creation of art. The list of books bearing Smirnov's name on the title page is endless. These include the collected works of Shakespeare, Marlowe, Stendhal, Mérimée, and Maupassant, and translations of national epics such as *The Song of Roland* and *The Poem of the Cid*, as well as Irish and Icelandic sagas, to name just a few.

Not infrequently, a well-known name is added to a list of editors to heighten a publication's prestige, even though the bearer of the name has never even glanced at the manuscript. In Russian, this is called "inviting a general." Smirnov never served as a general in this sense. He edited texts in old-fashioned good conscience, assuming responsibility for them. He edited, which meant he checked the text against the original, compared it with earlier translations, supplied explanations for unclear passages, found the sources for citations and checked every one of them.

The practice of obligatory editorship was first introduced by Maxim Gorky with the publication of *World Literature* in 1918. During that period, scholars and literati such as Mikhail Lozinsky, Korney Chukovsky, Viktor Zhirmunsky, Akim Volynsky, and Vasily Alexeyev worked alongside Gorky. One of the most active and reliable of these was A. A. Smirnov. His colleagues at *World Literature* departed for various other disciplines, but Smirnov remained an editor. This was the chief occupation of his adult life and became his most important contribution to Russian literature.

What was it, this culture that Smirnov brought to the studio, to the collected works of foreign authors, to his university courses on Medieval and Renaissance literature?

Above all else, it was a deep understanding of different civilizations, an appreciation for what was unique and irreplaceable in each of them. By "civilizations" I mean the national and ethnological unities and, within them, the periods that succeed each other over the course of history. Furthermore, it was an understanding of all these different civilizations as the indivisible, inseparable totality of human culture within which each distinct civilization is enriched by those surrounding it. Culture is the consciousness both of variation in time and space and of the unity that this variation comprises.

It was precisely this culture that Alexander Smirnov possessed. He had acquired it during Russia's Silver Age, which was also his own formative years, and he brought it into the Soviet era—into Russia's publishing practices and its universities in the 1920s through to the 1950s.

He did have a difficult time. Like all his contemporaries, Smirnov had to destroy himself in adapting to the monopoly of the party ideology. Now that this ideology has receded into the past, one marvels at the primitive forms it assumed and what compromises scholars had to accept so as not to find themselves in disagreement with it! Smirnov tried honestly to search for opportunities to participate in the class struggle that comprised the sole impetus in the history of society and literature. He had a deep understanding of Shakespeare, and his interpretations were guided by a knowledge that was indispensable for reading Shakespearean chronicles and tragedies. But he was required to bring in the class struggle. He therefore stuck the labels expected by party authorities onto the tragedies and chronicles. In his monograph *Shakespeare's Works* (Leningrad, 1934), we read, "For the class that had given birth to Shakespeare in the days of its first flowering, this Shakespeare became dangerous in the later stages of its development, culminating in its decline and dissolution. He turned out to be acceptable only if redrawn in a particular way. But we need Shakespeare, the real, revolutionary Shakespeare, and he is needed by a proletariat fully capable of fulfilling the aspirations that . . ." etc. (165-66).

Such run-of-the-mill formulations were concessions to time and place. Speaking at home with his friends and students, Smirnov laughed at the compulsory "class struggle," adding a quote in his favorite Franco-Russian *Volapük*:

> Sans la lute des classes
> They wouldn't publish us!

At the end of the 1930s, a four-volume collection of Shakespeare was published by Detskaya Literatura publishers under his editorship. The censor was particularly vigilant at the time. In his editorial article and commentaries, it was obligatory to have a "socialist adherence to the party." He gnashed his teeth, but of *Hamlet*, for example, he did write, "Shakespeare here makes manifest the soullessness, abasement, and hypocrisy not only of the English court, where such vices showed themselves in particularly vivid hues, not only the aristocracy of his time, but also of bourgeois and aristocratic society in general, where crude violence, the cult of money, and the cynical pursuit of profit reigned supreme. Yet we know that these traits, horrifying to the best minds, to all the humanists of the sixteenth century, are to a greater or lesser degree characteristic of any society based on exploitation and especially to bourgeois society at every stage of its development" (vol. 1, [Leningrad: M. L. Detgiz, 1938], 500–1).

Sans la lutte des classes . . .

More than anything else, he valued the publication of new translations instead of older, outdated ones. He sometimes commissioned new ones from surprising literati, close acquaintances from prewar days, or, more precisely, from prerevolutionary times. Among these were Mikhail Kuzmin, Tatiana Shchepkina-Kupernik, and, most importantly, Mikhail Lozinsky. He realized the historical significance of Alexander Druzhinin, Pyotr Weinberg, or Andrei Kroneberg, but was convinced that their translations belonged to the past, to the decades of the nineteenth century, which had been dominated by prose, and that, after Bryusov, Blok, and Gumilev, only those with an atrophied artistic taste could read Pyotr Weinberg. Smirnov's publications of Shakespeare were distinguished by the fact that through them he reactivated an entire contingent of translators. He mobilized the last luminaries of the Silver Age. That fact was his pride. But the paste-on "class struggle" labels depressed him. He once handed me one of the volumes of *Children's Shakespeare*, saying as he did so—in his characteristic manner, half-smiling, his lower lip protruding, pronouncing the consonants with a foreigner's accuracy—"Shakespeare in Time of Plague."* After this risky joke, he immediately added, "I wanted to write that as a dedication to you but was afraid to. Better to leave no traces."

His Shakespeare collaborators would occasionally visit the studio and talk about themselves. At one point, Alexander Alexandrovich warned us, "Next week, we will have a visit from the *grande dame* of poetic translation." The plump Tatiana Lvovna Shchepkina-Kupernik did stop by, astounding everyone with her youthful dynamism [she was over seventy] and her

---

* The title is a reference to *A Feast in the Time of Plague* (1830), a short play by Alexander Pushkin (1799–1837), in which the hero mocks death.

cheerful spirits. She read us her just-completed translation of *King Lear*. I have always remembered her translation, amazing for the relevance of the Fool's rhymes:

> Have more than thou showest,
> Speak less than thou knowest . . .
> Learn more than thou trowest,
> Set less than thou throwest,
> Leave thy drink and thy whore,
> And keep in-a-door . . . (*King Lear*)

On another occasion, Mikhail Leonidovich Lozinsky visited the studio. He read us his paper on the art of poetry translation that he had recently written for the All-Union Conference on Translation (1936). I still recall how Lozinsky maintained that sounds had no expressive quality in themselves and gave the example of two lines from Pushkin, where the repetition of the "ah" sound produced different effects:

> You waged attacks on the Kremlin of Kazan . . .

Lozinsky observed, "Those three stressed *a*'s illuminate like three bonfires quite a different picture than, let's say, in this line":

> My life was brief, and rapture was scarce . . .

Twenty years later, it fell to my lot to publish Lozinsky's paper for the first time (in the journal *Druzhba narodov* [Friendship of peoples]) and then assemble and publish a small volume of his selected translations titled *Bagrovoe svetilo* [Crimson sun], in which the article was also included. And the whole time, I remembered with excitement my first encounter with him, at the Writer's House in Smirnov's studio. Lozinsky's funeral took place in 1955, arranged by the Writer's House itself. His casket, along with his wife's, stood just where we used to meet with him in 1935. At the funeral service, Nikolai Pavlovich Antsiferov, author of the widely praised book *Dusha Peterburga* [The Soul of St. Petersburg], observed, "As these two caskets stand here side by side, they resemble the medieval tombs of a knight and his wife." Antsiferov was profoundly correct, and this resemblance was not only superficial. M. L. Lozinsky was a knight of poetry, of poetic translation. His wife, Tatyana Borisovna, had ended her own life. She did not want to, and was not able to, outlive her spouse. This, too, was an echo of a different historical era. Like Lozinsky, his closest collaborator on Shakespeare, A. A. Smirnov was a true knight of culture.

Conquistador

By the beginning of the 1950s, A. A. Smirnov had begun to decline rapidly. He could no longer shoulder the literary burden that had been laid upon him so long ago: editing poetry and prose translations from numerous languages, writing introductions and commentaries, supervising dissertations, and participating in defenses. The cause was not old age per se, but rather the excessive baggage of the Soviet times. He was not a Jew, but the antisemitic persecutions of Stalin's latter years had been painful for him. By the way, ironically, intelligent students doubted the fact that he was *not* a Jew. A joke made the rounds in which three Russian literary men were named Smirnov, V. Alexeev, and Balukhaty. It went like this: "Smirnov is a kike, and Alekseev is too. Now what about Balukhaty? Isn't he a scabby one?" We understood this rhyme as a parody of antisemitism. It was said, moreover, that Smirnov's father had in fact been Jewish, a banker named Soloveichik, and that as a boy he had been brought up by his adoptive father, Senator Smirnov.

No one verified such rumors. For us in the 1930s, this had no meaning. A. A. Smirnov was a model Russian intellectual. In our circle, we defined this concept, that of the Russian intellectual, in this way: a person able (and inclined) to engage in selfless intellectual work—in other words, a knight of culture.

When I came to see him as usual in his apartment on Peter Lavrov Street, he told me with sadness about his steadily growing fatigue. "Could you perhaps find me a sensible assistant and secretary?" The requirements were very high. The assistant should know several languages and understand how translation works—particularly for prose and poems, if possible—and be conscientious and hardworking. You don't find people like this often. Smirnov hinted that I would meet all of these conditions. But no, I could not, since I was teaching full-time at the Pedagogical Institute after several years of "cosmopolitan exile," as well translating and writing a lot. Moreover, of the romance languages, I knew only French well, but a knowledge of Italian and Spanish were also essential.

After giving it some thought, I thought of Yury Korneyev. He seemed to fit the requirements. A few days later, I told him about A. A. Smirnov's proposal, and he agreed instantly. A meeting was set up. The three of us met in Smirnov's office, and the discussion lasted for about one and a half hours. Korneyev impressed us with his knowledge of languages, his literary awareness, and his energy. He read to us a few of his own translations of Leconte de Lisle and Alfred de Vigny, which Smirnov relished. A contract was drawn up.

I was satisfied. I had succeeded in finding a real assistant for Smirnov, someone who would help him in different areas, but I was also worried. Was I doing him a disservice? My worries turned out to be not unfounded.

From 1947 to 1949, I gave a course on French literature at the Leningrad Institute of Foreign Languages. The majority of the students were girls aged eighteen to twenty. Among them, there was one tall lad who wore a faded soldier's tunic. I did not conduct any seminars, so I did not really know my students. At the end of the semester, the students had to take exams on the course. The girls came one after the other, anxiously took the slips of paper with the exam questions, turned them over, and after reading them, sat down to prepare. Most of them took a long time to prepare and were timid. They spoke with difficulty and stammered. Then Korneyev came in, wearing that soldier's tunic, took an exam question slip, snapped his heels and launched straight into what he had to say. "If you would please allow me, I wish to stand."

"Please, stand," I answered, surprised.

He continued with the same directness. "I will answer without preparing," he said, and added, "I would like to speak in French, if I may."

I started to feel uneasy and said: "You know, everyone here is speaking in Russian . . ."

"But all of my examiners have allowed me to do so."

"Oh, alright, do it in French."

The question was on Ronsard. Korneyev, without once stumbling over his words, gave a monologue with quotations from Ronsard. I don't remember whether there was a second question. I just remember that, having listened to Korneyev and having watched him, I was struck with fear. I thought: This is a tank, and he could roll over any of these girls, and of course, me. His answer was brilliant. Korneyev mastered French easily and knew sixteenth-century literature like the back of his hand. He was absolutely confident in himself and his knowledge.

Around four years later, when I had returned to Leningrad from my exile in Tula and had already become a member of the Union of Writers and even a secretary of the department of translation, I decided to organize an evening of Yury Borisovich Korneyev's translations. By that time, he had managed to complete quite a few translations and had them published. While preparing my introductory speech, I asked him where he had worked after the Institute of Foreign Languages. He answered with his usual succinctness, "In the Special School for State Security."

"Is that how it should be announced?" I asked again. "Perhaps we should not mention the KGB?"

"Why not?" Korneyev asked, surprised. "Anything there to be ashamed of?"

I thought again about the tank. The evening was a success. The translations of French and Spanish poetry were very professional, strong, and sophisticated.

Has the reader understood why I was worried about helping to set up a collaboration between Smirnov and Korneyev? Smirnov understood everything. In talking to me, he would ironically call Korneyev "your man in the SS," and as time went on, he became more and more dependent on him. Korneyev edited and prepared drafts for publication, corresponded with publishers and authors, produced books and journals, prepared materials for articles and doctoral defenses. All this lasted until A. A. Smirnov's death in 1962.

Around the same period, Korneyev made a name for himself. In the Union of Writers, he became the secretary to the party organization. The people at the top valued him: His peasant appearance fit the party's ideal. He was able to speak their language of official bureaucracy. For him, this was a kind of stylistic game.

He knew how to be tough, even merciless, when he made decisions. On the other hand, he was disciplined in carrying out orders from above. He was irreplaceable when you had to deal with foreigners.

However, this was not his main job. He translated an astounding amount and always to the highest professional standards. In a relatively short span of time, he had penned a large number of European literary epics. *The Song of Roland*, *Cantar de mío Cid*, *The Song of the Nibelungs*, Shakespeare's tragedies, including *Macbeth* and *The Tragedy of Coriolanus*, plays by Lope de Vega and Calderón, Christopher Marlowe and Corneille, the poems of Rabelais, Vigny, Aragón, compositions by seventeenth-century French moralists, and many other works by French, Spanish, Italian, German, and English writers. He worked tirelessly and was very productive. In terms of quantity, he printed more than Lozinsky and Pasternak. However, it was difficult not to compare his production to that of a conveyor belt. You could feel the factory stamp in many of his works. But one should also admit that there were great successes in this poetic repertoire, for example, Vigny's poem *Moses* and Aragón's *La Rose et le réséda*. He died early, in 1995, having lost his vision almost completely. Very likely it was the result of the inhuman pressure under which he worked for the four decades of his career in translation. He was finishing a collection of poems by François Villon, his last work, knowing that he did not have much time left. It is amazing that he translated (for the first time ever) Villon's poems written in "color" (thieves') jargon. How did it happen that he had such a brilliant knowledge of it?

> Do not be chickenshit on a stickup,
> Bro, get the sucker and let it rip.
> If you get busted, dude, then man up,
> Don't snitch on you bro, keep a tight lip. *

Y. B. Korneyev was an enigmatic individual. Many things about him remain inexplicable. He became a successor to A. A. Smirnov, continuing his patron's work in many respects. But how different he was from Smirnov! He was different in that he worked in the Special School of the KGB and was not ashamed of it; he built his literary career, plowing ahead like a tank; he was able to be a party secretary of the Leningrad division of the Writer's Union; he was able to translate the biblical poems of Alfred de Vigny and the thieves' poems of François Villon almost simultaneously. Whereas A. A. Smirnov had the integrity of global culture, Korneyev was a brilliantly gifted person who despised everyone around him with overt cynicism.

---

* This translation was taken from *The Jargon of Master Fancois Villon, Clerk of Paris A.D. MCCCCLII, Being Seven Ballads from the Thieves' Argot of the XVth Century*, ed. Jordan Herbert Stabler (Boston: Houghton Mifflin, 1918), 17.

Looking through the Walls

> ... I see him, marching through mountains of Time,
> whom no one can see.
>
> V. Mayakovsky

In 1961, contrary to any logic, an intriguing poem titled "Memoirs of A. R." by David Samoilov was published in the anthology *Pages from Tarusa*. I noted the following lines:

> He was a wretched invalid
> Not of a past but of a future war.

And suddenly, I guessed it. A. R. was Alik Rivin! Samoilov had in mind a poem that had not been published, just like everything that Rivin had written. I recalled its opening during the war years:

> Here comes a monster war
> We'll crawl into the cellar
> Mixing our hearts with silence
> Lining the floor with cadavers.

He probably died of starvation during the blockade in 1942. He was only about twenty-five years of age. Or maybe he committed suicide. But he could have died of starvation even without any blockade, even during the most prosperous times in the prewar period.

He would come to our house unexpectedly, place his battered suitcase on the dinner table, and say, "Gib geld!" (Give me money!) We had no *geld*. Our two monthly stipends only barely met our needs for one or two weeks, and we—Katya and I—were rarely full. We gave Rivin empty bottles. He placed them in his suitcase, where he usually already had a cat, and left to do business. He would sell the cat to the university laboratory for three rubles and take the bottles to a collection point.

It seems that Rivin was able to live on this *Geschäft* (that is what he called his simple form of commerce). I don't recall that he had any other source of income. Two women sometimes supported him: Tamara Yurievna Khmelnitskaya, a critic and translator; and Raisa (Leyla) Frenkel, a scholar in Germanic studies. It seems he had been romantically involved with the latter. His writing about it was course and vague:

> Leave me alone, I'm a good, simple guy
> All my life I've done the same as you do,
> Mixing up love, like galoshes in the hallway,
> Canoodling with Lyolka on the Neva's steps.

As for Tamara Khmelnitskaya, she believed in the genius of Rivin, having heard his dramatic reading of the poem "Eternal Fish." She simply purchased the manuscript from him—those greasy paper tatters smeared with soot on which crooked dancing letters formed lyrical couplets:

> Little breamy, little fishy!
> So bulbously your fins are curved,
> Your fine-meshed scales, so moist and swishy
> By a skillful cutter carved!
>
> Like a battered, flattened barrel,
> Like a slender bulging leaf,
> Like a tiny shiny nickel,
> Like a glassy optimist.
>
> So intricately sculpted!
> Little breamy, darling boy,
> Like some silver pieces melted,
> Like a shiny, bright decoy.
>
> Here you lay—your gaping mouth
> and your moistened fins ablaze,

> While life in its swooshy pants goes south
> spitting in your fishy face!

He hummed these lines softly and sadly, then suddenly, without any pause, he began yelling hysterically, in a voice that rose higher and higher.

> The year will not pass,
> The year will not pass,
> The year will not pass,
> The day will not pass,
> Before a change in the weather,
> A change in the weather,
> A change in the weather,
> Crumples me altogether!

He had trouble pronouncing *r*—it sounded like *kh*—and hard *l*—it would come out as *oo* ("Pooavnikami ko *oo* y *kh* aya . . ."), and he spoke with a lisp and nasal twang. But there was a magnetic power in his reading. It drew listeners in, deafened and frightened them, and at times suggested something close to despair. When he appeared at our house for the first time, in February 1940, we actually became really frightened. We were frightened by the frozen gaze in his dark eyes, his mutilated right arm waving in the air, by his deafening voice as he wailed his poems of nightmarish visions, where you could hear the strong determination to end his own life.

> Headfirst, headfirst, thrown down
> To gobble the corn of cobblestone!

"The corn of cobblestones"—is it possible to describe in a more precise and frightening way the cobblestone street that someone ready to commit suicide sees from the window before taking a fatal leap? In Rivin's poems, this pre-death image is a constant: It is the last impression that someone has when he is doomed to be executed. Or determined to commit suicide.

We had an easy life, even a happy one. We were just over twenty. We loved, composed parodies, sang funny songs, read novels from our course on the French Enlightenment, and played poker. The country was drowning in blood, and our youth tried, or at least made the effort, not to see it. I am writing these lines in February 1994. This morning, fifty-four years later, still not knowing what I would write, I read N. I. Yezhov's last words, which had been published for the very first time (in *Moskovskiye Novosti* [Moscow News]). He spoke those words at a meeting of the war tribunal on February 3, 1940, and he was executed on February 4. Yezhov, who had been responsible for the torture and execution of hundreds of thousands of people who were not guilty of anything, was himself subjected to beatings and torture. ("At the initial investigation, I said I was not a spy, that I was not a terrorist, but they did not believe me and subjected me to the strongest beatings.") He admitted his guilt as he understood it. His crime was that he had not punished enough enemies. ("I had cleaned out fourteen thousand Chekists. But my biggest mistake was that I had not cleaned out enough of them.") The meeting took place on February 3, which is exactly the time I am talking about. In those days, Rivin would visit us and, squinting, he would sing or sob in a broken voice:

> It happened under a black sycamore
> On a path where toads sing,
> Where a towering Cupid froze
> In the intimate dark of the green.
>
> There the braids were coming undone
> Over a golden blimp of a face,
> Two black rings in a throbbing race
> Span in the astonished, slanted eyes.
>
> They collided and rolled up in unison
> Under eyelids and into the whites,
> No longer desiring anything—
> Not love, not flowers by the riverside.

And then followed the stanzas presenting highly concentrated memories of the Great Terror of 1937–39. They even reflected the fate of Yezhov himself, saying in the last line, "I admitted to all accusations because by nature I could not tolerate violence done to myself.

> I picked up a dazed dip-pen,
> I looked up through a stifling smother,
> squiggled a signature on paper
> and swapped one fate for another.
>
> And they laid me down behind walls
> On the frigid stony slabs.
> I was given a change of bedding
> and a crooked and wobbly desk . . .
> After death the butchers from earth
> Will set out to live on the moon . . .

They did not imprison him. He did not see the cellars of the Lubyanka or Shpalernaya. Could Alik Rivin have known that, during the period when he was losing his mind from horror, when he was wailing out his nightmares, thousands of people were being killed each day in Russia, at least one per second? As he was crossing Liteyny Avenue, would he have been able to guess what was happening below, under his feet? There were torture and execution chambers, and streams of blood ran along special pipes into the sewage system and into the Neva. Let us imagine for a moment that God's eye could see what was happening at the same time on the same day, that is, on February 3, 1940. There is Rivin, who is reciting his nightmares out in a rhyme, wailing; the half-dead Yezhov who, awaiting execution, is confessing his own liberalism in a whisper; and Professor D. D. Pletnev, who is writing about these days to Voroshilov:

> They used incredibly foul language on me, threatened execution, pulled me by the neck, held me by the throat . . . threatened to pull out my throat and with it my confession . . . Because of all this, I am paralyzed in half my body.

Only a poet could become such an eye of God. He is given insight—the ability to feel and experience what others cannot. People of Rivin's age played poker, and next to them, in the same three-dimensional space in which they lived, there was an ugly boy who wandered around, who sold stray cats and empty bottles, who looked through the walls and saw mountains of corpses, and streams of blood, where others saw parades by athletes and *Swan Lake*. Pushkin did not invent anything in *The Prophet*. The poet hears "Sea monsters moving in the deep, / The growing grapevines in the vales." The poet guesses what will happen in the future ("I see one passing through the mountains of Time . . ."), and his vision penetrates the thick of the earth and the walls.

In some inconceivable way, a poet is able to know what is hidden from everyone else. One should not dismiss this truth—it is more important than anything that literary studies can reveal. Mandelstam said a lot to people, but what can compare to what he guessed in the 1930s? He begged fate to take him to the places where you could see "no coward, no splashing dirt, no bloody bones in a wheel." In 1932, he already knew about bloody bones. And Mayakovsky knew what the "year of the Great Break" was. He, too, had looked through the walls. That is why he shot himself. That is much more significant than the demise of a "love boat" that "crashed against everyday routine." That Jewish boy whom I remember perished without having become famous or seeing even one printed page. But he was a poet, in the truest sense of the word. He was a seer of the truth. To the people around him, he seemed either mad or strange, since they lived in different worlds. They gathered in the evening, sipped wine, and sang a carefree song by Lebedev-Kumach that had been popular in the late '30s, to music by Dunayevsky from the film *Children of Captain Grant*:

> Fearless Captain, fearless Captain, smile, Sir!
> Like a flag, a smile flies over the wave.
> Fearless Captain, fearless Captain, cheer up, Sir!
> For the ocean surrenders to the brave!

Rivin lived near them and saw *Children of Captain Grant* with them. But he had looked through the walls and felt that Lebedev-Kumach was just a disguise and that behind that "smile," which was the ship's flag, there was a steep drop into black terror. He sang the same song of the 1930s differently. Injected with a dose of the Jewish grotesque, his *Captain* freezes the blood in your veins:

> Fearless Captain, fearless Captain, smile, Sir!
> Kush in toches* is the ship's flag's worth . . .
> Our ship sails with no flags or seigneurs.
> In the universe, our ship is the earth.
>
> And the stars are splattering wild,
> And the comets are oars meant for us,
> But our ship is lagging behind
> And we're late for the train, alas!
>
> Over life, over death, over waves, Sir,
> Over stars of crushed glass set your sails.
> As you stand at the helm, O smile, Sir!
> Catch the waves and step on their tails.
>
> No wave before it rises—it's a seesaw,
> No star without light—it will fade.
> O, Fearless Captain, do you get it, Sir?
> Before life, you couldn't speak of fate.
>
> Over life, over waves, over death, Sir,
> Over the crushed glass of stars you sail,
> Immortality deserves your best smile, Sir!
> As you step with your heart on its tail.

Is it possible to forget that V. Lebedev-Kumach wrote this little "Song About the Captain" in 1937? Also "Happy Wind" and "Song about the Volga," where the whole meaning comes down to these lines:

> Our happiness, like us, is young.
> Our power cannot be crushed.
> Under the happy Soviet stars
> It is good to work and live.

I repeat, the year was 1937. Song verses that were written at around that time sound like parodies today:

> At international competitions, the best Soviet violins sounded out,
> Nothing could beat our Soviet girls' smiling pouts.

---

*   Kiss my ass (in yidish—Ed.).

And in Leningrad, Alik Rivin wandered along side streets and through courtyards, reworking the songs of his contemporaries in his own way. The rows and rows of triumphantly optimistic participants of the First of May demonstrations were roaring out the "Kakhovka" by Mikhail Svetlov, which perpetuated the romanticism of the civil war—the best legitimization of the regime.

> Kakhovka! Kakhovka! My country, my rifle!
> Scorching-hot bullet, fly!
> Irkutsk and Warsaw, Orel and Kakhovka—
> Stages on the great road's way.
>
> Remember, Comrade, how we fought together,
> How thunder enclosed us in its arms?
> Then her blue eyes
> Smiled at us both through the smoke . . .

Rivin opened a window to another world:

> Remember, Comrade, how we fought together,
> How the sky overhead raced us with rain
> How maelstroms of rain were whirling and swirling,
> And we said to the rain: Let us wait.
>
> And it came up to us and licked our hands
> And battered our knees
> with its toothless face . . .

The romanticism of fratricidal battles gave way to an eternity of universe. Many of Rivin's poems were derived from couplets or lines that were known to everyone. His poems continued to develop them in new ways, each time departing from their conventional iterations. Who does not remember Pasternak's poems, which led someone to ironically nickname him "genius cottager"?

> One day years hence in the concert hall
> They will play me Brahms, wrenching me with longing,
> I'll give a start, recalling our six-hearted company,
> Walking, swimming, a flower bed in the garden.

Genius? Of course. But doubtless also a cottager. Rivin was least of all like a cottager. His rehashing of the Soviet songs of the time presents a worldview that is tragic and imbued with a sense of inevitable homelessness.

> One day years hence in the concert hall
> Boris will play me his latest chorale,
> And I will scream like a mushy-hearted sheep
> Like time screams, like Kerensky bellowed.
>
> Leave me alone, I'm a good, simple guy
> All my life I've done the same as you do,
> Mixing up love, like galoshes in the hallway,
> Canoodling with Lyolka on the Neva's steps.
>
> One day years hence in the concert hall
> I'll run into Boris and Lyolka together,
> And later, at the "Europa" over dessert,
> We'll settle it all without women.
>
> And the stroke of Boris's doglike gaze
> Will fall on our eyes, our living souls,
> And dismissing womankind, we will weep,
> It's no go without women, and no go without music.

I don't remember who Borya was in these verses—it could have been Pasternak (I probably asked, but forgot). Too bad Rivin's poetry never reached Pasternak. He would have valued his work, both as poems and also as a path into the unknown. But then again, another wonderful contemporary, David Samoilov, remembered it. The poem "In Memory of A. R.," with which I started, reads as follows:

> There once lived in Leningrad, an odd fellow.
> Melancholy, gloomy, not well
> Talented in no small measure
> And I knew him before the war.
>
> He kept a strict reckoning of offenses
> Carried the burden of no one's fault,
> He was a wretched invalid
> Not of a past but of a future war . . .

We awaited victories and fame
The thunderous bravura of brass
While he foresaw only disasters
And the picture of his own wretched corpse.

The howling waves of bombers
Left him staggering about;
The frost of the coming siege
Draped him in grayness.

When we read his strange ballads
We didn't recognize in him
A prophet of Leningrad's siege
Drawing nearer day by day.

Where was he killed? In what cellar?
How did his earthly days end?
And who were the people who served him
His final drink?

What line weighted with suffering
Was his still to write?
What unhappy man fed his verse
Page by page into the stove?

His poems were probably all burnt.
There was little in them of warmth,
While the perpetrators have grown old,
The course of their lives ran out.

And he disappeared. In all the world,
There is nothing of his that is left.
And we do not mention him ever,
As if he never was.

The Double

Nina, the colonel's secretary, came running in the morning. The chief of the Political Administration of the front, General Rumyantsev, wanted to see me at 14:00. Why did he need an ordinary translator from the Seventh Directorate, this insignificant officer in the military hierarchy? At the appointed minute, I stood at attention before him in the roomy office (and why are there these buildings in the middle of some provincial Soroka, which is now Belomorsk?). Clicking my heels with exaggerated diligence, I said: "Second-rank technician quartermaster Etkind, at your command!"

The portly Rumyantsev rose, approached me, and said, "I called you to, well, um, so to speak, finish things in the Seventh Directorate and hand the papers in to the chief of staff—that would be, what, Bergelson? Tomorrow you will leave for the division, so to speak, well, to Kandalaksha. Understood?"

"Understood!" I roared, although I did not understand anything.

It turned out they were sending me from the Seventh Directorate of the front down to a place where, to be honest, I had nothing to do. There was no department for propaganda targeting the enemy army in the division. Why would I go there? Of course, being a technician quartermaster, they would find some use for me, maybe somewhere in the housekeeping unit, where I could count foot bindings or issue boots. But I already had a military profession, even a rare one. In a year and a half or two, I had learned to write German leaflets, publish a newspaper for the enemy, address the enemy on the radio, interrogate prisoners, and even obtain their trust: They openly told their Jewish interlocutor about their circumstances at home and their unit's situation.

I was listed as a simple translator, even though I knew that I did something that required much more responsibility. But I could not count on a promotion—I was not in the party, same as my closest comrade in EPS (the editorial and publishing section) of the Seventh Directorate, Igor Mikhailovich Diakonov. He was an experienced expert in Eastern studies and a brilliant literary specialist at the time. He was also doomed to the position of a translator.

The "intelligentsia" was ruled by the "party authorities." In reality, this certainly was not always the case. The head of our EPS was Grisha Bergelson, a longtime friend from the university philology department, and one of our colleagues was Anatoly Borisovich Lokhovits, a well-known lexicography expert and a co-author and editor of German-Russian dictionaries. Sukher Itskovich Goldenberg, a Jewish writer, worked at the newspaper *Frontzoldat*. They were all educated and true members of the intelligentsia. However, party membership helped further their military and political careers. Class enmity did not become an issue that came up between us, even though we were fed so differently in the dining room. Grisha Bergelson and Sukher Goldenberg were given caviar for appetizers.

In some ways, I was ahead of my brothers in translation. For example, by contrast to many of them, I wrote German verses easily. Besides the regular newspaper *Frontzoldat*, we also published a satirical monthly *Michel im Norden*—this title had been translated from the name of chocolate candies (which had been forgotten during the war), called "Mishka in the North." For this publication, I wrote funny couplets regularly and was particularly proud of a comical long poem titled *Der Führer und der kluge Hund* (The Führer and the clever Dog). I remember that another long poem began with a quatrain, dedicated to the same miserable Mishka in the North.

> Michel der Gefreite
> Stehet vor dem Stab;
> Seine linke Seite
> Fror ihm gänzlich ab . . .
>
> (Michel the corporal
> Before his staff he stood;
> Meanwhile his left flank
> Had totally frozen off.)

I didn't simply enjoy the work in the Seventh Directorate. I was fascinated by it. For me, there was happiness in being with those who were most important to me, even though it was an unendurably difficult time, a period when our relatives were dying of hunger and bombing in Leningrad. Here in the Seventh Directorate were Igor Diakonov, Grisha Bergelson, and Shura Kasatkin not so close to us but still one of us (though an incorrigible pedant). Another university colleague, the historian David Pritzker, worked in Belomorsk—not in the Political department but still at headquarters. My young wife, Katya Zvorykina, who was twenty-four at the time, worked at the Belomorsk Military Hospital as a nurse. In spite of the obstacles of the war period, we were lucky enough to be able to meet at least once a week. Sometimes, it was with everyone together, but occasionally, it was just the two of us.

And I would have to drop all of this tomorrow morning, when I would take a little plywood suitcase and hitch a ride to the division headquarters, where the boots and socks would be waiting for me (but would they be waiting?). Why? Saying goodbye to my wife at the hospital, I returned to the "red barracks," told my friends, then packed my suitcase. That evening, I was close to suicide and overcame the temptation with difficulty. I remember that I walked in the darkness along the canal, saying Blok's verses to myself:

> I'm drawn to it and gaze into its depths
> Wedged between dark granite.

> It flows, it sings, accursed thing
> It beckons to me like a lover.
>
> I come close and I pull back
> And freeze in indecision
> Just one step and I'll cross over . . .

That evening, I did not cross the line, although I came very close to doing so. I was incredibly young. The destruction of my Belomorsk life seemed like a catastrophe. For, at once, I was losing—and maybe forever—my wife, my friends, my job, and the only job that made it possible for me to remain connected to the country that was in the throes of a massive war effort. My own place in the common cause—how important that was in 1942–43! Leningrad was dying, Moscow was under attack, and everything was hanging by a thread. Could I remain on the sidelines? An unknown power was pushing me to the side and depriving my life—on both the personal and the social levels—of any meaning. Walking in the darkness, I compared the events of the past few weeks, and suddenly, suddenly I understood what had been a mystery to me that morning. I did not understand everything yet—the rest would become clear later, after the war. And yet . . . That's what I would like to speak about now.

The war on the Karelian front was being fought based on positioning. Prisoners of war were rare. We mostly had a few deserters, each one of whom we befriended and indulged in our attempt to extract from them what was essential for us. Not long ago, a simple-natured Austrian, Joseph Robinet, came to us in the Seventh Directorate. He was by profession a pastry maker: cake recipes attracted his attention much more than military events. For New Year's of 1944, he found flour, milk, and sugar and baked us a cake that left us speechless. He helped write leaflets (true, he didn't astound us with his literacy), where he called on his comrades to surrender. Occasionally, he spoke on the radio, although he lisped badly. We even liked that—it made it more natural. In February 1944, I was sent to accompany him to the faraway port of Polyarny on the Barents Sea. There, he was to broadcast for the German sailors. The very first evening, having left him in the hotel, I set off for the officer's club, to dine in freedom. A tall naval officer sat at a neighboring small table, watching me with curiosity—in Polyarny, you seldom met infantrymen. Taking a seat, he asked where I was from, where I served and in what capacity, and what I was assigned to do in Polyarny. I name-dropped my superior, Colonel Suomalainen.

After he heard this, his expression changed, and he asked an entirely inappropriate question: "Were you ever on a submarine?" No, of course I had never been even on a plain war ship, except when I visited the historical "Aurora." "Come for dinner tomorrow—I'm the commander of a submarine cruiser. I will treat you to dinner and show you the ship." He explained where his vessel was, and we agreed. The next day, when I came, he was waiting on the pier.

Captain Avranov—that was the name of my new acquaintance—led me through his cruiser and, after sitting down at a table in his mess hall, poured a full tumbler of vodka for each of us. "To our meeting," he said, raising his glass. But then, suddenly, he set it back down onto the table. "Wait, don't drink. If you drink, you'll forget what I'm about to tell you. I want you to remember this and tell it to your colonel, so that he knows under what conditions his name was bandied about."

And he started his detailed story. Half a century has gone by, but to this day I still remember not only the voice of Avranov, not only the details of the story, but even the names of the key players.

Olya Parayeva was a hot young woman. Avranov lived with her for a few months, but he got really bored with her. What was to be done? He tried to break up with her, but she did not get the hints. He did not want to be cruel or rude. Once, after spending a long time at sea, he returned home and came in unexpectedly. Olya was writing a letter. He looked and saw what it was immediately: a love letter. That seemed to him to be unexpectedly fortunate. He pretended to be very jealous, yelled and even slapped her, apparently. She suffered his ire without protest, then said quietly, "It's not what you think it is." Avranov got even more angry, until she confessed, "It's a special code. Suomalainen is my boss." That night, Avranov asked her in a whisper while they were in bed, "Who do you work for?" She avoided answering him, but he understood: for the Finns. In the morning, he reported his discovery to the Special Unit. Olga Parayeva disappeared.

Some three months passed. He bumped into Olga on the street. "I know everything," she said. "I read your denunciation. Silly, how could you believe that I was a spy?"

Well, spy or not, he had gotten rid of her, and he was glad of it. "Tell it to Suomalainen," he repeated. "Let him know."

After returning to Belomorsk, I told my friends all of it. They were confused and alarmed. Colonel Suomalainen, head of the Seventh Directorate, was in charge of propaganda for the enemy troops, which in Karelia mainly meant the Finns. He regularly published not only leaflets but also a newspaper for them. He was able to transmit any information to the Finns, encoding it in, for example, an editorial, which he always wrote himself. Can you imagine better conditions for a secret service man? Suomalainen was a strange personality. I remember once—it was in September 1943—I reported about astounding news that we had just heard over the radio: Italy had capitulated. "Is that all?" Suomalainen asked coldly, without showing a hint of happiness or satisfaction or even raising his eyes toward me. I felt a sense of hatred for the indifference of this incredibly fat, imperturbable Finn. The outcome of the war was clearly of no consequence to him. My coworkers strengthened the suspicions that I had had of Captain Avranov. In addition, they remembered what seemed to be a funny episode, which had taken place while I was in Polyarny. A medical commission had visited the Seventh Directorate. They had examined everyone, one after the other. One of the doctors, who had a drink with the guys, revealed with a laugh that Nina Ivanova, the colonel's secretary, was in fact a virgin. This was rare in the army. Moreover, each one of us had to take turns to go on night watch. We knew that at night, Nina went upstairs to Suomalainen and returned to her place only by morning. What were they doing? Her virginity made us look at both of them differently—that is, we now believed that they were most likely encoding some materials. Our theory seemed irresistibly convincing. In essence, this was the only possible explanation that we could come up with. Olga Parayeva was at one end of the chain, and Nina Ivanova at the other.

The war was still going on. The impunity of a spy could cost our army innumerable lives. Having guessed what Suomelainen was up to, I had become his accomplice. My friends unanimously supported my plan to report my suspicions to the Special Unit. Getting involved with SMERSH* was disgusting, but I saw no alternative. The next day, I let Lieutenant Colonel Leontiev, with whom I was somewhat familiar, know that I wished to be granted a meeting with him. A meeting was set for two or three days later. I told him about Avranov, Olga Parayeva, and her strange coded letter to Suomalainen, the submarine cruiser, and the glass of vodka. Leontiev listened calmly and seemingly indifferently, then began running around the office. Suddenly, interrupting me, he said loudly, almost shouting, "Do you realize what you're telling me? We'd guessed this long ago, but we couldn't find the evidence." I told him from the very beginning of my request not to wait for my comments. I told him everything that I had come to know. I did not want to get into the meaning of what had occurred. That's what counterintelligence was for . . .

Leontiev listened until I was finished, nervously walking from one corner to the other, and said to write it all down—right there, without leaving his office. I wrote for about two hours, then returned. The guys were waiting. They knew where I had gone and had begun feeling concerned. What will happen now? Will Suomalainen stay or fly off and perish? Time passed. Those on duty observed each night that Nina Ivanova was still disappearing into the colonel's room and reappearing the next morning.

---

*   SMERSH, a name coined by Joseph Stalin for the counterintelligence organizations in the Red Army. The name was a contraction of смерть шпионам, death to spies.—Ed.

One could not read anything from Suomalainen's fat face—it remained shallow, self-satisfied, superior, and unmoving, as always. He spoke as he usually did, with brusque interjections, without expressing approval or disapproval. What did that mean? Had we made a mistake? Or was the spy network larger than any of us could imagine? Finally, that day came, the one with which I began my story. Rumyantsev called me in and declared, "Tomorrow, you will leave for the division, so to speak, well . . ."

I did not reach the division: I got picked up by the commander of the Twenty-Sixth Army, Lieutenant General Lev Solomonovich Svirsky. He knew that I was a translator and left me with his staff in the intelligence section. During the war, a general had the right to dictate his will, especially regarding officers under him. He paid no attention to my dismissal from the Seventh Directorate. For him, as for all staff commanders, political departments had no business with the actual army. He clearly despised political instructors and other commissars, or in any case, ignored them. "Now, war will start for you," he said condescendingly; and added, "Until now, you've been playing at leaflets." He was not right. Further events showed that our efforts in propaganda were not in vain. When the German army stopped winning, the Germans began capitulating to become prisoners of war in droves. Quite often, they came with our leaflets, which, as stated in the text, served "as a ticket to become war prisoners." I was lucky. They could have shot me. After all, I had been privy to a dangerous military secret. Colonel Suomalainen was in fact a secret agent. He worked for the Finns, and at night he encoded editorials for the Finnish paper he published. However, he did that on the instructions of the Soviet command. On the surface, he was informing the Finns about our headquarters' military plans, but in reality he was misinforming them, and they believed him. Feeding disinformation to the enemy was part of his duty as a secret agent. In essence, he was playing a double agent and doing so for the benefit of the Soviet Army. During the war, it was common to remove those who accidently entered this protected area of work belonging to secret service double agents. They spared me and decided to limit themselves to "banishment" to a division. I wound up in the intelligence section of the staff completely by luck and by the will of General Svirsky. I learned the truth about Suomalainen only after the war, when there was no longer any need to keep it secret. He himself did not hide it. Did Olga Parayeva find out the truth?

Ferenc, Count Batthyány

"You ask him," Colonel Potapov said. "I can't understand what he's blabbering about." He left us. Before me was a young, nice-looking officer in Hungarian uniform who resembled a girl. His epaulettes hung like rags, and his buttons had been torn out. He sat without moving, with his hands on his knees, and carefully glanced at me. He spoke German without an accent but very slowly, choosing his words. That was strange. Prisoners were not usually very concerned about the form of their answers and tried to quickly find favor with the Soviet officer from whom one could expect anything. My interlocutor had been brought up well and, most importantly, exhibited an inborn dignity.

The man before me turned out to be Ferenc Batthyány, a descendant from a line of counts that included Hungarian ministers, generals, and scholars. He had been mobilized recently. Earlier, he had been discharged because he had been sick. It had not been his wish to fight on the side of the Germans. Nazi politics disgusted him. He had long sympathized with the Soviet Union. All of his friends were from the left-leaning liberal circle of the intelligentsia. He had waited for conditions to become at least slightly favorable and crossed the front line at night. Russian soldiers seized him, took him for an intelligence agent, and beat him cruelly before delivering him to headquarters (he had a bruise under one eye and an abrasion on his forehead). From the regiment, they sent him to the division, and from there, they handed him to the army—and now he sat before me in army headquarters, in the intelligence department. Nobody had yet had the time to question him. I became his first military investigator. He gave me no reason to doubt him; the story he told seemed truthful. He was a trustworthy deserter. I talked with him for a long time. He knew nothing about military matters. He had spent time on the front at Lake Balaton, but only a few days. He lived in Budapest and talked about the mood in the city. According to him, everyone was waiting for the war to end. They did not like the Germans and would greet the Soviet Army with relief and even joy. The population of the Hungarian capital had become much more fearful than they had been in a long time. People had never been so deathly afraid of bombardment and had never been so ready to pile into shelters together. Why? It was very simple. The end of the war was close, and no one wanted to perish in the last weeks—that would be too absurd.

He had crossed over not due to cowardice. He was not trying to save his own skin. He wanted to help Hungary as much as he could. "I know all the roads in this area," he explained insistently, trying to maintain a dignity that had been damaged because of his torn-off buttons, unshaven state, exhaustion, and hunger. He smelled bad—he was aware of it, as he himself told me later. He was ready to disappear into the ground from shame. He knew the local roads, even the paths in the woods, from his childhood. The family had had property near the lake. He had lived there more than in Budapest. "I could be useful for propaganda, too," he offered, getting ahead of me. "Every Hungarian who knows even a bit of history knows the name Batthyány. You can imagine how convincing it would be for all our people to hear the words 'Ferenc Batthyány.' My example would be followed by many others who cannot agree to act because of a false understanding of honor. I am firmly of the view that a man of honor cannot fight for Hitler and Himmler." Later, he told me in detail about his relative, Lajos Batthyány, who had led the first Hungarian government during the 1848 Revolution, who had fought for the independence of Hungary from Austria, who had been arrested by the victorious Austrians, and who had been executed by shooting in Pest in 1849 following the military field court's sentence. He had been just over forty. Understandably, he became a legendary figure in his country. This was the person from whom Ferenc Batthyány had inherited a sense of honor.

Colonel Potapov, as was expected of the chief of the Soviet information section, blurted out, "He's lying!" He had trouble understanding that a young Hungarian could have civic ideals. It was clear that they had sent him to smell out our plans, memorize our positions, and count our weapons. "You'll see. He'll take off and go back."

"But we can expect to get real help from him!"

"Nonsense!" Potapov said, in fact using stronger language. "As for the roads, we'll figure them out ourselves!"

I tried for a long time to convince the vigilant colonel that Batthyány was essential to us. First of all, his name would be irreplaceable for propaganda among the Hungarian population. Second, I did not speak Hungarian and neither did Kotlyar, yet we would have quite a few Hungarian prisoners. Kotlyar and I would only be able to interrogate them with the help of Batthyány, who spoke German. Third, he was not a prisoner but a deserter. What reason did we have not to believe him? Potapov waved it all aside. As for the propaganda, let the politicians of the Seventh Directorate worry about that. It had nothing to do with us. "I will not let him be a translator. How can you be sure that he will not trick you?"

I had difficulty convincing Potapov; he hated me. Suffice it to say that our boss was after the attractive Musya Kotlyar, the second translator at headquarters, who had clearly rejected him, while I was considered by Potapov (not without some reason) to be a successful rival. He did not abuse his power (we were to him grateful for that), and he tried in any way he could to humiliate me in front of her. Once, having invited both of us to his office at the usual fireworks in celebration of our victories, he asked me to translate the content of some document that had been captured and, interrupting me, said, "Drink up, then tell us." I gulped down my drink and tried to say something but couldn't—my voice was gone. It turns out the glass had been filled with pure alcohol, which had burned my throat. Potapov laughed triumphantly, glancing at Musya. She didn't smile. Was he able to feel sympathy for me? To him, I was—as he liked to say it—an "overeducated sissy."

Still, Ferenc Batthyány was allowed to remain my assistant. In the housekeeping section I found a soldier's shirt, trousers, and an overcoat that was well-worn but still in a good condition. The count washed and shaved, and on the third day, he seemed revived. He ate in the officers' mess hall and came to have the same rights as the rest of us. He really became my translator when questioning Hungarian soldiers. You had to see their faces when they learned who was speaking to them. Count Batthyány? Could it be that this fellow in the Soviet shirt bore the most famous name in the country? A Frenchman would probably have experienced a similar shock if he had seen the Duke of Orléans or General Bonaparte in similar circumstances.

Count Batthyány was not only amused by the reaction of his compatriots; he constantly felt his responsibility toward them and, perhaps, toward history. He spoke with each at length, without my involvement, and did not so much question them as attempt to convince them. He told them in private the same things that he had said over the radio and in leaflets. By continuing to support Hitler, Hungary was shaming itself. The Soviet Union was defending justice, and France, England, and America—all the democracies of the world—were fighting alongside it for humanitarian ideals. Do not believe the fascists' lies about the Soviets mishandling their prisoners. I, Ferenc Batthyány, can attest to the fact that justice and humanity are important ideals among the Russians here. By becoming prisoners, he told the soldiers who were still fighting, you will free yourselves from the terrible responsibility for Hitler's crimes. You will save your health and your lives, which postwar Hungary and your families need so much . . . This was incredibly valuable, particularly since the war in Hungary was coming to an end and you could count on the enemy's being reasonable. What Batthyány did led to visible results. The number of prisoners grew. Most of them alluded to the arguments that they had heard over the radio or read in the leaflets. The name Batthyány had a magical impact.

We lived in the same house and often talked in the evenings. He trusted me and was deeply grateful, yet he never tired of being surprised at our customs, which were foreign to him. Can you really drink so much wine, and vodka especially? Can you really live in such a way that you never—really never!—need to lie down sprawled over a couch, relax, or take a nap? He was astounded by our tirelessness, our inability to have a rest, even when there was an opportunity, or by our ability to stay calm with regard to danger. He observed all of this constantly, and he liked all of it. Overall, he continued to believe in the generous spirit and dignity of Russians and in the fairness of our society and even the system.

About two weeks passed. Once, in the evening, he told me what was tormenting him constantly. When he was preparing for his escape, he had buried a Batthyány family watch given to him as the last member of his generation, in the ground in the woods. The watch had been handed down from generation to generation. It bore engravings of the count's coat of arms and the name of his great-grandfather, its first owner. He would be able to find the tree where the watch was buried without difficulty. It would be easy to get to it now, as the place stayed in the rear of the advancing Red Army. He asked to be given a car for an hour or two—it was so important for the whole family! In the morning, I presented this request to Colonel Potapov. "What? Have you gone mad?" He answered. "A car, to this scoundrel? I told you, he'll take off to join his people. He'll tell you anything! Does he think I'm an idiot?" I knew Potapov; I knew all the important Soviet officials, civilian and military. They were all the same. But this time, Potapov surprised me with his inhumanity. Ferenc worked sometimes at night with us and for us, honestly, even selflessly. His request could be fulfilled easily, and it was so understandable! I tried to talk about postwar Hungary.

"We really need to have loyal friends there! After all, he is Batthyány. He might become the minister of foreign affairs. He will come to Moscow and say that he will never forget Colonel Potapov who . . ."

"Who sent him—do you know where?" the colonel said, and this lengthy dialogue concluded with that short word without which Potapov was unable to speak.

Something had to be said to Ferenc. I was not sure what. Should I tell him about my conversation with Potapov? To my surprise, a sense of patriotism came over me, a feeling that had been reinforced in every one of us during the war years. I definitely did not want to present our army and our commanders to him in a bad light. How could one understand Potapov's refusal? I myself could not explain it sensibly. Was it cowardice? Vulgarity? Indifference? Sadism? Animosity to all who spoke a different language? Class hatred? Racism? Probably all the above, which he expressed with one phrase: "Oh fuck off." Count Batthyány wanted to believe in Russian generosity, and I valued his naive illusion. I put together something incomprehensible: The driver was sick, so as soon as he gets well. . . . We will go together. I would like to take part in this event. Yes, and it was dangerous. I was afraid to let him go without me. . . . He appeared to believe, and I was ashamed. Each time now, I felt ashamed when we were alone together.

But this didn't last long. A few days later, I was saved by the order regarding the redeployment of the Twenty-Sixth Army's headquarters from Sárszentmiklós to the Austrian town of Bruck an der Mur. The operations in Hungary were behind us. Ferenc Battháyny was no longer needed, and they placed him in the group of POWs being sent to the rear, to a camp. I found out about this the night before it happened. "What, by foot?"

"They'll get there, don't worry," they told me at headquarters. "They all get there."

But I knew that Ferenc did not have shoes: all the army shoes were too large. His feet were small, delicate, like a young woman's feet. At headquarters, he was able to move around. But walking several hundred kilometers? That was certain death. I managed another conversation with Potapov, and again, he finished with the same: "Fuck off." All I could do was accept the inevitable and get footcloths for him.

The next morning, Count Batthyány wrapped his feet awkwardly, taking a long time. He understood what lay ahead. He also understood that they were treating him inhumanely. He no longer spoke of his family clock. Obviously, he was more perceptive than I had imagined. Before his departure, he said to me, "If you happen to get to Budapest, find my wife. Her maiden name is Esterházy. She lives in her parents' house. (He gave me the address; I believe it was on Esterházy Street.) Tell her about me, about how we worked together, how I wanted to help them, and what came of it. Tell her that I will not forget her and our loved ones. . . . But will I return? Will I make it? I am afraid that I will not. But don't tell her that."

We embraced. He left. And I went to Bruck an der Mur. It so happened that two or three weeks later, I was in Budapest—this trip had occurred suddenly. I took off to the address given me by Ferenc. I found the home without difficulty; it was quite a prominent mansion. In the courtyard, a woman with a bucket met me. I asked—in German—where I could find Mrs. Batthyány-Esterházy.

She looked me over nervously and said, "I don't know. I don't know."

"Excuse me," I insisted. "Excuse me, madam [*gnädige Frau*], I have to return to my unit shortly. I would like to tell her about her husband. I parted with him just recently."

She set down the bucket and said, "Let's go," and almost ran ahead. Following her, I entered the living room. Then she demanded, "Tell me."

I told her in detail, withholding almost nothing. I only kept quiet about the family watch and about how Ferenc went without footwear on the march. She ran her fingers over something, maybe a rosary—I would remember this gesture forever. I also remembered her question: "Do you think he'll live? Will he come back?" I assured her: certainly.

After the war, I tried several times to find out about him, or her, or about the family. It was in vain. No one would help me. Did Ferenc Batthyány reach the camp? Did this young woman, who had been fingering the rosary beads, get to see his return? More than once, I remembered him, his fate in the bloody days of the Hungarian uprising of 1956. I knew that this uprising had been provoked by the Potapovs. They had overcome

Hitler's fascism, but still, they resolved all of life's other difficulties with the motto "Fuck you."

In 1996, I became a stipend recipient of the Berlin Research Center (Wissenschaftskolleg zu Berlin). Once, I happened to dine at the same table with a young Hungarian writer, Péter Esterházy. I knew his prose. We had published something in *Vsemirnoe Slovo*, a St. Petersburg version of the international journal *Lettre Internationale*. I told Péter the above story of Ferenc Batthyány and, almost as a joke, asked if he happened to be a relative of his wife, Madam Esterházy. Péter answered, "Wait a few days, and I'll explain." A week later, he brought me a note with the address. "Amazing thing, she turned out to be my aunt! Her husband is alive but very ill."

I wrote a letter immediately. I hoped Ferenc had not forgotten me. We had experienced a lot together. Finally, I was able to track him down. The answer came immediately from Baden bei Wien, but it was she who wrote. Ferenc could not reply. He had had Alzheimer's disease for a while and could not remember anything, neither from long ago nor from more recently. "Do I remember you? Every word that you said about Ferenc, I can repeat now, more than fifty years later. We often talked about you. Now, I will wait for you. Come."

From October to November 1997, I had to give lectures at the University of Vienna. We arrived, Elke and I, in Vienna. My first phone call was to Baden. A few days later, we found their house, and so it was that I saw Ferenc Batthyány after half a century.

A rosy-cheeked man with a friendly smile appeared at the meeting, greeted us pleasantly, and asked, "Where do you live?"

I answered, "In Paris," and tried to remind him of our friendship at the end of the war. He listened carefully and said,

"A beautiful city, Paris." He had not heard or noticed anything else. About ten minutes later, he repeated, "Where do you live?"

And he did this several more times. I took a close look at his elderly yet childlike features. It was him, yet not him. There was almost nothing left of the former Ferenc Batthyány, although there was a familiar shadow of him on this face, which produced a sense of horror by its combination of a self-satisfied well-being, a good upbringing, and the complete absence of thought. His wife, who introduced herself as Maritta, was a respectable elderly lady who bore no resemblance to that young woman whom I had found in Budapest in 1945. She sat on a small sofa, and above her hung a colorful, poetic portrait of that young wife of the count who had been forced into a camp, who was fingering the beads—yes, that very one. Looking at her now and at her portrait from long ago, you would believe that it was she. Life had not been kind to her, but it had also not disfigured her. She sat Ferenc down at a separate small table, tied a napkin around him, and, placing a can before him, said, "Drink your beer." He drank his nonalcoholic drink, and his wife said, "It isn't easy with him since he can neither read nor watch television. He does not understand. He did not recognize you and will not. He sometimes asks me, where is Maritta. And yet, he used to speak of you so often and so warmly."

And, not bothering with details, she told us about his life after they had sent him from our headquarters to the POW camp in March 1945. Ferenc Batthyány had walked as far as Romania, and then he was sent to Siberia. There, in one of the far-eastern camps, they put him on trial. In August 1950, he was sentenced by the tribunal to be shot, for spying. At the time, as we know, Stalin had done away with the death penalty, and death by firing squad was commuted to twenty-five years imprisonment in a camp for Ferenc. He served five years of his term in a Soviet hard-labor camp. He was sent home in November 1955 together with the German POWs, who were returned by agreement with Adenauer. What had he been sentenced for? What had they accused him of? He did not like to speak about that. It was too sickening to remember the stupidity and awful cruelty of the Chekists who had played the military judges. During the trial, the prosecutor asked, "So, are you in fact a count?"

"Yes, a count."

"Well, tell us in detail how you mistreated the laboring Hungarians, how you exploited the proletarians." "I was not able to mistreat anyone or exploit anyone. I was studying in a university, then I worked for a short time as a lawyer."

"But you are a count?"

"Yes, a count."

"That means you mistreated and exploited others. Tell us!"

The questioning about spying was conducted in the same spirit. "What task did you come to us with, to our military division? Why did you cross the border?"

"I was against the criminal war. I wanted, as much as possible, to help the anti-fascist powers."

"You are lying. We know everything. If you don't confess, you may be shot."

"I have nothing to confess."

A sentence was issued immediately: capital punishment.

"Ferenc came back. That was a miracle. We had lost all hope. We lived for a year in socialist Budapest, where counts were not loved, then the uprising of 1956 came, and we left, abandoning everything. We understood that our family was under threat after the defeat of the Hungarian Revolution. With our lives in danger, we went on foot, along secret paths, and crossed the border. When we ended up on the other side, Ferenc found work as a lawyer in the Ruhr area, and we spent over twenty years there. When the Communist regime collapsed and Hungary became independent, they returned some of what had belonged to us. Both the Batthyány and Esterházy families had owned estates. We were able to buy this house near Vienna."

Is it any wonder that Ferenc Batthyány, who was by now eighty, had become physically and spiritually destroyed as a human being? We should wonder at the endurance of this noble aristocrat. Here are the milestones of his life: fierce battles at Lake Balaton; transfer to captivity; ten years of Soviet concentration camps; persecution as a former count in socialist Hungary; escape over the border; twenty years as an emigrant in Germany. . . . To survive all that, you have to be a titan. Ferenc Batthyány survived, and he broke only at the very end.

Before me is a copy of an official document presented to me by Maritta. It was issued by the head of the Central Archives of the Hungarian Defense Ministry.

Contents: Confirmation of Length of Imprisonment

On the basis of information available to the Command, Dr. Ferenc Batthyány (born 1915) was a prisoner of war from 08.02.1945 to 28.08.1950 and a convicted prisoner in the Soviet Union from 29.01.1950 to 22.11.1955.

The present attestation is issued with the aim of receiving material compensation based on your petition of 06.11.1991

Budapest, 20 April 1992

Signature

(Charady Josef, Lieutenant Colonel)

Ferenc Batthyány did not live to receive any material "compensation" in time. About half a year after our meeting, we received a funeral notice:

> Remember with love
> Ferenc, Count Batthyány
> von Német-Ujvár
> Born 4 October 1915 in Kittsee
> Died 16 June 1998 in Baden

Perhaps Maritta Esterházy-Batthyány will follow my insistent suggestion and write a history of our ruthless century. And I, remembering Ferenc, come back to one and the same thought: They did everything in their power to turn their supporters into irreconcilable opponents and friends into enemies. For what? For nothing!

Ebensee

In March 1995, I received a call from Vienna. A woman's voice asked me whether it was true that I had taken part in the liberation of Ebensee concentration camp fifty years ago. I was indeed in the camp in May 1945. The woman who was calling turned out to be the director of a TV documentary. She invited me to Austria for the filming, which was to mark the fiftieth anniversary.

Once again, I saw what had stunned me there that May long ago: the incredible, divine beauty of the dark-blue lake and the grand rocky mountains above it. There were now comfortable houses surrounded by gardens, with roses flowering and lawnmowers humming. The remnants of the tall concrete gates, rounded off on top, stood only in one place, on the eastern side, I think, of this colorful and tranquil settlement.

"I Remember You"

In the beginning of May 1945, there was a pile of naked bodies to the right of the gate. They seemed to be the corpses of young people. I later realized they were victims of starvation, skeletons enclosed in dry skin. In war, there are some things that you are forced to see. The most terrifying memory was that of a dead soldier who kept being flattened by caterpillar tracks. I will not forget the crunching of bones and the view of flattened flesh. And now—these piles resembling wood, of what were until recently people.... I was no longer a boy. I had turned twenty-seven in February, but I was not prepared for this, even after three years of living in war. Not backing away, I looked and thought about my father dying of hunger in Leningrad, about my brothers and mother who had outlived the terror of the blockade...

The operator moved the camera toward me, and they asked me to share some memories. I told them what I could about what there had been earlier and what had shaken Second Lieutenant Etkind. Several people stood behind the camera, including a small, dashing old man in an Austrian hat with a feather. When I stopped talking and the camera moved off, he came up to me and said, "I remember you." That seemed ridiculous to me: How and what could he remember? Half a century had gone by. The young Soviet officer had grown old with time—and where was he from, my unexpected interlocutor?

The old man with the feather introduced himself: Władysław Żuk, a Pole. He had been in several camps: Auschwitz and Mauthausen, and he was sent to Ebensee, which was officially called the "Cement Labor Camp." The prisoners—there were up to twenty thousand—they broke through the rocky mountain to create tunnels. Weakened by hunger, the people worked in freezing conditions for eleven to twelve hours, prodded by guards. Those who fell were trampled with boots and whipped to death. The corpses were thrown into a common pit or burned in a crematorium. ("Want me to show you where it stood?") The head of the camp was Obersturmführer Anton Ganz, a sadist who was always everywhere. He walked with an enormous dog, which he set against the detainees, and when he was drunk, he would shoot his pistol at whomever. "We tried not to catch his eye. He was capable of shooting or slashing your face with a whip, just for fun."

Władysław Żuk stopped talking—we had gone over to the memorial graveyard, where there were monuments to victims from many countries: Poles, Italians, the French, and Hungarians. As for ours, for decades, nobody memorialized them. Stalin considered all prisoners to be traitors. Only when perestroika began did they erect a rusty tower, a memorial to the Soviet soldiers and officers who had perished here. And there, amid the misery, had stood the crematorium. Not a trace of it was left. The camp land was sold off cheaply after the war. Houses in the vicinity were built by people who were not very well-off. The crematorium was taken apart and its stones used for foundations. I saw two monuments with an inscription in Hebrew by the wall of the cemetery. They had started bringing Hungarian Jews here at the very end of the war (I remind you, the Germans annihilated more than six hundred thousand of Hungary's Jews, out of a [total] population of ten million!) and almost all of them perished here.

Władysław Żuk offered to show me the tunnels. I had seen them only from a distance earlier. He opened the massive gates to one of them where there was now a museum. It was some ten meters tall. We walked into it for more than one kilometer. It seemed there were twelve such hallways. The German command gave them a great strategic significance after the Allied aviation began to direct massive bomb attacks systematically at German military centers. There were plans to put factories here in the massive tunnels in Ebensee, to produce "secret weapons," which Hitler's propaganda machine called the V2 (V for *Vergeltungswaffe*, or weapons of vengeance). However, the rockets never went into production. Instead, they installed oil-refining machinery in the tunnels. But they ordered the mountain to be hammered out at maximum speed, so that the trolleys taking out the piles of stones had to run at a high speed. Żuk led me from the damp darkness into the light and fresh air. We again went through the camp gates. Żuk stopped. "Here was the *Appellplatz*, the assembly place." We sat on a bench; he continued.

"Meine Herren! . . ."

"On May 5, they herded everyone who could walk to this place. There were about ten thousand of us, more than six thousand were sick and dying. We lined up as usual by barrack, but a lot happened differently on that day. For example, no one counted us. Lagerführer Anton Ganz had gone up onto some kind of platform. He was surrounded by a chain of SS guys with automatic weapons. That used to happen when they hung some camp inmates during the roll call to frighten the others. This time, they didn't hang anyone. But there were a lot of SS people, and that scared us. What was Ganz up to? Machine guns were aimed at us from towers surrounding the *Appellplatz*. We kept looking at each other. They were capable of anything. Based on messages from supportive informants that had come to us the night before, we knew that the American and Soviet armies were approaching from two sides.

"Finally, Ganz began to speak. Next to him stood Hrvoje Makanović, a young Croat who was translating German texts into several languages. The Lagerführer said hoarsely: 'Meine Herren! Gentlemen!'

Sobbing was heard. We had not heard that form of address for a long time. After all, we were the last remaining scum. And suddenly, 'Meine Herren!' That meant that they were done for.

"In short, it came down to this: It had become known that the Americans were planning to bomb the camp. We have decided to save our prisoners from certain death. We propose moving to the tunnels. There, you will be safe, and we will get provisions . . .

Those who were gathered all shouted in unison, 'Nein!'

"We had heard several days earlier from one of the guards who had treated us with sympathy that they were planning to drive us into the tunnels and blow up the entrances. We would all be doomed to perish in huge graves. And we shouted, 'No!' We yelled in all languages, 'No!'

"It was a decisive moment. We understood that our 'No!' was an open revolt. The camp inmates ceased to be prisoners. We still didn't know how this sudden burst of courageous decisiveness would end. Ganz could give orders to open fire from the towers. They could force us into the tunnels. There were a lot of SS officers, not less than six hundred well-fed, healthy, armed fellows. Could we resist them? Moreover, there were the *Blockälteste*—heads of the barracks, many *kapos*, who were soldiers of the Wehrmacht—by their side. The Lagerführer was not prepared for disobedience; such things did not exist. Several minutes passed. We thought they were endless. Ganz approached a group of SS guys who stood behind him. He consulted about something with them. We couldn't hear them; they were standing some thirty meters from us. Finally, Ganz reluctantly and with difficulty found the words (Makanović translated them slowly). He said that if we did not want to go over to the tunnels, then we didn't have to. 'We thought of saving you. You prefer to die under the bombs? That's up to you. We will not be responsible for the consequences.'

"Everyone breathed a sigh of relief. Ganz ordered us to disperse to the barracks. We understood: he no longer had power. All he could do was pretend that he was still the master. And he left, surrounded by SS officers. And we realized—suddenly, we realized that it was not only he who had left but all of them, forever. And we also realized that we were free.

"Happiness? The word *happiness* does not really express much. The weakest among us fell dead from the sudden emotion. Those who were able to danced. We sang 'The Internationale' and 'The Marseillaise' in multiple languages, and then we started to sing different national anthems: of Italy, Hungary, Poland, Czechoslovakia, Greece, Spain . . . "

Vengeance

Władysław Żuk reluctantly described what happened later, after the celebrations transitioned into slaughter. It was painful to remember. I will tell you briefly, using what he told me along with some eyewitness accounts that I managed to read.

First, scores in the camp were settled with the *Blockälteste*, the head of one of the barracks, the terrifying Ludwig X. He was famous for his sadism and perverse loyalty to orders. If he noticed any stain on the clothes of an inmate, he would whip him with a heavy belt that he always had by his side. Hrvoje Makanović, the translator whom I have already mentioned, told the commission that was conducting the investigation a few months later into "The Camp Cement Case" about the weekly "bath days." Ludwig X had been responsible for them:

> In winter, at temperatures of minus 15 to minus 20 degrees, the inhabitants of the barracks would get undressed completely. All they would have left on were their wooden shoes, and they wrapped themselves up in their thin towels. Under the instruction of the head of the barrack, who was armed with a heavy club and accompanied by fierce helpers, the inmates were to march to the bath house, about eight hundred meters away, in groups of five. All this occurred after a twelve-hour workday,

dinner, and the evening roll call, which lasted not less than an hour, so that they were washing themselves late at night. Then, another hour's wait for their turns in the frost. Then, having washed themselves in the stifling space with intense heat, the majority would wait naked in the snow until all the barrack's residents had lined up. Together, they walked back in a column.

Those who got pneumonia died. If Ludwig saw lice on a prisoner, he would whip him with his heavy belt. The authorities valued the headman's zeal. The *Lagerführer* put him in charge of flogging. By combining jobs, he became an executioner. It is understandable that he was the first to be the subject of the ire of the prisoners. A Czech, Dragomir Barta, the only one who had succeeded in writing a secret diary and who later wrote about the resistance in Ebensee, spoke about this:

> He came to our office and began shouting wildly, protesting that they had removed him from the position of head of the barracks. Talk turned into a fight. Ludwig pulled out a knife and attacked us like a wild animal. We had no weapons and had not expected an attack. Ludwig, in his frenzy, stabbed to the right and left. There was blood everywhere. Almost all of us were wounded. Only after we rallied and armed ourselves with tables, chairs, and anything else that was available did we manage to deal with Ludwig. Finally, we got hold of his knife and threw him out the door. Everyone in the camp hated him. He had caused many people's deaths. A group of prisoners stood in front of the office. Seeing him covered in blood on the ground at the entrance, they understood right away that the situation in the camp had changed and that power had now passed to them. They threw themselves at Ludwig, dragged him to the *Appellplatz* a few meters from our office, and tied him to a pole. Many inmates gathered, about twenty. Everyone wanted to spit in his face. They carved him up, and he hung there for a long time, tied to the pole.

They dealt with the gypsy Hartmann, who had terrorized everyone, in a similar fashion. And with Otto, who had the blood of many victims on his hands. The Spaniards took care of him: they threw him into the stove of the crematorium alive. Many camp leaders who had distinguished themselves by their beastly cruelty were drowned in the reservoir. Altogether, more than sixty camp officials who had tortured others were killed.

Leprous

Władysław Żuk continued his story. The next day, May 6, the American forces entered the camp. The Third Cavalry Squadron (named "cavalry" by tradition; it was a motorized infantry unit).

> We met our liberators with elation, joy, and love. We threw ourselves at the tanks and tried to climb onto them, and we wanted to embrace and kiss the tankmen. . . . The Americans looked with astonishment and fear at the wild, half-naked crowd of monstrously emaciated people, pushed us off the vehicles, tried to pull off the hands that held fast to their shirts, and, pressing down on their gas pedals, increased their speed. I understood later why they took such fright. The Americans didn't know where they had come to and whom they were liberating. They, or most of them, had not received an explanation ahead of time. Looking at us, the soldiers thought they were among lepers. They had heard nothing about German camps. It is understandable that they were horrified when lepers threw themselves at them. The only thing they wanted was to get away quickly from this evil disease.

Here is a fragment of an official American document. It's a report from Third Cavalry Squadron headquarters:

> The 3rd Cavalry Squadron continued its movement in a southerly direction that day at six zero five, encountering no resistance on the part of the enemy. In its path, prisoners of war were again encountered who were occupying large areas of the liberated territory. At one o'clock, the advance detachments reached the settlement of Ebensee and reported that there was a concentration camp in the town. Then, information was received that there were sixteen thousand political prisoners in the camp and that the conditions were terrible. Approximately three hundred people died from hunger and untreated illness every day. The prisoners lived in filth and stench. The fact that they were prepared to eat the dead among them was not surprising. The camp could be compared to Buchenwald or Ohrdruf.

And in an essay on the history of the same military unit (published in 1946 in San Diego), it says:

> On May 6, military detachment A [. . .] was given the task of penetrating the region of the Austrian Alps. It was moving south of the city of

Gmunden along a picturesque, dark-blue lake and came to the city of Ebensee. At the end of the latter, a concentration camp was found, separated from the city by a rushing stream. One cannot describe this camp. Words cannot convey the stench of rotting human flesh and the horror of the conditions in which the hungry human mummies existed. Not one person from the 3rd Cavalry Squadron will forget this concentration camp.

I will return again to Władysław Żuk. Not sparing any details, he told us how quickly the Americans left from this hell that had opened up, from the stinking crowds whom they had mistaken for lepers. He repeated the phrase that had surprised me: "I remember you!" He continued:

> The Americans had already gone, leaving behind authorized personnel, who began to organize hospitals and kitchens. We were discouraged by our liberators' indifference, no, worse, by their squeamishness, and even disgust. And so, after a few days, I saw two Soviet officers come into the camp. They came on foot, past the dead corpses, shook hands with the living, kissed these half-corpses, these lepers. I remember both of you with gratitude and admiration.

Żuk, of course, remembered not me but simply two Soviet soldiers whose behavior had astounded him, by contrast to the frightened Americans. I listened to his excited admission with wonder and—I don't want to hide it—with pride.

In the Camp's "France"

It is time to speak about my own impressions of that day. On May 12 or 13, I, a translator, was called in by the deputy head of army intelligence, Lieutenant Colonel Nikiforovich. He said, "You'll go with me to the German concentration camp. The Allies have informed us that some of our people are there. We will liberate them." The headquarters were situated in Bruck an der Mur, not far from Graz. The trip to Gmunden and its neighboring town of Ebensee was about two hours. We drove the army M-1 along a road of tremendous beauty. At some point mid-journey, we met another vehicle. On it was a tricolor flag. A bearded, middle-aged fellow stepped out of the vehicle, stopped our M-1, and asked in broken German, "Where is the road to Italy?" He was on his way home. These first days were a time of returning. Walking toward us were lines of recent POWs—Frenchmen, Italians, and Soviets. We arrived at Ebensee and entered the territory of the camp through the gate I spoke about earlier. What was stated in the American report was correct. There were no words to convey the horror we saw. I will not repeat it.

There were many Soviets remaining—several thousand. In documents published later, I read that on the day of the camp's liberation, there were 5,346 Poles, 4,258 Soviets, 2,263 Hungarians, and 1,147 Frenchmen in Ebensee. There were almost no Jews there; they had been exterminated first (of the Jews who died in 1944, ninety-four percent came from Hungary, and four percent came from Poland).

Nikiforovich gathered a bunch of Soviet prisoners around him (there were also many civilians who carried signs on their sleeves with the letters *RZA*, for *Russische Zivilarbeiter*) and spoke with them for a long time— about what, I don't remember. I was too shaken by all that I saw. But here's what should not be forgotten: It turned out that the man who had previously been Nikiforovich's superior in the military was among the prisoners. He had been the commander of the company when the future lieutenant colonel had commanded the platoon. Their meeting appeared incredible to us—they themselves shook hands in disbelief. Nikiforovich immediately sat his comrade into our M-1, and, with another three, sent the car to Bruck. They never got there: on the way, they each drank a glass of vodka, which turned out to be methanol. Everyone died; only the driver survived.

A young prisoner in a striped shirt came up to me and asked if I spoke French. "How wonderful!" He shouted. "We invite you to France. There will be a feast to celebrate the liberation [1-é festin de la libération]." To France? I did not understand. What had happened was that immediately after the SS left the camp, the prison population divided itself by country. You could see signs and inscriptions on the camp territory: Italy, Hungary, Poland, France, Luxemburg, USSR, and even Germany. All of Europe was at camp Ebensee. Nikiforovich was busy with our people (there were many Soviets among the sick as well), and I went off to France. Tables were pulled out from the barracks and placed in a large rectangle. The camp inmates gathered outside and inside, lifted up glasses filled with champagne and celebrated their freedom. Iron cups filled with murky water stood in for the champagne, and there were containers with camp soup on the table, but the French being the French, they put on a festive banquet with talent and spirit. On that day in May, I saw real Frenchmen for the first time. Before that, I had come across only French teachers who had become Russian long ago (except for our beloved university instructor, Madeleine Geraldovna Melluppi; in the eyes of her students, she was the epitome of the best of the nation). And then, I became aware of their innate and immutable theatricality. How they believed in their champagne, how with every gulp, they became more intoxicated and happier, how they got louder and friendlier as they sang "Sur le Pont d'Avignon," "Le temps des cerises," the "Marseillaise," "L'Internationale"! In later years, I would frequently remember this amazing spectacle. I have lived for a quarter of a century in France, and I see over and over how important theater is for this country. The French Revolution, the county's National Convention, their public guillotines—were they not theatrical? Or the grand spectacle of the empire (and before that, its Consulate), when the whole French nation played the resurrected Ancient Rome? Even the butcher at any French market guts chicken with true artistic virtuosity.

At the "liberation feast," I was the only observer. Many looked in my direction, smiling amiably, and did not stop thanking me. I was happy and understood that they were giving their thanks for good reason, because in coming to this place, to Austria, the Red Army had left mountains of dead soldiers behind them.

Victory made me drunk. I was proud that we—we, Soviet soldiers—had brought back freedom and life. If I had been able to look into the not so distant future and had seen how the half-starved slaves who had been tortured by the Germans and their own traitors were now surrounding

Nikiforovich; and how my compatriots who had miraculously survived would be transported from a German concentration camp into a Soviet one—if I had been told that they would be sentenced in their fatherland to serving in the camps for the fact that they had been captured by the Germans and served their German hard labor in Ebensee—would I have believed that? But that is actually what happened: they were herded from Ebensee to Kolyma, from one slave camp to another slave camp.

My Pride

On that day in May, I was filled with pride. Now, it is no longer easy to remember my feelings at the time with certainty, but I'm sure that as for most important things I will not be mistaken.

I was proud that I belonged to the Red Army. Ebensee concentration camp was liberated by American tanks, but they arrived in Europe to a done deal. They had disembarked in Normandy a year earlier and moved southward, encountering little resistance. We already knew at the time that the Germans would put up a bitter resistance in the East, while they were preparing to open up a front in the West in order to surrender not to the ruthless Soviet Union but to the USA and the Western democracies, which were capable of compromise.

I was proud that we were freeing the world from a terror that was much more terrible than any plague. It was enough to walk through Ebensee concentration camp, past the decaying wall of the dead, to understand what we rescued humanity from. Did I know about Soviet camps? I knew something. But the euphoria of victory and the happiness of feeling that we were liberators were stronger by far than this vague knowledge, which was being pushed inward.

I felt proud of the fact that in this mixed, multinational camp, people of different nationalities and classes spoke of "Ivan"—that is what they called Vladimir Sergeyevich Sokolov in the camp, the Soviet colonel, the former railway man. They talked about how wise and knowledgeable this giant was, this man who was a head taller than everyone else on the *Appellplatz*, who carried a double load and who shared generously whatever he could or could not. This was the man who became the leader of the armed resistance. No less popular was another Soviet colonel, Yakov Nikitich Starostin (his actual name was Lev Efimovich Manevich). He came to Ebensee from the camp in Melk in the middle of April 1945, and during his three short weeks there, he managed to win the respect of many people (he was one of those very rare Jews who was able to hide his nationality). How could I not feel pride for such compatriots? I remembered both of them later with despair. Could it be that these heroes of the camps' underground movements, these proud anti-fascists, were sent to rot in Stalin's torture chambers?

I was also proud of everything I was told about the part played by Communists in the resistance. The French gave the most frequent and best accounts of this. One-tenth (about 120 people) were involved in the camp's *Résistance*. They waited until they could act, and then they did. At the head of the French groups—which had been isolated from one another as a protective measure for their conspiracy—there were a few Communists, about whom people spoke with sincere admiration. The first was Jean Lafitte, who later became a writer and the author of the novel *Nous retournerons ceurillir les jonquilles* (We will return to pick snowdrops, 1948) and of the memoir of Ebensee concentration camp, *Ceux qui vivent* (Those who live, 1950). The title of this book takes a line from Hugo's poem "Les Châtiment" (Castigations): "Those who live are those who fight" ("Ceux qui vivent, ce sont ceux qui luttent"). The second mentioned was Henri Koch, a sixty-year-old shoemaker and member of the French Communist Party since 1924. Everyone called him "papa Henri" and liked speaking of his selfless generosity and remarkable bravery (the shoemaker's workshop where he repaired prisoners' wooden shoes and the boots of the Germans was a conspirator center for the camp resistance). The third Frenchman who enjoyed everyone's love and gratitude was the doctor René Kenuville, who saved many weak inmates from death and who contributed significantly to creating an "International Camp Resistance Committee," which formed itself as an underground organization in May 1944. Here are a few lines from the diary of Dragomir Barta about the meeting of three leaders of the committee, including himself, René Kenuville, and Hrvoje Makasović in July 1944:

> We are returning from the hospital. Fresh mountain air, a deep impression from our parting. A wonderful symbol of the human relationships among the representatives of various peoples. As a matter of fact, three generations—the doctor, Hrvoje, and I were 64, forty, and 23 years old; different nations—Frenchmen, Croatians, and Czechs; different social backgrounds and different professions, personalities, experiences, and worldviews acquired by each of us. We found a common ground—humanism. In addition, today is exactly July 14, Bastille Day. Meeting with Hrvoje and Vinko Verno in a corner of the garden in front of the barracks at 11 pm. After discussing some business, we spoke about French culture and then about the Soviet Union. I thought about the doctor for a long time, about how fresh he seemed for his age. Fresh in the sense of young. How flexible in his mind was. I cannot stop thinking about the final minutes of our parting.

Yes, I was proud of all that I have recounted. I can say even now, half a century later, that I was proud for good reason. But what has become of all the things that I was so proud of, that we all admired? The victory over Hitlerism took grotesque and ghastly forms. The feeling of freedom was first stifled by the Zhdanov Doctrine in 1946, and then everything else that happened under Soviet despotism. The sense of international solidarity died under the pressure of savage nationalisms. The noble cause of the Communists gave way to their union with the Nazis. The anti-fascist movement degenerated into open fascism. That is how we can sum it up in 1998, at the very end of the twentieth century.

Two Years Later

In 1997, I found myself again in Ebensee. I came by car with my wife. With some difficulty, I found my friend Władysław Żuk. I wanted to know everything about him that I didn't have time to and indeed was unable to learn at our first meeting. Why and how had he remained in Austria, and why did he stay in Ebensee? He told us in quite decent German:

Every so often, a free woman came into the camp to work in the kitchen as a dishwasher. We had exchanged glances from a distance. There was obviously no question that we could meet. After the liberation, many of us wandered through the town, and I, too, walked through the streets, hoping to run into her. And just imagine, I saw her. More than fifty years have passed. We are still together. We have five sons. No, I only have three. Two she had from a previous marriage. Her husband was killed in the war. But all five are my children. We now sometimes travel to Poland. My wife and children learned Polish, and, as you can tell, I manage to speak German. In Ebensee, I try to do everything I can so that people will not forget, but they would like to forget. The old people try not to remember how they had failed to notice the factories of death next to them, how they had convinced themselves that the people walking around in striped clothes were only criminals and murderers. The young don't want to hear about the unpleasant past. They are much more interested in soccer and discos. I have to go against these as well as others. It is hard to play this role. They have called me many times on the phone, threatened to beat me and hang me, called me a traitor, claimed I sold myself to the Jews and Communists. There are quite a few neo-Nazis here. I used to be afraid of them. That's over now. I know that I'm stronger than they are; that we are stronger.

"On the Sly"

> *Creeping stealthily ahead,*
> *Time is killing Mom and Dad.*
>
> —Joseph Brodsky, A Performance, 1988

For about twenty years consecutively, in the 1950s and 1960s, I would visit him without fail in Moscow, at his tiny apartment on the MKhAT Proezd, where I was familiar with every design on the wallpaper and every photograph on the wall. Now in 1971, I came to him again—to his dead body. The coffin stood in the Small Hall of the Central House of Writers. Lena stood frozen by the coffin. With the passage of time, she had grown more like her father. Next to her, some man was crying, covering his face with his hands. Later, I looked at him again. He was marked by wrinkles and had a face exhausted by years and bitterness. "Who is this?" I whispered to Lena. She told me his last name, which meant nothing to me—at first. Then, I remembered.

I arrived at the Belomorsk headquarters of the Karelian front in April 1942. The Seventh Directorate of the Political Administration—they worked on "propaganda among the troops of the enemy" there—was situated in the vicinity of the nineteenth lock of Belomorkanal, in a dirty wooden house, which all those of us who worked there mockingly yet affectionately called the "red barracks." It was mentioned for the first time in a poem by Igor Diakonov, which included this stanza:

> Like a sickness on my mind,
> Desolate North, the land of dark.

I'm unable to leave behind
Those barracks red and stark.

This, however, is a special topic. We are talking about something else right now.

I had spent only a few days in the "red barracks," when one morning, Igor Diakonov called me to the window. A group of prisoners in greasy padded jackets were marching along the street in the direction of the nineteenth lock. Igor pointed one of them out: "You see the one with a black beard? That is Levin, Fyodor Markovich, the critic from Moscow. He was arrested recently."

Major Levin was a literary worker in the editorial department of the newspaper for the front, called *Into the Fight for the Fatherland*, which was situated across the road from the Seventh Directorate. He wrote reports from the war theater, which was actually quite peaceful, as our war focused on positional tactics. Suddenly, Levin disappeared. This occurred not long before I arrived, under mysterious circumstances, as was always the case. Now, we saw him from the window, as he was marching to work with a convoy. Dark rumors were circulating about the reason for his arrest. People were seldom taken from the army, especially from headquarters, and especially political workers. There had been some vague discussion about his friendship with Isaak Babel who had long ago—at the end of the 1930s—been arrested. Levin had actually written enthusiastic reviews about *The Red Cavalry* and *The Odessa Tales*. Other writers categorized as "enemies of the people" were also mentioned: Boris Pilnyak and Bruno Jasieński. Now, was Levin imprisoned because of them? Incidentally, we were aware of the fact that people such as Levin were certainly "repressed" in 1937–38. He had been a Communist since 1920 and had studied at the Institute of Red Professors. He had never doubted the truthfulness of not only Marxist teachings but also of Leninism. In the years of the Great Terror, that was enough to end up in the camps or even to get the death penalty. Levin was lucky; he had survived the Great Purge. Now, with the war underway, *they* were cleaning up. Igor Diakonov and I talked about this and much more as we wandered along the canal in the evenings in the bitter northern winds. ("The hyena is howling," we would say.) Igor felt sorry for Levin. He had become attached to this extraordinary and brilliant teller of tales, this kindhearted man. We had no doubt that Levin had disappeared forever. It had already become well known by then: The authorities do not make mistakes. There are never any mistakes in their work. These mythical assertions applied all the more so to the army's "Special Units," which during the war were known by a frightening name, Smersh, meaning "death to spies." They said that this cannibalistic brevity had been thought up by the Supreme Leader himself. Most likely, that really was the case; it would be like him. Several meanings are contained in that abbreviation. First, inevitable execution; second, immediate procedures without trial; third, someone arrested by the NKVD was by definition a spy. All of this taken together was the foundation of Stalinist justice—and not only during wartime. And so, Levin wound up in the hands of Smersh. In the best-case scenario, they would send him to Vorkuta, where he would perish from beatings or starvation.

In 1942, we knew little, yet we understood enough so that we were in no doubt about the fate awaiting Levin.

A few months later, they sent me to Murmansk from where we, of the Seventh Directorate, broadcast messages by radio to urge German soldiers to give themselves up. I spent the night at Hotel Arctica, which was fragile and shook from any disturbance, even the most distant bombs. At times, we ran five, six times a night into the cellar to wait out attacks by German planes in the unreliable bomb shelters. Still, Hotel Arctica had comfortable rooms. Sheets and warm blankets covered the beds, and there was the fantastic smell of foreign cigarettes everywhere. They were smoked by American and British sailors. During the break between the bombings, I fell asleep. I was awoken by a persistent knocking on the door. It was late at night, so I became frightened. A military man who was not that young stood at the door. He had a major's insignia on his patch, an intelligent face with a wide, humped nose, expressive eyes, and deep wrinkles. He was embarrassed and took a long time to excuse himself. There were no rooms; even the easy chairs were occupied downstairs. He had heard about me earlier and decided to ask to stay with me overnight. Besides the bed, my room had a couch. Then, he introduced himself: It was Fyodor Markovich Levin. He had been freed several days ago. Freed. . . . Well, of course, they'd freed him—he wasn't guilty of anything! He spoke in a deep, rumbling voice, constantly looking up at the ceiling. In those times, we didn't speak openly under ceilings. The probability of microphones, especially in hotels for foreign sailors, was too great. Still, we talked until morning—about literature, our families, and our journalistic work. We discussed the most important topics the next day while walking around Murmansk. Levin was exhausted from the long imprisonment and the work on the canal. His imprisonment and hard labor had lasted for over half a year. They had freed him "for lack of the commission of a crime." He had returned to the editorial department of the newspaper *Fighting for Our Fatherland*, and so he came to Murmansk on a business trip. We established a relationship right away that deepening with time and lasted for thirty years. I was much younger. He immediately called me by name, "Fima." For me, he remained "Fyodor Markovich." As fate would have it, our friendship survived many difficult times.

A few weeks later, already in Belomorsk, Levin told me what he had withheld in Murmansk. He had been arrested on the basis of a denunciation by colleagues in the editorial department—three literary people in Moscow, including the poet Kovalenkov, prose writer Kurochkin, and the critic Goltsev. The denunciation had stated that Levin had carried on defeatist discussions, expressed indignation at the country's lack of preparation for the German attack, criticized the supreme command for a panicked retreat and huge losses in manpower and technical equipment, and expressed a lack of faith in victory. Why had they given such a damning denunciation to the Special Branch? Probably, Levin suggested, they were afraid of each other. Each person who had taken part in those conversations, which everyone had at that time, could feel safe only by signing a denunciation. The three of them preferred this base result to the constant fear of each other. In addition, they were convinced that the victim of their disclosures would not return and that no one would find out about their loyal report.

However, a miracle occurred: Levin returned. To the same rank, the same position, the same newspaper. And he appeared in front of the same three people. Fyodor Markovich said—without any hint of malice, but rather with sadness—how they saw him as having dropped out of the sky. The first to run into him was Aleksandr Kovalenkov, smartly dressed and, as always, confidently brash. He stopped dead in his tracks, then, turning pale, jumped through the closest door. Levin bumped into all three later, in the officers' dining room. They had apparently now prepared to meet the ghost from the other world. They greeted him and began talking as if nothing had happened (how would they have known that he had been shown the denunciation at the hearing?), and he had to reply, feigning ignorance (the investigator had broken the rules, and he could not be thrown under the bus). The painful game lasted for a long time, but in those times, we all led that kind of life. The editorial team of *Fighting for Our Fatherland* became a tiny microcosm of Soviet society where, in accordance with Gleb Semyonov's formula, those who "had been convicted and those who convicted them are all one under the red banner!"

Fyodor Markovich wound up with a reasonable and good-natured investigator, who, from the first inquiry, understood that the man before him was not guilty of anything and that he was no less patriotic than probably he himself. Levin was a victim of his colleagues' cowardly treachery. The investigator decided to do everything in his power to acquit and release Major Levin. After a few months, he succeeded. He called on the detainee for a final conversation. "Fyodor Markovich," he said, handing Levin a sealed envelope. "I can free you today. But I want to set one condition: give me your word that you will open this envelope only in three days, not before." Levin was surprised but gave his word. He returned to the editorial office. He introduced himself to the colonel, the editor of the paper, who looked at him as if he had returned from beyond the grave. The colonel remembered a detail that was characteristic of military life. Major Levin had a canvas belt on and a canvas sword belt over his shoulder. Understandably, leather belts were the main and perhaps even the only sign of a well-groomed front officer. They had been taken away when he was arrested and were not returned.

Three days later, Levin opened the envelope. In it was the report of his son's death. The investigator, who had come to develop a sympathy for Fyodor Markovich over the course of six months, had wanted to give him at least three days of untainted happiness.

After the war, they met in Moscow. Both were inveterate chess players. To maintain a friendship with F. M. Levin was dangerous. He was considered one of the cosmopolitans. In all the newspapers, he was attacked as an enemy of Russian literature. The former investigator ignored the danger and stayed friends with the man whom he had saved in 1942. It was he who was crying at the coffin, covering his face with his hands.

Yes, to be friends with F. M. Levin in those years—from 1948 to 1954—was risky. The campaign against cosmopolitans crushed him with all its might. I remember the editorial in *Literaturnaya Gazeta* titled "On the Sly." Levin, who in fact had for many years thoughtfully followed the development of Soviet literature and in his reviews took note of all the new works, according to the paper had been undermining it "on the sly." One of the greatest accusations against him was his alleged attack on Anton Makarenko. F. M. Levin, who had been one of the first to praise Makarenko's *Pedagogical Poem*, tore apart his unsuccessful book *Flags on the Battlements*. During a writers' meeting, where they branded Levin an "antipatriot" and "cosmopolitan" (that is, a Jew), they shouted to him from the hall, "You're the killer of Makarenko!" Makarenko died in 1939, soon after the discussion on *Flags on the Battlements*, but Levin's review had no connection to his death. Levin was blamed for persecuting Russian writers and for allegedly praising only Jewish writers, such as Babel, that enemy of the people and of socialist realism. Oh, the things that were written in newspapers in those years! Every time I read these vilifications, it seemed unbearable to me; it was heartbreaking. All this was that much harder for F. M. Levin because he continued to be a believer in Communism and a dedicated Leninist. Not long before his death, he wrote in one of his memoirs on Petrograd in 1922–24, "Remembering the past, I do not blame myself. I could not think differently then. For me, it was completely natural to demand that the revolution and the fight for it be not only the foremost but the only subject for writers during those years."

Today, in 1994, such a position may seem absurd, unworthy of an intelligent and honest person. Levin's generation viewed life differently: devotion to the doctrine of abstract socialism—despite its insidious and even monstrous distortions—was for them a matter of honor. In the days of Khrushchev's thaw, Levin was reinstated to the party, and he, already knowing much about transgressions and villainy, considered it a victory of historic justice. Did not the best people of Levin's generation and even those much younger, such as Tvardovsky, react in a similar way to the phenomenon of Khrushchev, to his report at the Twentieth Party Congress, his support for Solzhenitsyn, his order to publish Tvardovsky's poem "Tyorkin in the Other World" in *Izvestiya*? It was not without reason that *Novy Mir* was close to Levin's heart: Solzhenitsyn's stories, which were printed in 1962–63 and, most importantly, *One Day in the Life of Ivan Denisovich* and "Matryona's House," elicited not only his approval but also his enthusiasm. The literary and political movement of the 1960s gave him more hope. But the literary process was now passing him by. Levin appeared more and more archaic and inadequate. Today, his articles and books seem naïve and old. But let us be fair. The simple belief in the inevitable victory of the good carries light in itself.

F. M. Levin was a talented person. His actual gifts, however, lay beyond the boundaries of literature, and here we are talking not only about chess. After being freed, he would come to us, in the Seventh Directorate and, seated at a table, tell us about French and American films he had seen before the war at closed viewings. Later, I became convinced that his stories were often better than the films themselves. During the war, he was in love with a very young girl who worked at headquarters, and quite a few of his poems were dedicated to this girl, the pretty Valya. I carefully keep the notebook where he wrote them down in large and distinct handwriting, which looked as naïve as his worldview. The poems were romantic in an old-fashioned way, but they were imbued with his personality and love. Here is one of them, dated March 22, 1945, and written in the Hungarian town of Szegvár:

> I foresee, once this war is over,
> that you and I will come to part
> at any random hour, even though
> it has been fated from the start.
>
> Still, I'll be overtaken by surprise
> when the inevitable day arrives
> In some German village, in a hut.
> And we'll begin our separate lives.
>
> It will happen in great haste; all in vain,
> wrong, all wrong, no matter what I say,
> and later I'll recall with piercing pain
> we never said goodbye in the right way.
>
> The end. There'll be no future meeting.
> The day has passed. The queen of spades
> was dealt me, just as fate was dealing
> the cards by its fortune-teller's hand.
>
> I smile awkwardly and wave goodbye
> for one last time, and stand there bereft,
> as you disappear, you move away—
> and nothing—nothing's left.
>
> Your image slowly fades away,
> Your voice grows faint, the words you said
> are lost, and night, like ocean's waves,
> descends and closes on my head.

This wartime love was a great and painful passion for Levin, and not only because it was unrequited but also because he continued to love another woman, another Valentine, who was waiting for him in Moscow. He was tormented by what he wrote in the poems addressed to her in the same year, 1945:

> The letter speaks to me in a familiar way
> but still it's deaf and mute.
> Separation covers the past like clay,
> like ashes, like the dead sand.
>
> Reach me! Even if in a dream!
> I'm summoning up spirits, high and low.
> Love, will you return? Life, will you come back?
> I don't know, I don't know, I don't know . . .

He was a courageous person. That revealed itself in the war, when he walked calmly from one company to another at the front; and in postwar times, when his recent comrades shouted to him at meetings that he was Makarenko's killer; and in the last weeks and days of his life, when, knowing that he was dying, he said goodbye in poems written with a trembling hand:

> You often came to see me off
> and bitter was our separation
> but this time my departure
> is from no ordinary station.
>
> As I leave for my final destination
> Not from the Kursk or Yaroslav station,
> It is you, my only love, I am asking
> To scatter Russian soil on my casket.
>
> You came to meet me many times,
> this once you will not wait for me,
> The time has finally arrived
> to sail away from the last quay.
>
> A stranger among strangers,
> Unguarded by me, and all alone,

"On the Sly"

you'll find living hard, as if
cast into water like a stone.

We'll never see each other again . . .
We do not buy religion's lure . . .
But may the past light up your way
and give you strength enough to endure.

How We Lived

There was a knock on my door. I peeked out from behind the curtain that separated our sink at the end of the hallway and called out, "I'll finish shaving and come. . . . Sorry!" The institute hallway was half dark. I stuck out my soapy face once more and was able to see this time: a military man with blue epaulettes stood at my door. "Just a moment!" I repeated, realizing that my life was over.

"Keep shaving, I'll wait . . ." said the soldier and sat down on the windowsill.

It was 1951. The Russian intelligentsia was swamped by a new wave of terror. At the center of attention were Jews this time. Everywhere, they were hounded and called "undocumented drifters," rootless cosmopolitans, antipatriots—all these invectives served as synonyms for "kike." Many were arrested, with the main accusation being "bourgeois nationalism." No one was surprised by the terms of imprisonment to which the court sentenced them—ten or twenty-five years. My friends went off to the camps: Akhill Levinton for ten years, Ilya Serman for twenty-five, his wife Ruf Zevina for ten. Our teacher and a man who was close to us, Grigory Alexandrovich Gukovsky, died in prison while under investigation (we received concrete information about this, not just rumors). His brother Matvei, a historian, was in prison. I was constantly on the alert for *them* to come with an order to conduct a search and to arrest me—but it was only at home, in Leningrad, that I prepared myself for their arrival. Here, in faraway Tula, my vigilance had slipped. I thought we were safe in a provincial pedagogical institute. I was mistaken. There, by the door, my fate was awaiting me.

It was embodied by a boy with shoulder straps. Twenty-five years in the camps—that was a death sentence. We could not count on an amnesty, much less on the fall of the Soviet regime to save us.

Behind the curtain at the end of the hallway, there was not only a sink but also the door to the room occupied by Alexander Petrovich Kazhdan, my closest colleague and friend in Tula. The door was not locked. I considered that fortunate. Sitting at the table, I jotted down farewell notes to my wife and mother: "My dears, you know yourselves what you have to do. Take care of our daughters. Perhaps, if I ever return, they'll recognize me. Masha's already big—she's five. I'll try to keep her father alive." I told my wife to take our daughters and immediately go to a faraway village. Only then would they be able to survive. "Leave everything—the books, the furniture—save yourself and the children." I tried to console my mother as much as I could: she still had two sons, and she had a grandson, Grisha, whom she loved dearly. I also wrote a few words to Kazhdan. "Farewell, maybe at some point . . ." I put all this under his pillow. Then, I cleaned the last of the soap from my face and, trying to appear brave and calm, approached the door. The State Security lieutenant rose to meet me. I unlocked my door with the key and opened it wide. "Come in." He let me go in first, stepped over the threshold, and slowed down.

"Please excuse me for bothering you at home," he said. "I'm an extension student. I have to leave today . . ."

I could have died right there, at the entrance to my room—the shift from death to life was too sudden. But I didn't die. I asked him, as if nothing had happened:

"You want to take the exam today?"

"Yes, yes, today. I have to leave. I'm prepared. I've read everything."

I told him we could do it in an hour, in one of the auditoriums on the third floor. I had just been doomed to be a victim, handed over to a boy with epaulettes. Now, it was I who had power over him. I was not yet camp scum but an associate professor, and he was a lieutenant of security services who was standing in front of me, timid and stammering. No, I did not take the agony that I had suffered during those ten minutes on the other side of the curtain out on him. After listening patiently to his answer, I gave him a four and went out to walk on the streets of Tula. I inhaled deeply and delighted in my freedom.

"The Blond Hidden in a Bottle"

It had been reported to the director of Tula's Pedagogical Institute that Professor Chemodanov was never sober when appearing before his students. Bogdanov became concerned. He knew perfectly well that he was in a dangerous position himself, that the minister of education could recall him to Moscow any day and remove him from his job.

The country was in a frenzy: the party was advancing against the cosmopolitans. They were being chased out of universities, research and pedagogical institutes, publishing houses, and libraries by the thousands. Director Bogdanov was well aware of what was going on behind this campaign: an operation was under way to clean out elements that were ethnically different, in other words, Jews, who comprised a significant percentage of the Russian intelligentsia. Cosmopolitans, as *Pravda* explained—along with other papers, which followed its lead—were antipatriots, people who lacked national roots, and who were therefore incapable of experiencing pride in the fact that Popov invented the radio and Yablochkov the electric lamp. The antipatriots were maliciously replacing Popov with the Italian imposter Marconi and Yablochkov with the American scoundrel Edison. They felt threatened by Russians being in first place. They mocked and dismissed the idea. "Russia is the fatherland of elephants"—that's how they laughed at the party's call for people not to forget that the sciences, technology, art, politics, and military matters were a matter of priority for every Russian.

The anticosmopolitan campaign had reached its almost implausible climax by the end of 1949, when the Leader and Teacher of advanced mankind, the greatest Commander of all times and all peoples, the Strategist of international Communism, celebrated his seventieth birthday. On this great day, December 21, I was called to the office of the director of the Leningrad Institute of Foreign Languages and was told that I was fired from the position of associate professor "for mistakes of a cosmopolitan nature." What these mistakes were, I had no idea. It appeared that I had said somewhere that *A Story of a Real Man* by Boris Polevoy was similar to stories by Jack London. For a charge of cosmopolitanism, this was enough. I was "worked over" at an open party meeting and dismissed from the institute. I sustained myself for a while by writing dissertations for barely literate party peons, producing them, as they said then, using "the client's material." The work was disgusting but not complicated. Only once did I encounter difficulties, when I had to write two dissertations on the same subject: "Criticism and Self-Criticism: Driving Incentives in Soviet Society." It was difficult to write the same thing twice in different ways. For one client, I openly confessed what my difficulties were and took a larger payment from him—he paid without grumbling. These scoundrels, becoming social science PhDs, quickly rose up the professional ladder. After paying the specified sum to "the negro" (that is, the Jew), they quickly forgot about him. And the poor cosmopolitan could barely make ends meet. I will note parenthetically that I was present at the defense of my clients a couple of time. They were not at all embarrassed in answering the examiner's questions with quotes from my text. Once, after such a defense, I was even invited to a banquet. Out of a sick curiosity, I stopped by the restaurant Quisisana, discovered about two dozen drunken goons there, and then fled to avoid temptation: I was afraid of what I might say if I got drunk.

  I contacted many pedagogical institutes looking for work. Short rejections came from everywhere. Suddenly, a letter came from Tula, inviting me to come for a meeting and discussion with the director Comrade Bogdanov. It was totally unexpected and unusually attractive. Ancient Tula, two hundred kilometers from Moscow—many trains going from Moscow to the south stopped there, close to Tolstoy's Yasnaya Polyana. I went right away. A. M. Bogdanov received me with respect, even friendliness, and he gave the order that very day to hire me for the position of associate professor, to teach courses on Western European literature. I was given a room in the institute's dormitory on the fourth floor of the building, next to the beautiful Tula Kremlin. A week later, I went back, this time to reside there permanently.

Many instructors lived on the fourth floor, and I soon came into contact with some of them. Among them were the Byzantine historian Kazhdan, Western historian Shusterman, and literary specialist Eventov. They, too, had been kicked out on accusations of cosmopolitism, and they had been hired by Bodganov. At times, when we got together in the evenings, we would be astonished by the bravery of the Tula director. Evidently, he was one of those few rare people in those times who would risk their own well-being for the sake of the flourishing of the matter that had been placed in their care.

Needless to say, Bogdanov did take a big risk. By accepting disgraced Jews to work for him, he had improved the institute but made enemies. Tula party members, who up until then had been thriving in an environment of provincial ignorance, felt offended. The recent cosmopolitans, without themselves wanting to, had pushed them to the back. The new associate professors were the authors of books and articles, had knowledge of foreign languages and experience of research and teaching at the university level. Many were well known, and not only in Russia. It was understandable that the Tula swindlers could not stand us. And in public they called the hated Bogdanov an opportunist "on the leash" of the antipatriots.

Bogdanov, for all his bravery, realized that trouble was brewing. His detractors were just waiting for any excuse to start a party case against him. Chemodanov's behavior could become one such convenient reason. They could say that the director encouraged poor behavior by allowing an alcoholic to behave disrespectfully in front of the students. Yes, and they were all the same. Our director's favorites were transgressors of socialist morals and preachers of bourgeois amorality.

First of all, Bogdanov needed to ascertain whether the accusations were justified. Did Chemodanov come into the auditorium while drunk? Bogdanov went to the next lecture on the introduction to linguistics himself.

The large hall was full. Chemodanov's lectures were aimed at first-year humanities students, but the director also saw biologists, physicists, and mathematicians among those present. He found a seat in the back. No one really noticed him. As usual, it was noisy, with students shouting to each other. Some five minutes after the bell rang, Chemodanov came in, held up by two boys. He walked on crutches—the consequences of suffering polio during his childhood. Yet one could not fail to notice that he was drunk. When he'd clambered up to the lectern, he dropped his head onto it. After straightening himself up with some difficulty, he started speaking. His speech, at first incoherent and unintelligible, became more and more confident and solid, He did not have any paper in front of him. Bogdanov had never seen anything like it. The speaker was looking into the hall and improvising, but it seemed as if he was reading an unseen screen. His elucidation of linguistic concepts was marked by precision and elegance. Moreover, his descriptions moved from one to another with perfect logic, forming a well-ordered concept. Bogdanov could not recover from his astonishment. The only thing you could hear in the huge hall, which was filled to the brim with attendees, was the sound of pen on paper.

In that year, in 1951, one could not speak of linguistics without mentioning Stalin's articles—they had recently been published and were called the "work of a genius on linguistics." Not mentioning them could cause a scandal. Bogdanov, fascinated by the lecture, was trembling with anticipation: Would they not go through the standard ritual? That would threaten the director with a party case . . .

Chemodanov lectured until the bell rang without mentioning the luminary of linguistics: ritual was unimportant to him. (Subsequently, he told us Bogdanov had asked him to come speak with him and had quietly insisted that he follow the rules of the game for the sake of the safety of the institute. And in a lecture soon after, Chemodanov brought in some quotes from Stalin. He was able to do it without denigrating himself and his audience. Bogdanov was delighted.) When the lecture ended, Chemodanov, with the help of the same boys, came down from the lectern and remained standing for a long time, leaning on his crutches as he answered questions.

Bogdanov didn't skip a single lecture by Chemodanov. Now the accusations could become even more threatening. Not only did the director know about the alcoholic's disgraceful behavior, he was also encouraging it with his presence. But his fascination with Chemodanov's lectures on the introduction to linguistics was stronger than his fear of informers.

I became close to Alexander Alexandrovich Chemodanov in my first few weeks in Tula. His room was on the fourth floor, the same as mine. I occasionally stopped by his place. It was a difficult experience. It became harder and harder to breathe—he would light one Belomorkanal cigarette after another, and he collected the cigarette butts on the table in the middle of the room so that they formed a tall pyramid. Did he eat anything? I don't know. At times, early in the morning, I would observe Chemodanov approaching the beer stall, which would have just opened. Leaning on his crutches, he would say, "One hundred fifty with a chaser." That is, vodka and a tumbler of beer. He would stand by the stall for a long time, then drag himself to the lecture. He taught four hours a week, two different courses. The entire rest of the time he would smoke, looking into the distance, and compose his next lecture.

With me he was open. He told me about his family, which had remained in Gorky ("relationships are difficult, one can understand my wife") and talked about the only woman he had ever loved. I hope that Nina Yakovlevna Diakonova will not blame me if I mention her name. Understanding the hopelessness of this love, Chemodanov spoke of her with tears of despair. English philology, which was his specialty, interested him, but he did not try to write or to get published. His whole creative energy went into his lectures. He was a genius of a lecturer; I've never met anyone like him. Perhaps, if at some point his students' notes are found, a book on what he said can be written. He built his lectures like an architectural construction. He added turns and transitions, asides and silences. A lecture was for him an end in itself, not something intermediate, as it was for many of us. If lecturing were an art form, he was a classic of this art. He understood that he was like an ice sculptor. The statue would melt, only a puddle would remain. What about it? He did not aspire to anything else. At times, he spoke about theater: the performance, too, would disappear forever only the audience's enthusiastic exclamations and the critics' vain attempts to make a concrete written record of the mise-en-scènes would remain.

We often spoke about these "statues of ice." I urged him to write down his findings, to record them more concretely—even just for himself, so that he wouldn't have to begin the following year from scratch. He would get angry. I won't become an ordinary craftsman, he'd say. I'd rather stitch shoes together than repeat myself every year! The meaning of creation was to create something anew each time! Otherwise, it would be better to drop it all and throw it all away. This motive of self-destruction came back from time to time, but I didn't take it too seriously.

Only later did I begin to understand the tragedy of his worldview. Our evening conversations were at times interrupted because, in the middle of our talks, he'd suddenly fall asleep, or drop a lit cigarette on a pile of newspapers, or sway on a foot stool and lose his balance. He spoke without regard for the person he was speaking to, looking into the corner and speaking in broken sentences but insistently, like a maniac. He was particularly tormented by the thought of the tyranny of collective ideas. "Can't you see, Etkind?" (He called me by my last name.) "Can't you see that the world is governed by madness? In the past years, they demanded that I teach students about Marr's primal elements. Do you remember them? Sal, yon, ber, and rosh. Well, Marr was crazy, what's that got to do with me? Now they require me to repeat other absurdities. . . . You know, Bogdanov called me in and asked me not to undermine the institute. . . . I don't care. I'll cite the luminary, but can you live that way? Everybody believed that Marr was a genius; now they believe that Marr is an idiot. . . . Yet they believe that the luminary . . . ah, why bother! You're a cosmopolitan, Etkind, and I'm a cosmopolitan, too . . . and everyone's repeating it, everyone's talking nonsense. Well, I don't care what they're saying. What frightens me is that they do it together in unison. Today they shout one thing, tomorrow they'll shout another. Yesterday for Marr, today against Marr. Let them shout. Why do I have to shout with them?" I'm citing this monologue using notes from that time. I only cleaned it of words that the linguist Chemodanov would call "expressive lexicon." He filled in his pauses and garnished them liberally with this vocabulary.

I traveled to Moscow from Tula often and left Chemodanov to our mutual friends. More recently, after his lectures in Oryol and Kursk, a young woman showed up. Every now and then, she'd come, feed him, air out his den, and throw out the pyramids of cigarette butts. This meant that she had a huge influence on him. We weren't even allowed to talk about this. The next time, returning to Tula, I found the fourth floor empty. I stopped at Chemodanov's. His room was cleaner than usual. The pyramid had disappeared, the room had been aired out, but there was some sweet smell there. The neighbor saw me and, in tears, told me that, the night before, that same woman had found a dead body upon opening the door. He had strangled himself, seated, by tying a rope to the heating unit. On the table lay a note addressed to me. I read it:

> Why, Etkind, hush! At our age,
> love takes second place
> to vodka! And Lethe's pace
> has cooled desires and cured the rage.
>
> A bottle shimmers, fanciful
> Like a hundred-carat diamond.
> And hidden in the bottle, a blonde
> is a hundred times more beautiful
>
> than any living one. Eschew
> lovers and friends in drunken piety.

What?! You're bumbling of sobriety?
Why, Etkind, Etkind! Shame on you!

I was told later that if there had been a sip of vodka that night, he would have still been alive. I don't think so.

I soon succeeded in getting transferred back to Leningrad. From time to time I would come to Tula. There were always flowers on Chemodanov's grave. His students did not forget him. Since then, more than forty years have passed. Do the students from those lectures still remember him, the students for whom he lived?

Triumph of Spirit

When the clapping quieted down, a female voice shouted, "Author!" There was laughter at the other end of the auditorium. It was not difficult to guess why: Byron's *Don Juan* was on. Yet the audience understood the meaning of the exclamation, and others supported it: "Author!" Nikolai Pavlovich Akimov, having come out onto the stage with his actors, once more shook the hand of Voropayev, who had played the title role, and stepped forward to the lights. A woman in a long black dress that looked like a monk's garment rose to meet him. She sat in the front row and now, responding to Akimov's gesture, came up to him onto the stage. Stooped, hopelessly tired, she was looking uneasily off to the side. The applause grew stronger. Several members of the audience stood up, followed by the whole orchestra section. They applauded as they stood. Suddenly, silence fell. The audience saw that the woman in black swayed and started to droop. If Akimov had not caught her, she would have fallen. They carried her off—she'd had a heart attack. Did the audience members, who had been invited to the dress rehearsal of Akimov's performance of *Don Juan*, figure out the play's origin? Was the call "Author!" just a spontaneous emotional response, or did the person who had called out this significant word know the story I'm about to tell?

Tatyana Grigorievna Gnedich, the great-great-grandniece of the translator of the *Iliad*, started a graduate course in the department of philology at Leningrad University (it was then called LIFLI) in the early 1930s. She concentrated on English literature of the seventeenth century. Times were difficult. Now and then, there were cleanup operations. "Enemies" were driven out of the university: yesterday the formalists, today the vulgar sociologists, and always the nobility, the bourgeois intelligentsia, draft dodgers, and imaginary Trotskyites. Tatyana Gnedich, engrossed in the works of Elizabethan poets, didn't notice anything around her. She was, however, brought back to reality at some meeting where she was accused of hiding her background as a member of the nobility. She was, of course, not present at the meeting, but upon finding out about it, she was sincerely bewildered. Could she hide her nobility? After all, her last name was Gnedich. Since before Pushkin's time, it was well known that the Gnediches were of noble heritage. And now, she was being dropped from the university for "showing off her background as a member of the nobility."

That was how the party leadership acted in those times: reality was clearly absurd. The only weapon in the hands of its victims—who were essentially helpless—was precisely this absurdity. It could destroy you, or it could, if you were lucky, save you. Tatyana Gnedich was somehow able to show that these two accusations cancelled each other out. She had neither hidden the fact nor showed it off. She was reinstated. She taught, translated the work of English poets, wrote poems in the Acmeist style, and tried to translate the work of Russian poets into English.

We lived in the same house. It was a famous building of "private apartments" in Petersburg, then Petrograd and Leningrad, at No. seventy-three/seventy-five Kamennoostrovsky Avenue (later called Kirovsky Avenue). This huge building, which had granite façades and towered over the Islands, housed well-known Russian cultural figures. They included the historian S. F. Platonov, the literary critic V. A. Desnitsky, and the poet and translator M. L. Lozinsky. I was born in this house—my father owned apartment No. 2, and I returned to live there again. Having just gotten married, we managed to get a room belonging to my young wife's stepfather in a large communal apartment. Tatyana Grigorievna Gnedich lived with her mother in an even more communal apartment along another staircase, with a room that smelled of mothballs and, I think, lavender. It was piled high with books and ancient photographs and filled with dilapidated furniture covered by small handmade rugs. I would go there to work on English with Tatyana Grigorievna, and in exchange I'd read French poems with her, which, by the way, she understood very well without my help.

The war started. I graduated from the university. My wife and I left for the city of Kirov, and I went with the army to the Karelian front. Regarding T. G. Gnedich, we knew that she and her mother had moved into a small wooden house on Kamenny Island before the war. Later, we learned that her mother had died during the blockade, and the house had burned down. Tatyana Grigorievna herself (according to Andrey Venediktovich Fyodorov) was mobilized in July 1942 to serve as a translator in the special editorial section of the Seventh Directorate at the Political Administration of the Leningrad front. However, she knew German only passively, so she was transferred to the Baltic Navy Intelligence Unit. We at the front sometimes received letters from her and often poems. But then she disappeared. She disappeared for a long time.

There was no news from or about her. I tried to get some, but Tatyana Gnedich seemed to have vanished from the face of the earth.

After the war, my wife and I came back to the same apartment in the building at No. 73/75. No former inhabitants remained; almost all of them had died during the blockade. Only on rare occasions did we meet ladies of the old regime, ladies in hats with veils who had survived by some miracle. Once—this occurred, I think, in 1948—someone came to us from apartment No. 24. Lozinsky asked me to stop by. Something like this seldom happened, so I ran. Mikhail Leonidovich sat me down next to him on a couch and, trying to keep his voice low, rasped, "They sent me a manuscript by Tatyana Grigorievna Gnedich from the Big House. Do you remember her?"

"From the Big House? From Liteyny? From the GB?" (Lozinsky, remembering the previous names of this organization, would use either the Cheka or GPU.) "What's going on? What do they want from you?"

"This," Lozinsky continued, "is a translation of Byron's poem *Don Juan*. The complete translation. Do you understand? Complete. In octaves, magnificent, classic octaves. All 17,000 lines. A huge volume of first-class poetry. And do you know why they sent it? For a review. They need my review of the translation of Byron's *Don Juan*. How are we to understand this?"

I was no less astounded than Lozinsky, possibly more, even. For we had not known that Gnedich had been arrested. What for? In those years, one did not ask "What for?" If such words were spoken, they were introduced with an ironic proviso: "What an idiotic question, 'What for?'" And where had *Don Juan* come from? Gnedich's translation was indeed phenomenal. I realized this when Lozinsky, who was usually quite reserved, read several octaves out loud with restrained admiration Commenting on them, he mentioned two preceding examples: Pushkin's "Little House in Kolomna" and A. K. Tolstoy's "Dream of Councilor Popov." And he repeated, "But here, there are seventeen thousand such lines, that's more than two thousand octaves . . . and what lightness, elegance, freedom, and precise rhyming, brilliant wit, refined erotic paraphrases, swift tempo of speech . . ." He wrote his review, but I didn't see it. Tatyana Grigorievna, as far as I know, received it.

Eight years passed. We had already lived for some time in a different communal apartment, not far from the earlier one, at 59 Kirovsky. Once, our doorbell rang. Tatyana Grigorievna Gnedich stood at the door, even more old-looking than before, in a padded jacket and with a tied bundle in her hand. She had returned from the camp, where she had spent eight years. On the train on her way to Leningrad, she had opened up *Literaturnaya Gazeta* and saw my article "Multi-Faceted Classics," about the new one-volume Byron, translated by different poets who were unlike each other. She remembered the past and, after finding our address at the old apartment in house No. 73/75, came to see us. She had no place to live, so she stayed in our room. There were already four of us there, and if we included the housekeeper, Galya, for whom we had constructed a bunk bed, there were five of us. When I hung her quilted jacket in the communal entryway, the many residents of the apartment raised a protest. The stench coming from it was unbearable. And it had to be said, this "blazer"—that is what Tatyana Grigorievna called this object—had absorbed prison smells from Leningrad to Vorkuta. We had to throw it out. There was no other one, and there was nothing one could buy. When we had to leave the house, we did it in turns. As for Tatyana Grigorievna, she sat at the typewriter most of the time. She was retyping her *Don Juan*. There were several versions of the story behind this translation. I will speak about one of them, the best-known one.

T. G. Gnedich was arrested on December 27, 1944. She denounced herself. What she told them was not very plausible (by the way, Tatyana Grigorievna liked to fantasize). However, it could have been the consequence of a strange wartime psychosis. According to her, she was at the time a candidate for party membership (in the intelligence unit, this was obligatory). She returned her party candidate's card to the party committee, declaring that she was no longer morally entitled to party membership after what she had done. They arrested her. The investigators tried to get her confession—what did she mean? They did not believe her explanations. (I also would not have believed her if I hadn't known that there was something of God's fool in her.) In essence, the explanations were as follows: Commissioned by Soviet radio, broadcasting to the Allies before the opening of the second front, she had translated a poem by Vera Inber, "Pulkov Meridian," into English using English octaves. An English sailor who worked with the intelligence unit and who had been seconded to her as a consultant, approved the translation and apparently said, "If you worked for us, you could do so much for Russian-British cultural relations!" These words created an impression. The idea of going to Great Britain stayed on her mind. She considered it an act of treason and turned into her party candidate's card. Even though she had committed no other wrongdoing, Gnedich was tried—at the time, it was already common to "go to trial"—and was sentenced to ten years in corrective labor camps for "treason against the Soviet Fatherland" (intentions not realized, according to Article 19).

After the trial, she sat in the inner prison of the GB on Shpalernaya, in a common cell, and waited to be sent to camp. One day, the person who had investigated her last called her in and said, "Why don't you use the library? We have many books. You're allowed to . . ."

Gnedich answered, "I'm busy; I have no time."

"No time?" he asked, not too astonished (he already understood that she was rather strange, to put it mildly), "What are you so busy with?"

"I'm translating," she said, "a narrative poem by Byron."

The investigator was in fact educated. He knew what *Don Juan* was. "You have the book?" he asked.

Gnedich answered, "I'm translating it by heart."

He was even more astounded. "How do you remember the final version?" he asked, revealing an unexpected understanding of the matter.

"You're right," said Gnedich, "that's in fact the most difficult part. If I could write down what's already been done. . . . Plus, I'm coming to the end. I can't remember anything more."

The investigator was about to go home. He gave Gnedich a piece of paper and said, "Write what you've translated. Tomorrow I'll take a look." She didn't dare ask for more paper and sat down to write. When he returned in the morning to his office, Gnedich was still writing. Next to her sat an angry guard. The investigator took a look. There was a piece of paper with the heading "Testimony of the Accused." It was filled on both sides with the tiniest blocks of stanzas, which would not have been legible even with a magnifying glass. "Read it out loud," he ordered. This was canto 9, which follows Don Juan's travels to Russia. The investigator listened for a long time, at times laughing, not believing his ears. At some point, he interrupted the reading: "For this, you should receive the Stalin Prize!" He did not know of any other measure of merit.

Gnedich said jokingly and bitterly, "You've already given me that." She seldom allowed herself such jokes.

The reading lasted for quite a long time. Gnedich had written no fewer than one thousand lines, that is, about 120 octaves, on the piece of paper. "Can I help you with anything?" asked the investigator.

"You can, only you!" Gnedich answered. She needed Byron's book (she specified the edition that seemed the most reliable to her, which included commentaries), an English-Russian dictionary, paper, a pencil, and, of course, an individual cell. A few days later, the investigator found a cell for her that was a bit brighter than the others. They brought a table and what she had asked for.

Tatyana Grigorievna spent two years in this cell. She rarely came out for a walk, and she read nothing. She lived on Byron's poems. She would constantly recite lines by Pushkin to herself, addressed to her distant forefather, Nikolai Ivanovich Gnedich:

> Alone you spoke with Homer for days,
> And for days we've been waiting for you.
> Then in glory you descended the mysterious heights,
> Bringing to us your holy tablets.

He had "communed privately" with Homer, and she, with Byron. Two years later, Tatyana Gnedich, like Nikolai Gnedich, came down from "the mysterious heights" and brought out her "tablets." Only her "mysterious heights" were her prison cell, which was equipped with a foul-smelling slop bucket and a window "muzzle" that obscured the sky, blocking out the daylight. Nobody bothered her. True, from time to time, when she walked from corner to corner in search of a rhyme, the jailer would open the door noisily and shout, "You've been told to write, and here you are taking a walk!"

Her talks with Byron lasted for two years. When she wrote the last full stop at the end of canto 17, she let the investigator know that the work was finished. He called her in, picked up the mountain of pages, and informed her that she'd be leaving for the camp only after the manuscript had been typed up. The prison typist took a long time to deal with it. Finally, the investigator gave Gnedich three copies to proofread. One he put in the safe, another he handed to her together with a security certificate ("In case of search not to confiscate or to read"), and as for the third, he asked who it should be sent to for a review. That's when Gnedich named M. L. Lozinsky.

In the camp to which she was transported, she spent—from start to finish—the remaining eight years. She did not part from the *Don Juan* manuscript. The precious papers were often in danger. "There you go rustling again. Can't you let us sleep?" Her jail mates would yell. "Get rid of your filthy papers." She saved them until her return—until that day when she sat down in our place on Kirovsky at a typewriter and began retyping her translation. Over a period of eight years, she made a multitude of changes; moreover, the old manuscript, after going through prisons and camps, gave off the same stench as her "blazer."

Soon after she was freed in the spring of 1957, the House of Writers held an evening in honor of T. G. Gnedich. She read fragments from *Don Juan*. Gnedich was particularly proud to receive generous praise from several masters whose opinion she held in high regard, including Elga Lvovna Linetskaya, Vladimir Efimovich Shor, and Elizaveta Grigorievna Polonskaya. About two and a half years later, the publishing house Khudozhestvenaya literatura published *Don Juan* under the editorship of and with an introduction by N. Ya. Diakonova with a print run of one hundred thousand. One hundred thousand! Could the prisoner Gnedich, who for two years shared a single cell with prison rats, dream of such a thing?

Tatyana Grigorievna received a substantial payment for *Don Juan*: seventeen thousand lines plus royalties (in those years, an initial print run for poems was ten thousand copies). For the first time in years, she bought herself some essentials and presents for everyone around her. After all, she had nothing: no pen, no watch, not even glasses.

"No. 2" is written on the copy of the book that was given to me. Who was given "No. 1"? Nobody. It was intended for the investigator, but Gnedich, despite all her efforts, could not find her benefactor. He really was too intelligent and liberal a person. Judging by the fact that he disappeared without a trace, it was likely that he was just disposed of by the security services.

Later, a new edition was published, improved and corrected. I'm proud that on the title page, T.G. Gnedich wrote me a poem in octaves, ending with words of gratitude for the help I'd offered her during some difficult days.

> How long it's been since we've kept company,
> Once having met, in an unbroken thread
> *"When she had twenty five, and thirteen he"**—
> Or something like, as Byron might have said.
> Though we have changed, no change in amity,
> despite the troubles passing years have bred:
> We both acknowledged what had pressed for truth:
> *"Your inexperience moved my gentle ruth."***
> I'll end then with a bread-and-butter note:
> I thank you for your loyalty and charm
> For the integrity with which you wrote.
> For preying on none weaker, for a warm
> heart—and for this: that critics missed the boat
> who called you talentless and wished you harm.
> And—damn it all!—for all high-flying brings!
> I love a friendship when my friend has wings!
>
> T. Gnedich

22 October 1964

*Canto I, Octave 69.

**Canto XIV, Octave 51.

The poem contains, as we can see, two references which allow us to understand the hints. The first is a reference to the stanza where Byron speaks of Donna Julia, a young married Spanish woman [canto 1, octave 69]:

> Juan she saw, and, as a pretty child,
> Caress'd him often—such a thing might be
> Quite innocently done, and harmless styled,
> When she had twenty years, and thirteen he;
> But I am not so sure I should have smiled
> When he was sixteen, Julia twenty-three;
> These few short years make wondrous alterations,
> Particularly amongst sun-burnt nations.

The second stanza [canto 14, octave 51] is dedicated to Lady Adelina, who was exercising her patronage over Don Juan due to her age seniority:

> His inexperience moved her gentle ruth,
> And (as her junior by six weeks) his youth.
> These forty days' advantage of her years . . .

This poem was on the title page of the book—a great honor. But even more priceless was that legendary page with the heading "Testimony of the Accused" where T. G. Gnedich wrote one thousand lines of her translation. She gave it to me. After all, this page is exactly what Pushkin had in mind when he addressed his friend Nikolai Gnedich:

> Then in glory you descended the mysterious heights,
> Bringing to us your holy tablets.

When the director and artist N. P. Akimov read *Don Juan* during his vacation, he was delighted. He invited Gnedich and proposed to work as co-authors. Together, they turned the poem into a theatrical piece. Their friendship led to another exceptional work of art: a portrait of T. G. Gnedich, painted by Akimov. It was one of the best in the series of portraits of his contemporaries created by Akimov. The show staged and designed by Akimov in the Leningrad Theater of Comedy, which he led, was very successful and stayed in production for several years. The first show, which I wrote about at the beginning of my story, ended in triumph for Tatyana Gnedich. By that time, the print run of the two editions of *Don Juan* had reached 150,000 copies, and there was a new publication of K. I. Chukovsky's book *A High Art*, in which *Don Juan* was cited as one of the greatest accomplishments of contemporary poetic translation. My book *Poetry and Translation* had been published, and in it I briefly related the history of *Don Juan*, judging it to be a masterpiece of the art of translation. Still, it was that moment—when seven hundred spectators rose as one in the Theater of Comedy and thanked the author who had been called onto the stage—that was the most visible culmination of the success of Tatyana Grigorievna Gnedich herself and her amazing creation.

After being freed, she lived for another twenty years. One would think that everything was fine. She even acquired a family: Tatyana Grigorievna brought home an old woman from the camp, Anastasia Dmitriyevna, who, after moving in with her, played the role of an aunt. And she also brought home a "camp husband," a master of all trades called "Yegor." A few years later, she adopted Tolya Arkhipov, a boy who kept his allegiance to his adoptive mother. Thanks to her care, he graduated from the university and became an Italian philologist. "It seems that everything is okay," I said. In actual fact, Anastasia Dmitriyevna turned out to be a grumbler who constantly fell into a dark mood, and Georgy Pavlovich ("Yegory") a heavy alcoholic who was incorrigibly foulmouthed. Tatyana Grigorievna managed to civilize him, but only superficially. For example, she taught him to substitute his favorite short obscene word with the name of an ancient Greek god. Now, he would say when his spouse's guest arrived, pointing at her, "Should we have a drink, folks? And if she objects, 'Phoebe' her!" He would sometimes hit his wife.

When I asked whether she was afraid of something worse, she answered reasonably, "Who would kill a chicken that lays golden eggs?"

Tatyana Grigorievna lived her last decades the way she had always hoped, in her favorite Tsarskoe Selo—in Pushkin, at the edge of the park. She dedicated quite a few poems to it, which remained unpublished, like most of her poems:

> It's good at least that the park survives,
> The contour of the Hermitage's still divine,
> The whiteness of its columns still alive,
> with the beauty of its capricious outline.
> . . . .
> It's good that we, the two of us, still sit
> In lindens' shadow in sacred admiration,
> the Lethe's waters silently we sip—
> a pure cup of thought and quiet inspiration.

The modest small apartment was furnished with old furniture that was reminiscent of the furniture in the house No. 73/75 when her mother, Anna Mikhailovna, lived there. The dining room was dominated by a huge oak sideboard covered by various embellishments. I don't remember whether Joseph Brodsky visited T. G. Gnedich in Pushkin, but it always seemed to me that he had in mind her nostalgic sideboard when he wrote:

> An old hutch from its inside
> Looks, at least to me,
> Exactly like its outside:
> Notre Dame de Paris.

Students used to visit her in Pushkin—Tatyana Grigorievna worked with them enthusiastically. The result of their work together were collections of translated poems. *Collected Poems* by the American poet Langston Hughes was published under her editorship in two editions. Many of her students became poets and translators. Here are the names of some of them: Irina Komarova, Galina Usova, Georgy Ben, Vasily Betaki, Vladimir Vasiliev. The chicken actually continued to lay "golden eggs." Gnedich translated Shakespeare's tragedies *Timon of Athens* and *Troilus and Cressida*, Grillparzer's drama *Sappho*, and many poems by Byron and other poets. In the 1970s, she remembered her Ukrainian roots and translated neoclassical sonnets by Mikola Zerov, who had for a long time been forbidden by Soviet censorship, into Russian. But she did not live to see his rehabilitation or the publication of her translations.

T. G. Gnedich died November 7, 1976. She was never able to return to the level of her *Don Juan*. Her own poems were published in a tiny book in 1977 in commemoration of her seventieth birthday, with an introduction by Mikhail Dudin. Dudin actively supported her; he will be credited for that in the next world. As for Tatyana Grigorievna, she also was partial to him. Once, she even wrote him a letter full of inadequately high praise of some poems of his, to which he answered, as he sometimes could—succinctly and expressively,

> My dear Tatiana Gnedich,
> You're giving me a head itch!

I will end this story about T. G. Gnedich with one of her most dramatic poems "Memory":

> Fate grabbed me by my shoulder,
> and deadly was its grip.
> And dark were sorrow's waters
> That rose up to my lip.
> And schools of fishes flocked and swerved
> Their gray-green bodies bare,
> Strange backs so maddeningly curved,
> when whipping past me everywhere.
> I dreamt I heard black thunder bore
> the firmament both day and night
> together march with Death the whore
> in a never-ending plight.
> And once again, I witnessed where,
> with side bangs on his narrow head,
> in Nuremberg, that same clown led
> his ashen troops onto the square.
> 1975

Up the Down Staircase

Abyssus abyssum invocate*

After reading that morning's *Leningradskaya Pravda*, I called Dymshits and said I was coming over. Did he understand why? It seemed that he did. He lived not far away, at the other end of Kirovsky Avenue. I arrived at his place half an hour later. "So quickly?" he asked, not greeting me. This could have been intended to mean: "I didn't have time to prepare. You're already here..." We went to his office. "Why did you do it?" I said with difficulty and, as I recall, without a questioning intonation. "You think about everything differently. I do know how you think..."

My words might have seemed bold. He was quite a bit older than I. Before the war, I was one of his students at the university—he was giving a course on twentieth-century Russian literature, and I took his exams. I was a boy at the time, and he was a young and very promising instructor. But then, our relationship changed.

In the mid-fifties, Alexander Lvovich Dymshits suggested that we collaborate. We did not know each other well. He seemed strange and distant to me. Even his appearance evoked antipathy. I felt a kind of class dislike of the quiet smugness emanating from his fat, pink face and of his bourgeois corpulence and comical little belly. I knew only a little about Dymshits's scholarly and literary career. It did not inspire trust. People talked about his doctoral defense before the war: it became a sensation in its own way. Dymshits worked on Mayakovsky. Didn't he realize that

---

* Lat.: "Hell calls to hell"—Ed.

this was ridiculous, this ludicrous combination of a small bourgeois man and a revolutionary giant? And the dissertation was about him. One of his externals, B. M. Eichenbaum, came out and said elegantly, "I will begin my remarks in the way one usually ends them: the candidate is completely worthy of the degree that is sought, that of a doctor of sciences. I say this at the beginning because—as the learned council will see—I will have difficulty returning to this later." Then, with the same kind and well-meaning smile and same quiet voice, he tore the dissertation to pieces, not leaving a single stone unturned. The voting was catastrophic. Dymshits did not become a doctor, the sumptuous banquet that had been prepared did not take place, and many canned goods and smoked sausages stayed in the refrigerator and outside the windows. The disastrous defense saved the family's life; the provisions bought for the "feast" came in handy during the blockade.

Dymshits's false revolutionary zeal disgusted me. I did not trust his eulogizing of the late Mayakovsky; I did not believe his infatuation with proletarian poets or the sincerity of his discourse on socialist realism. And still, I agreed to our collaboration. I found his intentions and, more importantly, the possibilities too enticing. The point was that we would be working together on publishing a single volume on Ferdinand Freiligrath. He wanted to write the introduction, and my task was to compile the volume, choose the translations, and, of course, translate the poems I myself chose. My decision was determined by yet another condition, which now, a few decades later, might seem improbable.

The Berliner Ensemble, a theater created and developed by Brecht, came to Leningrad in 1957. The performances brought to us by the ensemble won us over. Most of us were astounded by *Mother Courage*, where the main part was played by Helena Weigel, Brecht's widow, a genius of an actress. After one of the performances, there was a festive dinner at the Evropeysky Hotel. Someone raised a glass to the health of the man who had succeeded in getting the Berlin theater to come to us, Alexander Lvovich Dymshits. Helena Weigel, sitting at the table next to me, leaned over and said quietly,

"Do you know who Dymshits was to each one of us? He is our savior." Then, she recounted in detail what I already knew from other sources.

Immediately after the victory over Germany, Major Dymshits was made responsible for German culture. In the structure of the occupying powers, he was something akin to a minister. He made use of his authority to organize rations for the intelligentsia, who did not have enough food at the time. I heard about this at different times from writers, actors, and artists. Besides that, he was in charge of subsidies for theaters, publishing houses, and orchestras. His role in postwar Germany was in fact huge. He himself later asserted, laughing, that he had fulfilled the duties of Goebbels—or, more precisely, anti-Goebbels. After the dinner, Weigel called over Ernst Busch and asked him to tell us about Dymshits. Busch, almost in verse, repeated her words about Dymshits the savior. I found this convincing. Ernst Busch was a living legend. His unique, baritone-like bass created a song-like utopia of Brecht, generating the revolutionary atmosphere of the anti-fascist generation, "Und weil der Mensch ein Mensch ist / Drum will er was zu essen, bitte sehr . . ." I trusted Ernst Busch, and Helena Weigel for that matter. I believed them unconditionally. It meant that this Dymshits, too, did exist—a German one, a person who saved the culture of Germany and the creators of this culture. Later on, on more than one occasion, I would ask myself a question without an answer: how did the benefactor of German culture become a suppressor of Russian culture?

And so, I agreed to collaboration with Dymshits, the "German Dymshits," who had impressed me. After all, I myself had lived through the end of the war in Austria, which had been defeated. Through my own bitter experience, I knew how agonizingly difficult it was to convince badly educated Soviet generals of the fact that not all Germans were fascists. Besides, I liked Freiligrath. He had made a deep impression on me with his translation of *The Song of Hiawatha* by Longfellow (I compared his translation with Bunin's; both the German and the Russian versions were excellent, yet different) and revolutionary poems of 1848. I now read everything attentively and was fascinated by his pure lyrical poems. The

Germans had forgotten them, and I wanted to resurrect them in Russian. The first one that I did was a small poem, which turned out to be a practice round:

> Three gulls were flying high.
> I lowered my eyes:
> Without looking up,
> I know which way they fly.

A. L. Dymshits approved of my own attempts, as well as my list of recommended translators that included M. Zenkevich, L. Ginzburg, and V. Shor. We worked together amicably on the Freiligrath book. He did not impose anything on me, agreed quickly, and knew how to appreciate successful translations. The trim little blue book was published in 1956; we remained satisfied with each other, and he suggested that we continue collaborating. We were to publish another nineteenth-century German poet, Georg Weerth. I knew almost nothing about him. I read through his work and agreed. We knew Weerth as a poet close to Karl Marx. Such a biographical fact demanded special attention, which, of course led me to have legitimate suspicions. It turned out, though, that he was a decent lyrical poet. His cycle of poems *Love* was close to Heinrich Heine's *Book of Songs*. I translated him with perhaps excessive enthusiasm. Weerth came out in two editions with a short interval in between: at first in one volume, then in two volumes. We were praised. What was important was the fact that approval came from different literary camps. I remember reactions from V. M. Zhirmunsky and V. G. Admoni and letters from S. Marshak, I. Fradkin, and D. Samoilov. Dymshits was happy with the success of our books. Indeed, there was something to be happy about: for a long time, only the top German poets such as Schiller and Heine were recognized in Russia; second-rank poets were not known at all.

Working with Dymshits was still easy and fun. His introductions seemed superficial to me, but our collections were meant for the general public. It would have been unthinkable to delve deeper into aesthetic or philosophical problems. Yet bit by bit, I became more annoyed. My partner was too obvious in the way that he emphasized ideological and biographical details that were useful for publication, such as the closeness of our poets to Marx and Engels and to the labor movement and radical revolutionary spirit. Dymshits knew how to deal with the authorities. Georg Weerth's acquaintance with the "founders" was what got him his special position within nineteenth-century poetry. The same conversation would come up from time to time: this looks very much like demagogy, I insisted. Why do we need it? Dymshits laughed it off. Are we to explain to our *zhlobs* that Freiligrath gave new life to the poem *The Song of the Nibelungs* or that his poetics was connected to Longfellow's? But when you bring up Marx, they instantly understand: How can we not publish a Marxist poet? You want to publish a book? You need to meet them halfway.

The compromise that Dymshits suggested was basically acceptable. There would be a slight distortion of proportion in the introductions, but in exchange, there would be a respectable book of poems translated anew and published with a solid print run. Many other people did the same. Who would publish poems by Arthur Rimbaud, which were enigmatic and at times provocative, if you didn't stress the fact that he supported the Paris Commune? The same went for Verlaine. Would a Soviet publisher allow itself to publish the decadent aesthete Éluard if you did not emphasize in the introductory essay that he was a Communist? Even Bertolt Brecht would not have been approved by Goslitizdat if we had not provided a reminder that his poems honored the builders of the Moscow subway. Bad, even shameful poems served as the gateways to great plays: *Life of Galileo, Mother Courage and Her Children, The Good Person of Szechwan.* Dymshits was a virtuoso of this kind of compromise.

But one concession led to another. Once you start going down the staircase to the underworld, you can never stop. The introductions to Freiligrath, Weerth, and even Brecht seemed like more or less harmless diversions. But then Dymshits wrote an introduction to Mandelstam's poems. The book appeared in 1973, many years after it was prepared for publication.

When I read his manuscript and said that he had distorted Mandelstam's poetry, that the article was filled with false interpretations and fake information, he was beside himself. "You're all softies and snobs," Dymshits said to me, almost yelling. "I of course distorted certain proportions. Didn't you notice that Mandelstam is being published again after almost half a century? There was a publication in 1928, and now mine will appear. Say thank you: I sacrificed my good name for Mandelstam's poetry. I know, I know that I presented the poem 'For the Thundering Valor' inaccurately. But we succeeded in publishing it. Only this is important . . ."

Here's a reminder of what this is about. In this poem of 1932, the poet speaks about how he's "deprived of a cup at [his] fathers' feast, / Of happiness and of [his] honor"; he asks fate to move him further away from "bloody bones in a wheel": "Take me into the night, where the Yenisei flows / And the pines reach the stars / For by blood I'm no wolf / And only an equal can kill me." Piercing lines that condemn the terror of the early 1930s, Dymshits interpreted them as a condemnation of imperialism; Dymshits interpreted the line "The age like a wolfhound leaps on my neck" as the poet's being pursued by bourgeois ideologies and enemies of socialism.

"But you understand that you reinterpreted this poem and disfigured it beyond recognition?"

"I made it possible for it to be published," Dymshits repeated with pride, adding, "You pseudo-knights, you criticize me. . . . Each one of you, you democrats, would write an article, worrying about your pristine gowns. No one would ever see your articles. Which is fine; who's interested in your speculations? The trouble is that no one would see Mandelstam's poems either. But I published them. Russian literature owes me a lot. For its sake, I've received a lot of reproaches and even spitting from all kinds of hypocrites." I've cited his monologue very closely. I wrote it down at the time.

"Do you remember Leonid Andreyev's novella *Judas Iscariot*?" I asked Dymshits.

"Andreyev also praised Judas, who betrayed Jesus knowing that all the subsequent generations would curse him, but someone must play this role, otherwise Jesus would not complete his feat! Isn't that the way you see your function?" Dymshits, without stopping to think, said, "We live in complicated times. Those who do not want to publish Mandelstam and who do not understand him at all wield dictatorial power. Our task is to publish Mandelstam at any cost. At any cost . . ."

"If that is so, don't be surprised when people refuse to shake your hand."

"I accepted that," said Dymshits proudly, as before. "I knew that your wimps would reject me instead of thanking me. To hell with them. Mandelstam's poems will see the light of day, and that's to my credit."

Anna Akhmatova regarded such a standpoint with contempt and said scornfully, "And it's also profitable." In fact, Dymshits kept climbing up the ladder of the governing establishment. Despite his Jewish background, he became almost a deputy minister of cinematography and a member of various boards and secretariats. They accepted him as their own. And the liberal intelligentsia rejected him more and more emphatically. Z. Paperny, who was not a very consistent democrat but was unusually witty, said of him, paraphrasing Pushkin:

> On footpaths no one ever knew
> Are tracks of beasts no one has seen:
> A short-legged Dymshits—the oddest Jew,
> Who is on pogroms strangely keen.

I'll return to the conversation with which I began. V. Dudintsev's novel *Not by Bread Alone* had just been published, where for the first time the truth was told about the new ruling class, the governing establishment that was stifling everything that was alive. There were timid sympathizing responses in the press. Dymshits bore down on them and the novel. In his review, Dudintzev was accused of slander: he had not demonstrated the party's leading role in our society, the party that supported all that was progressive and worked tirelessly toward victory against reactionaries.

That morning, I understood that Dymshits's review had put an end to our collaboration and even our good relationship. After hearing me speak, he gave a long speech in his own defense. "Take a look at those two street lamps," he said, pointing out the window. "You will hang on one and I on the other if we rock the boat. Dudintsev doesn't understand this. He wants to start a storm. And those who praise his novels, they're stupid and suicidal. Only a strong power can protect us from the ire of the popular masses." This time, he pronounced for the first time a word that has stuck in my memory: "Zhlobocracy" [*zhlobokratiya*]. And he added, "This is exactly what has been built in our country and what is called socialism." I listened with astonishment: He understood everything so clearly. But what does his pen write in *Leningradskaya Pravda*, the party paper?

He kept descending the stairs to the underworld, and he kept rising up the ladder of establishment privileges. The lower he descended down one, the higher he rose up the other. Such was the law of our lives.

Postscript

More than thirty years after Dymshits's article about Dudintsev's novel and our estrangement—which the article had caused—I saw and heard Dudintsev for the first time. That was in Denmark, in Louisiana, near Copenhagen. In 1988, there was a meeting of our Russian and the émigré literati. I'd been commissioned to write one of the opening speeches. Among other things, I said that we've had to hate someone all our lives: either formalists, or Weissmannist-Morganists, or decadents, or Germans, or émigrés. How great that a different time has come, when understanding each other is more important than animosity! G. Baklanov, the editor of *Znamya*, attacked me, reminding us that not only hatred reigned in the 1930; it was a time of accomplishments and records: the epic "Cheluskin," the flights of Valery Chkalov, industrialization. I was embarrassed for him, but I understood that this was the price he was paying for being able to publish *Znamya*. After him, Vladimir Dudintsev spoke. He was already old, could barely speak, and got confused. He almost repeated the demagogic talk of Baklanov, only he added that no matter how difficult it was to remain dedicated to socialism after the arrest of, say, Babel, he, Dudinstsev, was able to stay dedicated. In the evening, one of the participants of the conference from the Soviet side, the historian Yury Afanasyev, told me how insistently writers in Moscow and in the Soviet consulate in Copenhagen had been instructed. They were told that they were to meet—for the first time!—émigrés, enemies of the USSR, and that, following the first émigré presentation, it was necessary to rebuff them. Baklanov and Dudintsev fulfilled the party's demand. It is bitter to remember and write about because Baklanov was the hope of the Russian democrats, and Dudintsev was the author of the novel *Not by Bread Alone*, which in 1957 initiated many things that happened in our country. I found it not only strange but also characteristic for the era. It gave birth to two-sided people. Baklanov was a two-sided person, publishing the freedom-loving *Znamya* and, for the sake of the journal, praising the accomplishments of the 1930s. Dudinstsev was also a two-sided person, who wrote a novel about the lethal aspects of Soviet socialism and spoke out in defense of this socialism in order to publish his new books. Both probably condemned Dymshits, who served the Communist regime. But Dymshits, too, was a two-sided person: a savior in Germany and a strangler in Russia.

It Turned out Okay

"I need two tickets for opening night," I said to the top administrator of the theater, Dina Shvarts.

She laughed, "Where would I get them? I can't find even one. Who'll give you tickets on the eve of the performance?"

She was right. I understood this well. BDT, the Bolshoi Drama Theater in Leningrad, was hugely popular at that time, in 1963. The public came in droves to see shows with Yursky, Basilashvili, Zinaida Sharko, Kopelian, Lebedev, and Lavrov. They admired the director of the theater, Georgy Tovstonogov, for the spirit of freedom that was alive in his shows. And the show, the one for which I had naively asked for tickets, was a Bertolt Brecht play staged by the Polish director Erwin Axer. Axer was known by his admirers from the press about Warsaw's Contemporary Theater (Teatr Współczesny), which he raised to the level of one of the top theaters in Europe. Brecht had already been shown earlier on Leningrad stages— *The Good Person of Szechwan* and *The Threepenny Opera* had earned him renown. The audience saw in Brecht an alternative to the official theater aesthetics. He seemed anti-Stanislavsky. People were attracted to him as to a liberator. I should note, by the way, that no one had anything against Stanislavsky—they considered him to be the creator of MKhAT and of the famous "system of physical actions," who nurtured a host of brilliant actors and authored the book *My Life in Art*. But everyone who hated "leader-ism," which under Stalin had become the principle of Soviet reality, rose against him. In every field, there had to be one—and only one!—indisputable authority or, to put it differently, a "monarch" or "leader." In biology, it was Pavlov; in prose, Gorky; in poetry, Mayakovsky; in farming, Lysenko; in botany, Michurin; in painting, Gerasimov; in sculpture, Vuchetich; in music, Khrennikov; and in theater, Stanislavsky. Everyone knew that Bertolt Brecht was close to Communism, that he had been coddled by the party and the GDR government, and that his theater company, the Berlin Ensemble, was the GDR's official government theater. But Brecht, in contrast to Stanislavsky, was creating a "theater as the art of a show," not as the art of experiencing, and he prioritized irony over pathos. That was sufficient for him to be sought as an ally in subverting the "stage monarchy." There was no politics in these other theatrical aesthetics—the politics lay in the anti-leaderism movement. The assertion of two truths rather than only one in any area meant victory of pluralism over dogma, democracy over dictatorship, free dissent over mindless obedience. That's why the intelligentsia was attracted to Brecht as early as the 1950s.

People really knew nothing about the play *The Resistible Rise of Arturo Ui* as it had not yet been published in Russian. There were rumors that in this play, which had been created in 1938, Brecht had in mind not only German racist fascism but also Russian fascism based on the class approach. Yet he had to hide the two-sided nature of his plays for tactical reasons. Rumors of this kind, which were spread by people who took part in the play, helped make it more sensational. Now, how could anyone expect to get "two tickets to the opening night" for something like that? I nevertheless repeated my absurd request for the tickets: "They're for Solzhenitsyn."

Dina Morisovna Shvarts pulled two tickets out from her little purse. "Take mine," she said. "One cannot refuse Aleksandr Isayevich." Then, laughing, she added that she wouldn't have given them to the Queen of England. But to Solzhenitsyn . . .

At that time, he was a legend. *One Day in the Life of Ivan Denisovich* had recently been published in *Novy mir* and had created a sensation. Advocates of the democratic renewal considered the book's publication to be a victory for their own movement, while those who wanted to preserve the status quo hurried to cozy up to Khrushchev's favorite. The press was bursting with praise; even the law-abiding Dymshits wrote an article applauding it. For the liberal intelligentsia, Solzhenitsyn became an idol. After Khrushchev's denunciations at the Twentieth Party Congress, so many steps backward and sideways had been taken that no one expected such a breakthrough. And here it had happened. What a miracle! And it had happened not in a political speech, not in a report by the leader in charge, not in a headline article in *Pravda*, but in a work of art. This suggested respect for literature, which was just about to be given up on. It appeared that victory for long-awaited truth was finally assured through genuine art. Solzhenitsyn would come to the opening of *Arturo Ui*—Dina Shvarts spread the sensational news throughout the entire theater, and expectations rose even higher for the opening performance.

He arrived at our house the evening before the performance. We knew about him a little earlier. Lev Ginsburg had once mentioned his last name to me, remarking, "It's hard to remember, but we'll have to." Then, some friends in Moscow gave us a manuscript with the title "Shch-854," typed without margins or spaces, and double sided. The author was listed as A. Ryazansky. Frida Vigdorova, to whom I was returning the folder that had stunned us, said, "Prose of a genius." After reading *One Day* once more in a magazine, my wife, Ekaterina Fyodorovna, wrote to Solzhenitsyn. I remember that in the letter she spoke about how the horror of the whole period was shown through one happy day of a Soviet convict, how the honesty of this narration resurrected the honor of our deceit-filled literature, how fortunate the readers were to live to see the holiday on their street (we would later see this letter in the folder of the most interesting reader's responses saved by the author under the title "Romantics"). About a month later, Solzhenitsyn called us on the phone and said that he had come to Leningrad for a few days and wanted to visit us so we could get to know each other and talk. We agreed on an evening. We waited nervously, and probably with some apprehension. On the only photograph that we knew of, there was a frowning, grim prisoner. He came with his wife, Natalia Alekseyevna Reshetovskaya. We could not get over our astonishment all evening: our guest turned out to be broad-shouldered, vigorous, and energetic. He spoke nonstop, smiled easily, and even laughed out loud. He also noticed little details. A poster for *The Resistible Rise of Arturo Ui* from BDT was hanging on the wall. He came up to it, read it quickly, saw that the play would be shown in my translation, and asked if it had been difficult. I said Brecht's drama was a parody, that it was written in Shakespearian verse, in iambic pentameter, and that conveying this five foot measure in Russian after Pushkin and A. K. Tolstoy had been fun. He glanced once more at the poster. "I don't go to the theater," he said. "Natusenka, when was the last time we went?" And, not waiting for an answer, he added, "So, shall we go?" Then, turning to me, "You know, this performance, I'd like to go. Is it possible?" He added something polite about his interest in my translation. Later, I found out that he had his own plans and wanted to give Tovstonogov one of his finished plays, either *Candle in the Wind* or *The Love-Girl and the Innocent*.

"Of course it's possible!" I said enthusiastically, suspecting difficulties ahead but knowing that I would overcome them.

Our seats were in the second row. In front sat the city fathers. I recognized them from newspaper photographs: there was Vasily Tolstikov, the shiny, fat-faced secretary of the regional party committee, known for his cruel stupidity, and Lavrikov, the secretary of the city party committee, who was more attractive and looked like an engineer; between them were their identically made-up wives. I did not get to tell Solzhenitsyn about our neighbors. What interest could he have in Leningrad party secretaries? Only at times, when he reacted loudly to the play, would I press his elbow. I feared his reactions mainly because Tolstikov appeared to accept the play officially. He could easily forbid it. The first half went by calmly. In the second half, however, I had to go up, at the invitation of Tovstonogov, to the side box of the theater stalls. Looking down, I was horrified. For comfort, Solzhenitsyn had changed seats to one in the front and had wound up next to Tolstikov. Now, each time he made his comments to our wives sitting behind him, he would turn his entire body. And he—probably rather loudly—reacted to the ambiguous passages, of which there were quite a few. At night, Arturo Ui sees an apparition of his brother in arms, Ernesto Roma, whom he had killed. His accusatory monologue can be perceived as a speech by Röhm, the head of the *Sturmabteilung*, addressed to Hitler, who made short work of him, but also as a speech by Bukharin addressed to Stalin:

> Don't touch your own, Ui! Don't. You hear me?
> Work your conspiracies against the world,
> But spare your co-conspirators. Trample
> on everything—but beware of trampling
> your own feet. Tell lies to everyone,
> But don't deceive the face in the mirror!
> You've dealt me a blow, Arturo!
> But it's a blow you've dealt yourself.
> I was your friend when only hired thugs
> knew who you were. And now, today,
> I'm a nobody, and you're on a first-name basis
> with the masters of the universe.
> Treachery has raised you up
> And treachery will be your downfall.
> Just as you betrayed Ernesto Roma,
> Your friend and helper, you'll betray
> us all, and in return, you'll be betrayed by all . . .
> . . . The day will come
> When those you have murdered
> And those whom you have yet to destroy
> shall rise again and come against you.
> Encircled by hate, you'll look for shelter . . .
> Yes, just as I did,
> And as I pleaded and cursed—
> Plead, curse!—The land will be silent.

From where I sat, I saw how my guest was moved listening to the monologue. He kept turning around and saying something. He especially liked the scene where Ui tries to convince the greengrocers of Chicago to vote for him:

> Appealing once again to you, Chicagoans,
> I say: you know me best, and so I trust
> That you will judge me on my merits.

> So who'll give me his vote? An aside:
> The one who won't will be my enemy. Beware!
> And this is all I have to say. The end.
> Now go and cast your vote freely!

The voting begins—some raise their hands. One asks (and here I cite the text of the play):

> So, sir, may I then step out?
> GIVOLA (GOEBBELS). All are free to do whatever they desire.
> (*The merchant hesitantly steps out. He is followed by two bodyguards. A shot is heard.*)
> GIRI (GÖRING). Right. Now, your vote! Who is your free choice?
> (*All raise their hands; each raises both hands.*)

Solzhenitsyn, laughing, turned back abruptly. Of course, I don't know what he said, but knowing him and my text, I was able to imagine. I no longer doubted that Tolstikov would forbid this seditious show. I felt as if I were in a dream—I saw everything and understood everything, but I was powerless to change the course of events. You couldn't shout or throw a note from above! We were in the hands of fate, which was embodied by the two audience members who were sitting side by side but did not know each other. And what if they knew, what if they could guess the future? Tolstikov would become an ambassador to China, and Solzhenitsyn, a Nobel laureate and the author of *The Gulag Archipelago*, who would then become an exile, then a victor . . .

The play ended. It was a huge success. Both secretaries left immediately—apparently backstage. I went to Tovstonogov's office. I was filled with bad premonitions and an awareness of my guilt about what I'd done to the theater: Why had I brought Solzhenitsyn? To show off my translation to him? To show off the fact that I was acquainted with him in front of the theater? My motivations seemed ignoble to me. Could it be that I had caused the death of a good play that was also good for society?

After a few minutes, Tovstonogov came in: "It turned out okay," he said somberly. "It turned out okay. Tolstikov didn't dare cause an international incident. The director's a Pole!"

"And he didn't ask to cut anything?" I asked, still trembling.

"Two things. He didn't like that Arturo Ui kept his hands on his private parts. Lebedev and I told him that that's just how Hitler held his palms and that Axer hadn't made up anything. He said, 'Get rid of it!'"

And second. Waiting for Arturo Ui in the garage, Ernesto Roma says to his assistant:

> . . . Only when
> I see the corpse of that damn bastard Giri—
> Then will I feel relief, as if I held it in
> And took a whiz at last.

"Tolstikov got very angry. His fine upbringing didn't allow him—and in the presence of his wife!—to hear such indecent talk. 'He held it in . . . and took a whiz at last,' he repeated, raging with indignation. Then, he added, 'Maybe in Poland this is acceptable. But you, you must understand that this is not in the tradition of the Russian theater.'"

"What should we do?" I asked.

"Well, nothing. He won't come again. There's nothing political in these remarks; we'll stay as we are!"

This farce was all that happened. The performance was shown more than three hundred times, and Arturo Ui continued to cover his private parts with his palms.

About the Axe

We stopped to stay overnight not far from Smolensk, near some village by the edge of the woods. We parked both vehicles further in, behind some bushes, then got ready for supper. Solzhenitsyn asked me to go to the village to get the blacksmith from the kolkhoz: "Find Konstantin Tvardovsky and bring him here." Half an hour later, we were sitting around a large stump and pouring vodka. Konstantin Trifonovich Tvardovsky turned out to be a good-natured, talkative giant (does my memory deceive me?), who quickly turned happy after the first glass. His speech was rich and lively. I remembered how he spoke about his brother: "Let's be honest—he writes well!" We talked about the family of the Tvardovsky brothers, about kolkhoz incomes, and then we began talking about axes. The blacksmith explained how they were forged. Solzhenitsyn added to the conversation with his knowledge about the matter. I was astounded by the number of words they both used. What did I know about an axe? Four, five words, maybe, but I heard over a dozen. That the blacksmith knew them was not surprising, but an instructor of mathematics, a camp prisoner, a literary man?

It turned dark. We saw Konstantin Trifonovich off to the village. When we returned, my wife asked Aleksandr Isayevich, "Do you know that many words about everything?" He began laughing. "For a window, let's say" she asked, "how many different words are there?" It became clear that she and I, and even Solzhenitsyn's wife, Natalia Reshetovskaya, knew at best five or six words. Aleksandr Isayevich drew a window and showered us with terms. It was an amazing linguistic experiment and, moreover, entirely improvised. The axe and the window had come up in conversation by chance.

Years later, I would keep recalling the evening by the fire in the woods. The lively wealth of words our fellow traveler possessed was unbelievable. He had a much richer vocabulary that any of us, even Ekaterina Fyodorovna—who I thought knew the most diverse "Russian languages" and was indefatigable in the area of folk phrases, sayings, and songs. And I recalled with special vividness that evening with Tvardovsky the blacksmith when I made painful efforts to read one of the volumes of the endless *Red Wheel*. I stumbled over the author's neologisms.*

I read this tortured prose, overcoming linguistic barriers every step of the way, and I could not for the life of me understand why he needs all these deformities. He who had at his command thousands of words that had been forgotten or were unknown to people? He who so clearly used to understand the difference between what was artificial and falsified on the one hand and what was natural and therefore real on the other? Poets and futurists, such as Khlebnikov, Mayakovsky, and Severyanin, often used neologisms. The avant-garde poets actually needed them, and the neologisms appear to have emerged effortlessly. But in his lifelike prose, how did he not see how strange and irritatingly artificial they were? Stepan Shevyryov at some point criticized Pushkin for his smoothness and felt that reading must be a difficult endeavor. Long before Shevyrov, Gavrila Derzhavin also arrived at an assertion of difficulty. All lovers of Russian poetry remember Derzhavin's ode "God" (1784), but it's doubtful that anyone rereads his other, later ode "Christ" (1814). Is it possible to fight through the piles of linguistic obstacles piled on by the poet?

> O, hear me, Thou God of love!
> O hear me, Father of clemency!
> And show me mercy from above
> And grant me, O Lord, some leniency

---

* There follows here a list of a number of these neologisms, which do not translate well into English.—Ed.

> for the sins of my guilty heart
> desiring to fathom Thy Deity,
> as Thou hast pitied Mary of Bethany
> who anointed Thy tired feet with nard.

Can it be that the tragedy of old Derzhavin did not teach Solzhenitsyn anything? Or did he not read him?

Last Meeting

In December 1976, my teaching in New Haven, at Yale University, was coming to an end. I was flying to Paris the next day. In the morning, the phone rang. Mrs. Rannit, the wife of the well-known Estonian poet and director of the university library, asked: "Could you find fifteen minutes to meet with a friend?"

"A strange question," I said, puzzled. "One should not limit one's time for friends."

"They said to tell you fifteen minutes. If you agree, come to the library. At exactly one o'clock, my husband will be waiting for you."

I immediately understood on whose behalf she was calling. It would have been difficult to mistake it for someone else. First of all, he had not himself picked up the phone to make the call but had instead told someone he knew to do it. Second, he had not called to ask me to visit him and or intended to drop in to see me but had instead specified a mysterious place to meet. Third, he had not identified himself and had apparently told Mrs. Rannit not to say his last name. Fourth, he had limited the meeting time to a quarter of an hour—not more, not less. All of this betrayed Solzhenitsyn—not only his conspiring habits, but his striving to keep things brief, his concentrated satiety, or, as he liked to put it, his density.

A bit later, the phone rang. "I was asked to say that it would be possible to make the meeting longer, up to thirty minutes."

I was surprised by the generosity of the anonymous friend, but I stayed silent and only expressed my thanks for the notification.

Another ring, the third, came not long after. "I was asked to tell you that the meeting is confidential. Come by yourself, with no one accompanying you."

At thirteen hundred hours, I came to the agreed upon entrance to the main lobby of the university library. Alexis Rannit was waiting for me and led me right to the vestibule. We went down two flights of stairs, and I saw Solzhenitsyn. He was nervously running around the small hall. Glancing at Rannit, he said angrily, "You're half a minute late!" I said softly, "Hello, Aleksander Isayevich!"

"Yes, yes, hello," he said, turning away from the embarrassed Rannit. "We haven't seen each other for a long time, at least a year. Let's sit here. Talk to me."

We sat in the library's wooden armchairs. Our conversation went quickly. He asked about my family, without hearing everything I had to say to the end, and suddenly, without a transition, he blurted out, "I will no longer give interviews. They don't understand me anyway." Then, he provided more detail. In Spain, he had thought highly of Franco's gesture in creating the only memorial (or simply a cemetery?) for the fallen on both sides, for the republicans and for General Franco's supporters. One should look to such Christian action as an example! . . . The journalists did not understand his, Solzhenitsyn's, aspirations for justice and accused him of supporting fascism. I said they had judged him mainly for saying something else—namely, that the crisis of humanity had begun during the Renaissance era, when people, filled with haughtiness, departed from God. Could one expect approval from people in today's Europe, in Spain especially, where they're proud of the Renaissance to this day? It was precisely in that period that great painting, grand poetry, and amazing theater were born.

The discussion became more lively. Now, a quarter of a century later, there's no need to reproduce it in detail (although it would be possible—I wrote it down then). Solzhenitsyn remained true to himself. Anyone who followed his thought could see how consistent it was. He asserted the same thing in various ways, whether he was talking about things that were earthly, as in the pamphlet "Our Pluralists," or the divine, as in many of his treatises. At the liveliest moment of our conversation, Alexis Rannit appeared. Solzhenitsyn glanced at him and said, as severely as before, "You're late again, by a whole minute."

He jumped up, put on a fur jacket and a cap with ear flaps, and, raising his collar, covered his eyes with dark glasses. Like a hero in a spy movie, he walked out onto the campus, separated himself from us, and walked past students toward the university, or maybe to a hotel.

I watched him leave, and I felt a bitterness that was not quite sorrow, not quite disappointment, mixed with hurt. Not long ago—two, three years earlier—we were still close. What had happened to him? When meeting me in Leningrad or in Moscow, he knew that he was being followed, that he was (to put it in his words) "on the radar." But still, he was just a normal human being. He didn't weigh each second of his time in gold, nor did he make his striving for "density" into a pathology . . .

That's how our last meeting passed. Thinking about it, I remember an earlier meeting, which took place in Moscow.

Aleksandr Isayevich had come to our place in Leningrad in the evening. Not long before, he'd met my friend, the oncologist Leonid Samsonovich Salyamon. Solzhenitsyn told his new interlocutor about a tumor that he'd had a long time ago, and how they'd operated on him during his exile using the most primitive surgical equipment, and how this homemade scalpel had saved his life. Stopping by again, he took a folder with x-ray films out of his backpack and said, "Here are pictures of my tumor from back then. Show them to Leonid Samsonovich. I would like to hear his diagnosis."

Dr. Salyamon looked for a long time at the x-rays and admitted that he could not give a definitive assessment. He promised to show them to his oncologist colleagues. A few days later, he told us, my wife and me, that he had spoken to the authoritative Professor Rakov in Leningrad (yes, there are such meaning-laden names!).* Rakov had studied the pictures for a long

---

* *Rak* is "cancer" in Russian.—Trans.

time and asked, "Leonid Samsonovich, perhaps you wanted me to admit this patient to our institute? I'll say right away, whoever he might be to you, I won't admit him. We have too many fatalities. This patient cannot be saved. His tumor is inoperable. He's doomed to die very soon."

Salyamon listened to the famed diagnostician's conclusion. He, fearing to offend Rakov with doubts about his competence, very delicately remarked that the pictures had been taken some twenty years ago, that the patient had survived after a successful operation, and that he'd been leading a normal life since then and even become a father to healthy children. Professor Rakov looked at the pictures once more and spread his arms: "Miracles do happen!"

Relaying the dialogue to us, Leonid Samsonovich said, "I've read works by oncologists—mainly American ones—about how sick people can heal themselves by will. I've never believed in such therapy. But now I understand that it's possible. Here's an instance of when you can believe in self-healing. By the strength of one's will, it's possible to overcome even inoperable cancer."

About two weeks later, I met Solzhenitsyn in Moscow and told him about Rakov's diagnosis and Salyamon's conclusion. He wasn't surprised. He simply said calmly, "And who would have written what I had to write?"

Solzhenitsyn the writer could evoke deep disappointment even in those who enthusiastically welcomed his *Novy Mir* stories and his *The Gulag Archipelago*. Solzhenitsyn the thinker could provoke fierce disagreement among democratically inclined readers. Solzhenitsyn the politician could make even moderate liberals, even careful republicans, go against him.

But—what can one say?—the will of this man, his courage, his single-minded determination cannot fail to evoke an astonished admiration in each of us, his contemporaries.

FAMILY, FRIENDS, COLLEAGUES

Etkind family, left to right: Efim, Mark Isaakovich (uncle Monia), Mark, Polina Mikhailovna Spevskaya (mother), Isaak (Sania), Language teacher, Grigorii Isaakovich (father), 1938

Igor Diakonov, Efim Etkind, Karelian Front, 1944

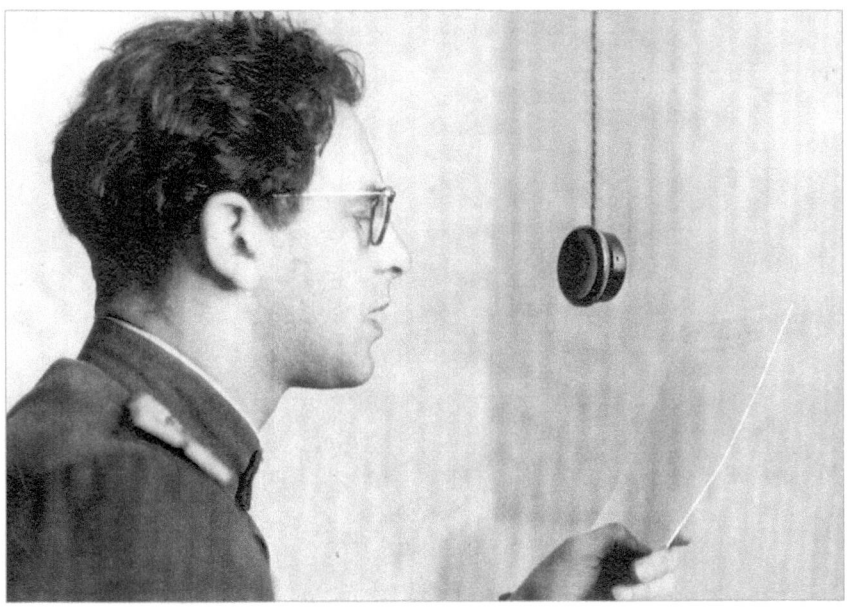

Efim Etkind, Karelian Front, 1944

Masha Etkind with mother Ekaterina Zvorykina, Tula, 1952

Efim Etkind, Valentina Levina, Fedor Levin, Moscow, 1956

Efim Etkind with students from Herzen Institute,
supervising summer agricultural works, 1956

Nina Diakonova, Ekaterina Zvorykina, Leningrad, 1966

Ekaterina Zvorykina, Greta and Leonid Saliamon, Natalia Zvorykina, Moisei Kirpichnikov, Ushkovo (dacha), 1969

Joseph Brodskii and Katia Etkind, Ushkovo (dacha), 1972

Catherine Etkind, Ekaterina Zvorykina, Efim Etkind, Suresnes, France, 1975

Ekaterina Zvorykina, Aleksandr Solzhenitsyn, Katia, Masha, 1967, Ushkovo (dacha)

Efim Etkind, Katia Etkind, Aleksandr Solzhenitsyn, 1967, Ushkovo (dacha)

Family, friends, colleagues 149

VPZR, 1970

Aleksandr Solzhenitsyn and Efim Etkind in Nida, Lithuania, 1967

With a graduate student and Irina Komarova (behind),
Leningrad, 1966

Natalia Dolinina, Mark Etkind, Yadviga Etkind-Kuks, Efim Etkind.
Departure—Farewell, Leningrad airport, 1974

Elena Chukovskaya, Efim Etkind.
Departure—Farewell, Leningrad airport, 1974

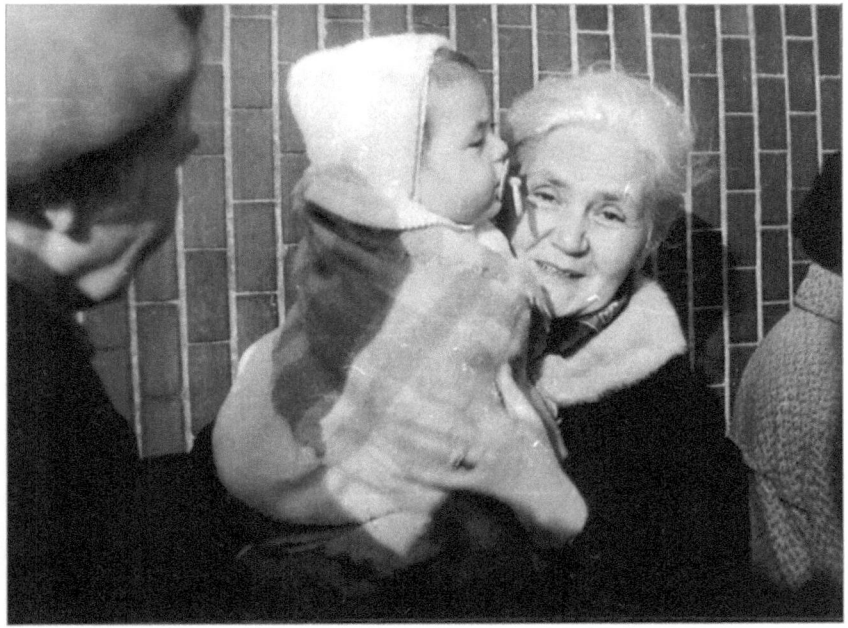

Ekaterina Zvorykina with granddaughter Asya.
Departure—Farewell, Leningrad airport, 1974

Tatiana Gnedich, 1960-s,
Tsarskoe Selo

Lev Kopelev, Catherine Etkind, Efim Etkind, Assia Shafrir,
Uri with David Shafrir, Raisa Orlova, 1987, Bellevue, Bretagne

Georges Nivat, Efim Etkind, Paris, France, 1988

Efim Etkind, Ilya Serman, George Nivat:
Editors of the *History of Russian Literature*, 1990

Masha and Efim Etkind, New York, 1978

Efim Etkind, Svetlana Elnitsky, Norvich symposium, 1992

Family, friends, colleagues 155

Andrei Sinyavsky (first from the left), Victor Nekrasov (fourth from the left),
Anatolii Gladilin (third from the right), Efim Etkind (second from the right),
Paris, 1985

Lev Loseff, Efim Etkind, Svetlana Elnitsky, Norvich symposium, 1992

Grigorii Bergelson,
Efim Etkind,
first trip back
to Leningrad, 1989

Efim Etkind and
David Bethea

Efim Etkind, 1978

Pavel Antokolsky: Generation of the Blind

*We, the recipients of prizes
That bear his name,
Did not flinch at compromises,
Were untouched by shame . . .*

I've remembered these lines for several decades already. Was the poem that begins this way published? It's not in the volume of poems by Antokolsky published in 1982 in the Library of Poets Large Series. I wrote it from memory in the autobiographical book *Notes of a Nonconspirator*, published in London in 1977, but this book did not reach Russia unless you count the individual copies disseminated underground during the Brezhnev era as *tamizdat*. This poem is not known, although it seems to me to be lyrical poetry's most significant response to Stalin's dictatorship.

How many loud but empty words are said about the necessity of "repentance"! Calls of this kind are false because repentance is an ecclesiastical concept. In Russia, which lived through seventy years of Soviet materialism, Christian church religiousness was impossible. Not only were churches destroyed to their core but also faith. It may take up to a century to restore them, if necessary. Present-day attempts at "repentance" are hypocrisy. There is no doubt that many Soviet people who honestly believed in Communist ideas became disappointed in them. The Russian Orthodox faith came to their service, and they grabbed it immediately. Why? First of all because they had grown up in an atmosphere of unconditional religiousness. The Soviet system would have been unthinkable without it. Catholics were known to accept the dogma that the pope is infallible. Looking at it from the outside, you cannot help but laugh. What kind of infallibility is there in such obvious criminals as Alexander VI of Borgia or Pius XII? That very Pius who knew about Auschwitz and never blinked, who supported the German aerial raids and the Croatian Ustaše. The dogma of infallibility is a principle of faith elevated to a grotesque and absurd level. In Soviet Russia, it was the cornerstone of the regime. To maintain that the party does not make mistakes, that its paper *Pravda* published only the truth, that its head was the leader and teacher of mankind was simpler than invoking belief in papal infallibility. There were no Lutheran Protestants denying Catholic dogmas. There was no press or any other form of public media able to counter the single party government propaganda. The USSR fell apart, as did Communist ideology, but the religious principle forming the consciousness of each Soviet person did not disappear. There was quite simply a reorientation. Thus, today's cult of the cross was formed, a caricature of devotion to metropolitan bishops and patriarchs, and an incredibly passionate love for church songs and the sounding of bells.

Pavel Antokolsky was a member of the Communist Party. Like many people of his time (and by far not the worst), he stoked a belief in its ideals within himself. Unlike his literary colleagues, he was well educated and knew French and French literature well. His favorite poets included not only such great writers of rhetoric as Auguste Barbier, Victor Hugo, and Aragon but also the great mystic Charles Baudelaire. These poets, together with Derzhavin, Lermontov, and Blok, formed his poetic world, which was diverse and rich. This fact alone already placed him on the same level as Akhmatova, Pasternak, Mandelstam, and especially Marina Tsvetaeva, who was tightly linked to him biographically. A poet of such cultural pedigree found it harder to share in the religious dogmatism of the Soviet populace than the not so well-read Zharov, Altausen, Svetlov, Simonov, and even Tikhonov and Tvardovsky. The poem with which I began this story in some ways continues Lermontov's "Thought," also written in the name of a whole generation. In Russian poetry, Lermontov was closer to Antokolsky than other poets.

I asked Antokolsky who "we" were for him. He listed several names: Simonov, Fadeyev, Tikhonov, Fedin. "And Zabolotsky?"

"No," Pavel Grigorievich answered. "Zabolotsky was in another category, and he received no literary award; he was far from the literary beau monde. Well, perhaps Marshak."

In the line "Calmly walking through time," the bitterest word is the first. It criticizes the passive indifference of a generation who you would expect to treasure the truth. Calmness is the same as complicity and connivance:

> We are all his comrades in arms
> Who never loosen our tongues;
> And from this craven silence stems
> Our nation's tragic wrongs.

With each line, the space widens, and the responsibility of "us all" for our country deepens.

> We kept secrets from one another
> and rarely slept at night
> while from our friends and brothers
> he was creating executioners.

The degree of blame, and even crime, grows: the recipients of *his* awards are guilty of indifference, silence, cowardice, and obedient submission to taking part in evildoing.

> From quarries of marble and stone
> What statues we would raise
> To bury the cries of suffering
> In an avalanche of praise . . .

To this very day, "we" were everyone, "all of us, the award recipients," the generation of law-abiding intelligentsia. Then sculptors or artists in general in the literal and figurative sense. Then, finally, singers and ode writers.

> We, of great and mighty truths
> The designated heralds
> Share blame for the blood of the Lubyanka
> And the darkness of penal worlds.

The responsibility was great, especially because the terror, it seems, was justified by a holy goal endorsed by the regime and supported by those who sang its praises.

> May our sons and grandsons
> Spare us no contempt;
> we are equal in our shame,
> No one is exempt.
>
> Truths self-evidently true
> Are plain to see.
> We shouldn't hate the man who's dead
> But our own complicity.

Can one call this poem a form of repentance? It is an act of exposure—of laying bare his generation and himself. This generation is pitiful, cowardly; it betrayed people and was blind. Not that it was actually blind; it just wanted to be blind. Antokolsky repeated the lines by Mayakovsky: "I'm alone, like the last eye / of a person joining the blind."

"Paul de Antokol"

Pavel Grigorievich Antokolsky read me these verses during one of his Leningrad visits around 1956. We met in the Writer's House. He rushed up to me and roared, "Let's go! Let's go!" He made me go to the embankment of the Neva. Here by the black water, looking at the forbidding walls of the Bolshoy Dom looming nearby, he cried out, "We are all award winners . . . " I had never heard him say such a thing before. I don't remember what I said to him, but two to three months later in Moscow, when I started talking about this poem, he asked sharply, "Where did you find the text?"

"I memorized it as you were reciting it to me."

He did not believe me. He was afraid that the text would be circulated by hand and that it would get to samizdat (which was already starting) and to "the authorities." Despite the thaw, the danger was, in fact, not small. I tried to convince him that the poem would remain in my memory. And it did for a long time.

Our acquaintance, which grew into a friendship, started in 1950. I had been dismissed from the Leningrad Institute of Foreign Languages as a cosmopolitan antipatriot and was teaching in Tula, near Moscow. Despite the disgrace and even my Jewishness, Goslitizdal had agreed to my proposal to publish a collection of poems by Auguste Barbier, a French romantic who had praised the July Revolution of 1830. Barbier had been translated a lot in Russia (the one by Benediktov was better than others, strange as it may seem). In the Soviet times, translations by Antokolsky, a poet close to me, were published. I was attracted by his unrestrained temperament, his keenness to play with sounds, and even the way he challenged common sense:

> We live in a green and beautiful land,
> We feast by night, we turn into sand.
> Zoom past us, the planets!
> But as you zoom past us,
> There's nothing to sate us,
> And darkness is at hand.
>
> So, honest to a fault and light of foot,
> We, like children, dream anxious dreams of pursuit
> And distant vexation—
> Just to feel the elation,
> The chill and elation
> of spring! . . .

What defiance, joie de vivre, and fire—even though fireworks sometimes! At our first meeting, Antokolsky professed his old love for Auguste Barbier as he ran around the cluttered office on Shchukin Street. He said the translations of his poems were the best that he had ever produced as a translator. "But those were the 1920s. Now I couldn't do it anymore!"

And to prove his point, he began reading Barbier's iambic verses in French. I, too, considered them unsurpassed since my youth. He wheezed:

> Ô Corse à cheveux plats! que la France étaitbelle
> Au grand soleil du Messidor . . .

These are the first lines of the poem "Idol," which had been dedicated to Bonaparte. Then, for the first time, I heard him reading his own poems. It was an unforgettable reading in which his talent as a poet and as a tragic actor came together. He rolled his *r*'s as if he were reciting a curse or saying the name of the Sierra Guadarrama mountain ridge, with growling to lengthen the vowels. Even the soft cadence of his raspy voice seemed irresistibly expressive:

> Remember France under the sun of Messidor,
>   young Corsican?
> France, untamed, with her fiery spirit,
>   Unbridled, unbound.
>   And, like a wild mare, her rump in foam,
>   steaming with the king's blood
>   She happily galloped, vigorously trampling
>   The free expanse of fields! . . .

This first phrase was read in one breath, with phenomenal speed and no less phenomenal pauses at the end of each line. In his reading, the words that contained the *r* sound (there were three or four rumblings), which were so important for him, united in an inseparable chain, which was buttressed by moaning, the *my-ym* sound.

His voice changed into another sound, another melody, which was now closer to something epic:

> No one's hand had yet raised over
> her head a master's whip.
> No one's saddle had yet rubbed her sore,
> To teach her a master's will.
> All aquiver, parading her youthful vigor,
> Flashing an intelligent eye,
> Neighing happily, she held Europe in thrall,
> And Europe listened, terrified.

And again, a sharp change, again addressing the Corsican. This time, it was not a row of exclamations but a tale of pathos about how free republics turned into empires and how Bonaparte became Napoleon. This new subject was read differently. His voice expressed both the pathos of jubilation and the sorrow of defeat:

> But taken with her playful gait that knew no rein,
>   You, bold little horseman, there and then
> took her by surprise and grabbed her mane,
>   And dug your spurs into her sides . . .
>
> But the horse couldn't bear the violence.
> And she collapsed amidst the hail of bullets,
>   Breaking the rider's back . . .

I already knew these verses of Barbier-Antokolsky's, but truly felt their rhetorical brilliance only when I heard him recite them. "You are saying that you can no longer do it," I said, "but I don't believe it. If you can read it this way, with so much spirit in every sound, then you can do anything!" My words were not intended as flattery but to convey my admiration. Antokolsky, with unexpected honesty, said that the 1920s, when his translation was born, was a time of revolutionary illusion and great fervor. After all, he himself had written enthusiastic poems at that time about the convent, about Jacobins, and about young generals of the republic.

"That was one complete whole: my own poems about the France of the Robespierre era and my translations from Auguste Barbier. That was my theater—I was the author, the director, and the actor. Now, everything has changed. Instead of Messidor, we have a somber November."

It was 1951, maybe one of the darkest times in recent memory. At the height of it was the persecution of cosmopolitans. Pavel Antokolsky turned out to be one of them. He was an enviable victim for those taking part in the pogrom, a rare example of an antipatriot. It was not enough that he was a Jew, of that notorious Jewish heritage to which his forefather, the sculptor Mark Antokolsky, belonged. In addition, he did not want to have ties with

Russian folklore. It seemed that France was closer to him than our native villages. The guardians of Russian national treasures who mocked him cited the same lines from the mid-1920s (from the poem "Sans Culottes"):

> My mother was a harlot or a witch,
> My father—some old aristocrat.
> His Excellency's ears were shut
> To her howls giving birth in a ditch
> and to how, to keep her son dry,
> She tore her skirt for swaddling cloths,
> While the autumn rain poured forth
> Not caring if he'd live or he'd die.

The accusers shouted in unison, "This is a translation from the French!" Sergei Vasiliev, a well-known parodist and antisemite in the 1950s, mockingly wrote about Antokolsky's poems:

> Here's where the Frenchman, the German, the Brit
> sleeps overnight and fornicates.
> All that is missing is the Russian spirit
> since Paul d'Antocole will not hear of it.

"Paul de Antokol.". . . Was there anyone who did not repeat this phrase? This might have made you laugh in a different era, but in 1951 it was a deadly stigma. Antokolsky's poems about France, about its revolution and its poets, were considered to be equivalent to the transgression that at the time was known as "toadying to the West." (Who made up such popular definitions? Can it be that we will never find out? Besides, now it is already too late.) P. G. Antokolsky was removed from teaching at the Literary Institute, where he had conducted a seminar with young poets that was enormously popular. They stopped publishing his work—they were even reluctant to order and publish his translations.

Is it therefore so hard to understand how by 1951 Antokolsky, who had been branded an antipatriot and lackey, had lost the revolutionary enthusiasm he'd had at the beginning of the 1920s?

However, there was something else that went back to an earlier time. Antokolsky told me about this later, when we became closer and he was able to trust me. In the 1930s, political trials were in full swing, and these invariably ended with all the accused being shot to death. The shootings made Antokolsky understand how the ideas of the Jacobins had developed. Revolutionary terror carried an aura of romantic theatricality even for Victor Hugo, the famous French poet and the author of the novel *Ninety-Three*. Antokolsky, like Hugo, admired this sense of theatricality. Saint-Just was no less appealing to him than Hamlet or Cyrano de Bergerac, the hero of his adored Edmond Rostand. We agreed on Rostand. I, too, was enthusiastic about him, particularly his drama *The Eagle*, which Antokolsky could talk about endlessly. He recalled more than once how Marina Tsvetaeva had loved *The Eagle*. He remembered the impact that the translation of this Rostand piece had on him. He remembered her reading and expressed his hope that the translation would be found. By the way, when he was saying goodbye to me in October 1974, when I was leaving for France, he said several times, "Look around in Paris. Find her translation of *The Eagle*. Find it for sure. The manuscript cannot have vanished!" Alas, I did not find it. Tsvetaeva's translation had apparently been hopelessly lost.

Stalin's terror of the 1930s and then the 1940s put an end to P. G. Antokolsky's passion for the romanticism of the French Revolution and the French Empire. The poet accepted Stalin's terror as a legitimate development of Jacobin terror (as Pushkin said, "replacing amusement with sinister terror"). He looked now at his own romantic declarations from the 1920s with mixed feelings: his regret for the past, contempt for his own naïveté, admiration for the talent of those years, irony, and even remorse all came together.

P. G. Antokolsky translated quite a bit for my collection of Auguste Barbier's work, published in 1953. But it could not compare to his own Barbier, created thirty years earlier. At the time, he was creating. Each line that he wrote followed Barbier and expressed his own revolutionary spirit. Now, he translated like a knowledgeable and conscientious professional. The romanticism of the revolution had receded into the distant past. But not the romanticism of France: Barbier ceded his place to Baudelaire.

Don Quixote

Pavel Antokolsky faded before my eyes. To be sure, he was getting old and resisted this with all his weakening might. Once, in a train compartment, he fell to the ground and, growling, began to bite the rug. He noticed the woman who served tea. She brushed him aside, and he suddenly sensed that as a man, he had lost his attractiveness. It was difficult for him to overcome such a blow. This episode was only momentary. I observed him in the days when a truly tragic event befell him: Zoya Bazhanova, his companion of many years, died. He loved her with all his soul—his unrestrained, crazy soul—and was proud of her like a vain young man. . . . She was fascinated with making sculptures out of roots—their large house on the Pakhra River was filled with the crazy devilish monstrosities she had made.

With childish happiness and amazement, he would show his guests the sculptures, which combined whimsical nature with the fantasy of an artist. Then, there was an exhibition of Zoya's sculptures, where he liked to lead his friends through by himself, praising her genius with words bordering on poetry. Zoya's death was the end of his whole life. The poems dedicated to her memory were least of all literature—they were the poetic howl of a mortally wounded man. His love would remain in memory, as it did for Laura and Lilya Brik. He dreamed about this more than about his own immortality because what he really experienced was love, a love that changed over time but never ceased.

> It's over. But there's no end to an end,
> And no beginning to our beginning . . .

On the eve of our emigration, in mid-1974, I came to him to say goodbye. For me, this parting turned out to be one of the most painful. He was old; there was no hope of ever meeting again.

Pavel Grigorievich tried to say something optimistic but couldn't. He just blurted out, "Without you, it'll be worse!" Then, he leapt up, jumped to the other corner of the office, and pulled out a small bronze statue of Don Quixote from somewhere. "Take this with you. You need it more." Even earlier, as he listened to the stories about my ordeals in the fights with party bosses, he would bring up the poor hidalgo: What can each of us do on our own? Even the trial of Brodsky, in whose defense a group of intellectuals stood up for the first time, did not convince him. He thought that each of us was fighting alone and that I was a Don Quixote by conviction. At times, he allowed himself actions of this kind—for example, when he wrote a letter in support of Solzhenitsyn, who had spoken out against censorship in 1967, to the Union of Soviet Writers. At that time, clinking glasses of the usual vodka with me, he repeated a grim toast that was popular at the time: "Let's drink to the success of our hopeless cause."

A fighter for justice he was not. His greatest fear was that they'd stop publishing his work. However, his letters arrived in France with amazing regularity. Until his death (four years later, in 1978), he wrote openly, not hiding his affection for us, not putting on an act. Such a faithful correspondent was rare in my life. Even old and close friends tried to move into the shadows, out of harm's way. If they wrote sometimes, it would only be when a safe occasion arose, and they would do so not hiding their fear. Pavel Grigorievich Antokolsky, who was so careful and so far from any dissident position did not know fear. Lines which he wrote some twenty years before we parted were not empty rhetoric:

> [We] share blame for the blood of the Lubyanka
> And the darkness of penal worlds.

Cousin

At the time—it was the end of the sixties—people seldom went abroad. France seemed to be the promised land, but it existed only in the poet's imagination. Igor Diakonov, however, had a business trip to Paris ahead of him. This wasn't easy to comprehend, particularly for me. I had been steeped in French culture since childhood, yet I had never visited France. "What shall I bring you from Paris?" Igor asked jokingly. He had no money and was not supposed to get any.

I answered, thinking realistically, "Look up Malama's address in a phone book. If you find it there, jot it down."

About two weeks later, Igor called. He had returned and had many impressions from his trip. He brought back the address, which I had forgotten about by then. Theodore Malama—that was the name of the man whom Igor had found in the telephone book. The next day, I asked my mother whether this name meant anything to her. "Of course it does!" Mother answered. "They had a son, Fedya."

Mama grew up in the family of a Petersburg shoemaker, Mikhail, or more precisely, Mikhel Spivak. There were four sisters, all very different. I knew three of them: Dora, a stern Jewish bourgeois lady who was a well-known dentist on our Petrograd side; Katerina, the kindest, an amazingly Russian woman in a headscarf, the devoted mother of a large family, and not in the least flamboyant or extravagant; and Polina, my mother. By contrast to her older sisters, she was a light-hearted and charming young lady who was delighted by expensive furs and worldly success. She started performing in concerts early, right after finishing at the conservatory. She was just over twenty. Mama was a contralto of rare beauty, and she sang mostly romantic gypsy songs. I was later informed they were all rather crass and that only a person with bad taste could be delighted by the romance—"We parted like ships on the sea." I didn't believe the rigorists who taught me to reject gypsy music. After all, I was like Alexander Blok in this delusion. Mama loved Blok. She sometimes sang verses that had been set to music by someone (maybe Johann Admoni?):

> And time and again I kiss the rings,
> not your hands. In the backward thrust
> of your shoulder are a dare and lust
> for freedom that parting brings.
>
> . . . .
>
> Farewell, and here, as a token—
> Another ring before we part
> To dress in shiny silver scales
> your dear hand and dusky heart.

These lines embodied for me what others with scorn called gypsyism. The combination of a "dusky heart" was connected in my memory to Pushkin's Mariula (not Zemfira, but specifically Mariula), with a habanera from *Carmen*, and with another poem by Blok—"Oh, yes, love is free as a bird . . ."—where there were phrases such as "your figure, all aflame."

This art was filled with yearning, longing, and passion, and in it, you could invariably hear the "ardor of freedom and of parting." And I would always hear my mama's voice in my ears and my soul, singing with restrained passion:

> As we part, tie a knot
> With the ends of my fringed shawl.
> Like them, we were once together,
> But now we are not.

I got diverted toward the gypsies, and here is why. The fourth sister, Anna, whom I never saw, was also a singer and performed in a gypsy choir. One evening—it happened, I think, in 1911—she disappeared after a concert.

They tried to find her but could not. About ten days passed. Her parents were desperate. Suddenly a carriage drove up to the house where they lived. A stylish lady alighted from it. It was Anna, the one who had disappeared. She had presents for everyone in the family. She had been abducted by a rich young man who was in love with her, the bearer of the ancient Moldovan Russian Malama family name, and she was already his wife. Sometime later, the young couple left for Europe and, after the revolution, it turned out they were emigrants. It was possible to write to them at first. Later, in the twenties, postal correspondence got worse, and the sisters sent greetings when they had the opportunity. Finally, in the thirties, having relatives "there" became deadly dangerous, and each year it became more dangerous. Mama no longer mentioned her sister who was abroad when she filled out forms. The three of us, my brothers and I, didn't know anything about her. We learned that we had an aunt in Paris for the first time only during Khrushchev's thaw. By then, this was considered something interesting even, and in any case, it was almost safe. What did she do there? How did she live? What family did she have? Mama had lost sight of her entirely, but now she didn't hide the fact that she longed for her sister. She loved Dora and Katerina, but apparently Anna was closer to her than the others.

When I showed her the address of Theodore Malama, she perked up: "This is Anna's son, Fedya, it is certainly Fedya. I'll finally find out something. . . . My God, we parted fifty years ago. . . . Is she alive? She should also have a daughter, Vera . . . Write to her right away, right away!" I wrote, adhering to all the rules of proper tone. And of course, I wrote in French:

> Monsieur,
>
> We are not acquainted. I was given your address in Paris, and I permit myself to write you for the following reason. If your mother is called Anna (I hope that she is alive and well), then she must know that her sister Polina lives in Leningrad and that she remembers her and loves her dearly. If so, I am writing not just to some Mr. Theodore Malama

unrelated to me, but to my first cousin from whom I hope to receive a quick reply.

Respectfully and sincerely,

E. Etkind

There was no answer for a long time. Finally, some three months later, it came, and I opened the envelope addressed from Paris trembling with fear. The letter turned out to be brief.

Monsieur,

My mother died a few years ago. She never said anything about relatives in Soviet Russia. I do not wish to violate her will, therefore I also do not wish to speak about this subject.

Yours sincerely,

T. Malama

He did not say the name of his mother—it would have been enough to write that she was called Heléne or Elizabeth to dispel our hopes. That meant that it was almost certainly Anna, and that he, Theodore, was mama's nephew and my cousin. Mama didn't doubt this, nor did my brothers and I. But why, why did he deny his family connections so adamantly? We could not understand that. An acquaintance who was a lawyer thought, upon hearing my story, that perhaps because Mama was a sister, under French law, she would have rights to a part of the inheritance. Malama may have gotten scared that she might have financial claims. Others thought he was a rabid anti-Communist—what good are relatives in Leningrad to him? A third person thought he might have been reluctant to help a destitute (undoubtedly destitute!) Soviet aunt . . .

Five years passed. I had to emigrate with my wife and daughters. From the end of October 1974, we lived in Suresnes, near Paris. In mid-1975, I defended my dissertation at the Sorbonne and became not only a Docteur d'État but also a full professor of the Tenth Paris University (this information will be necessary to further develop my plot). A couple of times, I called Theodore Malama at the number in the telephone book, but no one answered. One Sunday, we decided to visit him and try to understand. He lived, according to the same directory, on Rue Olivier de Serres. Ekaterina Fyodorovna accompanied me unwillingly and kept repeating with hesitation, "Are you willing to risk being insulted?" I was in fact motivated by curiosity and what seemed to me to be a legitimate interest. She came with me out of solidarity. The concierge indicated the staircase and the apartment we needed, and we went up. There was a small copper doorplate that read, "Theodore Malama." A woman opened the door. I asked in French for the master of the house, and she shouted loudly, "Fedya!"

Out came a very tall Fedya with a gray crew cut and a short moustache. "How can I help you?" he asked, bowing to the lady.

I said, switching over to Russian, "Mr. Malama, several years ago I wrote you. My last name is Etkind."

Without inviting us into the apartment or hesitating, he declared, "I answered you. I have nothing to add to that letter."

"Mr. Malama," I repeated. "You did not answer my only question. What was the name of your deceased mother?"

"I do not intend to answer that. Our conversation has ended."

What I did next was inappropriate, I'm aware of that. Taking my wife's hand, I stepped over the threshold of the apartment, entered his study—the door to the right of the entryway—and said firmly, "We don't need anything from you. We're probably richer than you are. I'm a professor at Paris University. We have no material demands . . ."

My wife tugged me by the sleeve and insisted louder and louder, "Let's go, let's leave . . ."

She was right, but I continued.

"I came to you to fulfil my mother's—your aunt's—wish. She asked me to find out when Anna Mikhailovna died and where she's buried. She would like to establish ties with your sister Vera. You are obligated to fulfil her wish."

"I am not obligated to do anything," said Malama. "And you are obligated to leave my house immediately."

He took a look at the gray-haired Ekaterina Fyodorovna, got confused, and said, "Excuse me, Madame, I allowed myself to be impolite, it is not my fault . . ."

He added something positive about her true Petersburg looks. The conversation continued for a while—that is, if the exchange of replies, or rather insults, can be called a conversation. In conclusion, he said his mother really was called Anna but that he would not say when and why she had died or where she was buried, and that he had a sister, who indeed was called Vera, who was in an old people's home. He would say nothing else.

Thus insulted, we left, not understanding anything.

Some old acquaintances, the Krivosheins, lived not far from Rue Olivier de Serre. We stopped at their place to recover. Nina Alekseyevna—she was already over eighty—met us in her usual style, with a welcoming acidity. Obviously, we immediately told them about what was overwhelming us, the story of our visit to Theodore Malama. Nina Alekseyevna, for all her aristocratic reserve, almost shouted: "You were at Fedka's? Why did you drag yourselves over to his place?"

"Do you know him?" I blurted out. "Maybe you can explain . . ."

"There's nothing to explain here. Why did you have to drag yourselves over to Fedka's? You should have told me earlier . . ."

What followed was something we couldn't even have imagined. Nina Alekseyevna turned out to be a relative of Fedka's—her mother was from the Malama family.

"Does that means that you're related to us, Nina Alekseyevna? I never thought, never guessed it . . . but why does he behave in this way?"

"And how would you like him to behave? Fedka is a well-known church member and antisemite. He was presenting his mother as a Russian gypsy. There's nothing good for a Russian nobleman about being the son of a gypsy, but it's much better than being the son of a Jewish mother. And you've come to expose him. If you're his cousin, then he's himself tainted and under current laws a full Jew. I would not be surprised if he hanged himself. Just imagine how it must be for an old Jew-hater to admit that his mother was Jewish? What was she called? Anna Mikhailovna Spivak? And not Anna, probably, but something like Khasya . . ."

I never saw mother again. She lived for another eleven years. I just tried to speak with her on the phone regularly. I wrote to her about meeting Fedka, without going into detail. Besides, she was almost eighty, and she was overwhelmed by her own difficulties—in particular, after the death of two sons, both my younger brothers—so her reaction was muted. When she died, we were not even allowed to attend her burial. The Soviet Embassy did not honor me with a reply to my request for a visa. About two years after that memorable visit, I read in the newspaper *Russkaya Mysl* that Theodor Malama "had passed away prematurely" in Warsaw.

"The Other"

> *I was born on November 7, 1917.*
> The beginning of an autobiography
> —D. P. Pritzker

David Pritzker was my friend or maybe an acquaintance. When we're young, we don't always distinguish between these two forms of male closeness. It so happened that the last we met was in 1972. Then, we met again only twenty years later, fleetingly and rather accidentally. A few more years passed, and I saw him in his coffin. Can what happened in 1972 be called a breakup?

In any case, the event that separated us for the rest of our lives was characteristic for its time, and David Pritzker was a most wonderful representative of his, our, generation. Is it not amazing that he was born on November 7, 1917?

First, though, about the event; then, about the era and the generation he represented.

VPZR in VPSh

In the spring of 1972, Solzhenitsyn and I came to walk along Voinov Street, which had earlier been called by the unforgettable name, Shpalernaya (which is what the prison on the corner of this street and Liteyny Avenue was called; during the thirties the grandiose granite complex of the Bolshoy House, which housed the NKVD, arose around the prison). Solzhenitsyn and I were walking toward Smolny Cathedral. This was a rare moment, an unexpected break. He'd just managed to finish something, and he'd not managed to start something else, and so he agreed on this walk, something unthinkable for him, a walk devoid of any meaning or practical goal. At least that's how it seemed to me at the time. Later, I understood that in choosing Shpalernaya Solzhenitsyn, as always, was deadly focused. He was planning on writing a series of books that would later be called *The Red Wheel,* and the action in many chapters were to take place in Tauride Palace on Shpalernaya, where the State Duma held its meetings. I had known about the idea of a multivolume epic—a fictionalized history of the revolution—for a long time, since 1967, when he let Katya and me in on his plan. (At the time, he had terrified us—we understood right away that there would be a catastrophe for the good writer, but that is another story.) We were passing by Tauride Palace, which in our day had housed the VPSh, the Higher Party School [Vysshaya Partiinaya Shkola], which was something of a special university for party activists. Solzhenitsyn, looking carefully at blind windows in the long, low building, said, "How I need to walk around in the palace, to look at the halls and corridors! It's hard to write without having seen it . . ." I answered that people who didn't belong to the party school were not allowed in but that I would try to arrange a completely legal visit of the former Duma for him. A close friend of mine was the head of the department of West European history, I think (it was called, as I later learned, the department of the international workers movement; it's a good thing that Aleksandr Isayevich didn't hear such a word combination—he would have spat on it).

"If it's . . . if it's possible for that to happen . . ." he repeated several times and reminded me again about it when we said good-bye. It was clear that he really needed this. He was to leave for his place near Moscow. I promised to do what I could.

The department in question was headed by David Pritzker. I called him, and in the coded language of that time, I let him know that VPZR . . . , etc. VPZR was the acronym for *veliky pisatel zemli russkoi* [great writer of the Russian land], which was what Turgenev had called Lev Tolstoy. We thought that the Bolshoy Dom would not know the jocular acronym, and, of course, we were wrong. Pritzker understood right away and, without hesitating, answered, "When he comes to the area again, give me a ring. I'll set a time."

A month and a half passed, and VPZR was again in Leningrad. Pritzker said to me, "Come together tomorrow, around six. I'll be waiting at the entrance." I brought Solzhenitsyn by car. Getting out with him, I didn't introduce him to Pritzker so as to avoid saying his last name—doing so was already dangerous then.

In the evening, Solzhenitsyn called to thank me. "That was essential. What I had imagined was so different. It's so important that I was able now to see, touch, and even take measurements."

"Was everything alright?" I asked, mainly to be polite.

"Well, not everything. . . . We'll talk later."

I understood that we shouldn't talk about the details on the phone and felt a little worried. That feeling became stronger when David Pritzker called the same evening and asked, "Tell me, was it a long time ago that you were at Suvorin's grave?"

"A long time ago," I answered. "But it's time to visit Aleksey Sergeyevich."

"Tomorrow morning at nine."

The next morning, we met at Suvorin's gravestone in the cemetery of Alexander Nevsky Lavra (I lived in the neighborhood). Pritzker, looking around attentively, let me know that he had managed to show his guest the large hall and several auditoriums and to give a brief commentary (and the guest had noted all this down assiduously in his very small handwriting), when suddenly, the building's chargée appeared.

Taking Pritzker to the side, he asked, "David Petrovich, who is this person with you?"

"A professor from the provinces," Professor Pritzker answered. "He's writing a dissertation about the Duma."

"David Petrovich," the chargée said, "see to it that in five minutes he's gone." He was silent for a moment, then added, "This is not my instruction. I was called higher up." He gestured toward the ceiling with his hand.

Pritzker understood everything right away. It meant that "the professor from the provinces" was being watched and that they had seen everything.

"You know," he said to his guest, "we have to leave—right away."

The guest understood as well—he had quite a bit of experience with "tails," which you couldn't always get away from. "I'll leave right away," he said. "If I could just see the oval hall . . ." Having managed to run into two or three more rooms, the visitor left.

"I was called to Smolny, to the regional committee," David said, almost in a whisper. "I wanted to tell you what my story would be. I will mention you, that you brought me an acquaintance of yours and then left without taking the time to introduce him. Now I can guess who it was but did not check. It seemed awkward to ask him, and I couldn't see you yet."

This tactic seemed reasonable to me. David Pritzker did as he said he would before the regional committee. They believed him. I guessed that they might have wanted to believe him. The majority of the people with whom he spoke in Smolny had studied under him at the Higher Party School. They owed him a lot, were delighted by his eloquence, brilliant erudition, talent as a lecturer, humor, and noble indulgence. Why not believe their favorite instructor? What he was saying was unlikely, but possible.

It was after this meeting at the grave of Suvorin that we didn't see each other for about two decades.

I don't doubt that David Pritzker experienced a certain awkwardness and maybe even pangs of remorse. Not because he had lied to the regional committee—that lie was a tactic, which was certainly acceptable against an opponent who held complete power. But I later found out that he had told friends of ours something similar, saying I had brought a visitor to him without identifying him and that as a result there were considerable complications. Upon discovering that his guest was Solzhenitsyn, he felt that he was on the edge of an abyss. What had started as a tactic began to look different in later instances. After all, what kind of a friend would put a man who was close to him in danger? David Pritzker, who was clever, discerning, and diplomatic understood perfectly the difference between tactics and slander and understandably could not forgive himself for this questionable overcautiousness. However, as usually happens in such cases, not only could he not forgive himself; he also could not forgive me.

In the middle of October 1974, I had to emigrate—the authorities, after many months of persecution, had driven me to such a decision. As a reminder, I'd been dismissed from the Herzen Institute as early as April. My academic degrees and distinctions had been taken away from me, they chased me out of the Union of Soviet Writers, and I was not able to work anywhere. On the eve of our departure, David Pritzker's son, Zhenya, who had tirelessly and selflessly helped us pack and send off books, brought me a typed letter from his father in which he said something like this: "I wish you success and hope for the best. Who's right and who's wrong—history will be the judge of that." History would probably find it hard to decide this, even if the note came into its hands. There was no addressee and no signature.

Since then, nigh on twenty years have passed, and this unsigned letter remains in my memory still like a painful trauma, like an unhealed sore. No, David Pritzker was not a coward, and at any rate was not a scoundrel. However, a man like him was unable to act differently. Why? To answer this question, I shall allow myself a digression.

A Digression about Jewishness

We grew up with a splendid scorn for national prejudices. David Pritzker's wife, the beautiful Maria Pavlovna (Musya) Rit, was Estonian. Her mother, the very kind Amalia Adamovna, spoke Russian with a strong Estonian accent. Musya herself hardly remembered Estonia. Did she consider herself Russian? It was enough for her that she was a beauty. And my wife, Ekaterina Fyodorovna Zvorykina? She came from Russian nobility on her father's side, and she was of merchant stock on her mother's side. She loved her family and her family history, but she lived in our circle, which—as we started to realize much later—comprised mostly Jewish boys: Erik Naidich, Misha Gabe, Lenya Salyamon, and Yasha Shokhor during our school years; and at university,

Vladimir Shor, Eleazar Krever, Dav Frankfurt, Akhill Levinton, Grisha Bergelson, Yury Lotman, Ilya Serman and David Pritzker. . . . They were all Jewish, but did Jewishness worry anyone or even interest them? In our group of Jews, there were also Russians: Alyosha Diakonov, then his older brother, Igor, Alexei Almazov, Anatoly Kukulevich. But they didn't feel the difference either. Jews were not *others* to them. There was a group of philologists, a bit older than we, who were fascinated by philosophical aesthetics. They all considered themselves students of Derdya Lukach and Mikhail Livshits. Among them were Yakov Babushkin and Volya Rimsky-Korsakov, and also Georgy Friedlander, Susanna Alterman, Nina Magaziner, Izrail Wertzman. . . . A person's national background was not important to any of them or to any of us. In the thirties, Soviet people did not divide themselves into national groups. The party authorities required that a ratio be met on admission to university, but what they required was not in relation to nationality but class—which was barbaric nonsense of a different kind.

During our student years, the Jewish last names of Soviet Russian intellectuals were famous throughout the world: chess players Botvinnik and Bronstein, musicians Gilels and Oistrakh, writers Ehrenburg and Grossman, Marshak and Pasternak, philologists Zhirmunsky and Gukovsky, journalists Radek and Koltsov, physicists Ioffe and Landau, composers Katz and Dunayevsky, performers Reizen and Mikhoels, film directors Eisenstein and Romm. Could you imagine our culture without them? We saw them least of all as Jews. For us, they were the pride of the Soviet land and Russian culture. They were on the same level as the brothers Vasiliev and Vavilov, Nikolai Tikhonov and Zabolotsky, Tolubeyev and Cherkasov, Stanislavsky and Mravinsky, Korchagina-Aleksandrovskaya and Michurina-Samoilova.

> But all has changed. You've seen the tempest's fury,
> The fall of it all, a union of mind and Furies . . .

When did it happen? When did the Jews all of a sudden become rejected? When did they become dangerous to the regime and even its adversaries? Vasily Grossman thought it was after the Stalingrad victory, which turned out also to be a defeat and the end of internationalism. That could be. However, it began with a lack of trust toward the intelligentsia in general. During the time of war, we were in demand mainly because we knew languages. We could study the enemy and communicate with our allies, but we seldom rose above the rank of major. True, there were Jewish generals; there was even Mekhlis, the head of the Political Administration of the Soviet Army. That evoked amazement. The "process of rejection" began, it seemed, when Stalin's Soviet Union drew nearer to Hitler's Germany, in 1939. It was then that the first prohibitions (in full reality) and limitations for people with Jewish last names appeared: diplomacy (that's what it began with), physics, military technology, upper-level army appointments, and on and on, in breadth and depth, until it led to the mass hysteria of 1948–53.

An important landmark was the war with the Germans in 1941–45, when something unexpected became clear to everyone, mainly to the party leadership: the attraction of Stalinist socialism was not so great that anyone wanted to die for it. (They laughed as they sang the popular marching song precisely for this reason: "And will all die till the last person in a battle precisely for this." Sure—*for this!*) After the first defeats of 1941, the optimistic speeches about the imminent arrival of the Communist future gave way to the glorification of the homeland, of Russia, and even of Holy Russia. Orthodox priests and Suvorov, Kutuzov, Ushakov, and Alexander Nevsky medals appeared in the army. The most popular poet and writer at the time, Konstantin Simonov, repeated, like a spell, the word "Russian":

> By Russian custom, leaving behind
> the torched and smoking Russian land,
> our comrades die before our eyes
> tearing their collars, as Russians do.
>
> The bullets have still spared you and me,
> but when I thought that my life was up,
> What I felt was pride for my dear land,
> My Russian land where I was born.

> I am proud that I'm destined to die in it,
> that a Russian mother gave birth to me,
> that seeing me off to the battle a Russian woman
> embraced me three times as Russians do.

Simonov's poems served their purpose. They raised the spirit of the devastated army. They resurrected the almost lost meaning of life and, most important, the meaning of death. Of course, a large majority of the army were Russian soldiers and officers. And what was living and dying like for those others who could not repeat Simonov's words? He was, after all, proud "that a Russian mother gave birth to me." And what of others, who were born to Jewish mothers? Until recently, there had been no such distinction.

Jews were pushed aside. If the war was fought for purely Russian values, for the Orthodox faith, for Holy Russia, Jews could only be outside spectators. More and more, they had to hear people say, "We Russians are fighting for our motherland, and you—you're fighting for your own skin." More and more, people would remember that Jews also lived in America, and so what ideals they were fighting for must be irrelevant to them. They were fighting not for Russia but against Hitler's Germany, which was annihilating Jews. Needless to say, there were many Jews who were brave and quite a few who were even Heroes of the Soviet Union, but theirs was a different kind of bravery than "ours."

It all began not with racism but with the crisis of socialist ideology, which had to be quickly (in French, *en catastrophe*, which approximately means "catastrophically fast") replaced by patriotism, until then arrogantly dismissed everywhere by Soviet ideologists. It was specifically Russian patriotism, called upon to stand up to German nationalism, that led to the alienation of Jews. Jews became the other and were shoved to the side, into the shadows.

The new shift occurred immediately after the end of the war, when those who were recently allies became enemies. The situation heated up, and Americans were now perceived as a hostile power. Understandably, this led to a worsening of antisemitism. Now, not only were the Jews the other; they turned out to be religiously and ethnically related to "the enemies of our land, our party, and our ideas." The same Simonov who had had an "absolute scent" now passionately denounced the new adversary in the cycle of "Friends and Enemies":

> I went through the gauntlet of war and learned,
> with my very skin and the knuckles of my fists:
> There are no black-, olive-, or yellow-skinned,
> Only us the Reds and they the Whites.

Besides, in Russia there was an old tradition of antisemitism, which was present not only among the less-educated masses and Cossacks eager to shed blood with impunity, but was also shared by a sizeable part of the Russian intelligentsia—from Gogol to Rozanov and Blok to Kuprin. As soon as Jews became different, age-old instincts flared up again. They made it possible to carry out the antisemitic "cultural revolution" of 1948–53, which was cunningly called the struggle against cosmopolitism, and to conduct a monstrous trial against "killer doctors." All this happened in Russia, where millions lived. It happened with the support of the population. One must not forget about this. These twists and turns defined the fate of several generations but above all the generation of David Pritzker, who was born, as if on purpose, on November 7, 1917.

Hero and Slave

The independent life of David Pritzker began in Spain: he was a translator during the civil war. He had a youthful love for Spain—for its language, customs, poetry, and songs. I remember him constantly singing "Dona Mariquita . . . Dona Mariquita de mi corazon." He later wrote about his Spain. The best of his published compositions was a passionate book *The Feat of the Spanish Republic*. Soon after Spain, the war started. Pritzker found himself on the Karelian front, in the intelligence unit. My position as a translator at the Seventh Directorate (Department of Propaganda among the Enemy Troops) in the political administration of the headquarters at the Karelian front was to a great extent due to David Pritzker. At the time, in 1942, we met frequently. Every week, I went with him and his wife to visit our only acquaintance who had a private home in Belomorsk, the Moscow writer Gennady Fish, who was at the time a military journalist, a "quartermaster of the second rank." My young wife, Katya Zvorykina, who was a hospital nurse, came too. Incidentally, among the guests was Yura, who usually looked quiet. Judging by some of his comments, he was quite an educated young man. He was hopelessly in love with Musya, David's wife. Much later, about forty years after this, I learned with whom it was that fate, with all its lavish inventions, had brought us together. It was Yury Vladimirovich Andropov, who would later become the longstanding head of the KGB (1967–82), and then, for just fifteen months, the general secretary of the Central Committee of the CPSU. In the sixties, it seems, Musya Rit went to him with some written request that was vitally important to her. He did not reply.

David Pritzker's work in the intelligence unit consisted of reading and translating trophy documents and soldiers' letters, interrogating prisoners, and gathering information about the enemy. He knew the opposing German units as well as he knew the multiplication tables. He knew the commanders of battalions and companies by name. He would write reviews and recommendations based on research for his supervisors. He was considered useful, especially when his superior turned out to be the dashing, even mischievous Colonel Ruzov, who resembled Suvorov (this is a separate story). Pritzker was appreciated, but he was a technical executor, an invisible captain doing everything for everybody. He was too intelligent to try to get into any kind of high position. In addition, he was a Jew. From 1942, that impeded careers. Every time I spoke with him, I thought how we would have fought the war better if only our superior had been David Pritzker rather than the poorly educated General Rumyantsev. Alas, that was unthinkable, even when Stalin admitted that those commanding the front should be not heroes of the civil war or big-mustached men such as Oka Gorodovikov and Semyon Budenny, but the highly educated generals

Rokossovsky and Zhukov, Meretskov and Chernyakhovsky. Of the four military leaders named, two were subjected to torture in the NKVD prisons and only by chance survived. We often did not know the facts (later, for example, we read about how the investigator had urinated in the face of the future marshal Meretskov, or how supervisors broke stools as they beat Rokossovsky), but I clearly remember that we understood the gist of the matter.

David Pritzker understood sooner than many that the catastrophic failure of the first months of the war were the direct consequence of the extermination, one by one, of the commanding staff in 1938 and that Stalin had done irreparable harm to the Red Army by killing Tukhachevsky, Yakir, and Uborevich, the experienced, independent-thinking military leaders. I remember a conversation one night on the street of Belomorsk, when Pritzker, who was clearly aware of the villainous actions of the German Wehrmacht, talked about the high military level of the top German generals, Field Marshals Brauchitsch and Guderian. He complained about the exorbitant power wielded by our so-called "members of the military council." Every commander had such a commissar, a party worker of a high rank who knew nothing about military matters but who was authorized to maintain the party line (Khrushchev and Zhdanov and Brezhnev were all "members of military councils").

Under normal circumstances, David Pritzker should have been a general. Or, at any rate, a minister of foreign affairs. His knowledge of languages—French, German, Spanish, English—his flexible and resourceful mind, his rare memory, and a charm that could win over any interlocutor instantly—all these talents would have allowed us to have a real Russian diplomat, people such as Chicherin and Litvinov. But we had the dogmatic Molotov, who was only able to follow his boss's orders, the sly sadist Vyshinsky, and the petrified Gromyko. As for Pritzker, he only rose as high as the department of the international workers' movement . . .

He died after a trip to Spain, where the sixtieth anniversary of the civil war and the creation of the international brigades were celebrated. Before that, he'd had a stroke and walked with difficulty, dragging his leg. "I'm a wreck," he said to me in 1989, when he came to visit me (after almost twenty years!) at the Leningrad Hotel. He came with a close mutual friend of ours, a comrade from the front called Grisha Bergelson. We found the time to talk briefly about events of that time. He expressed some hopes for perestroika but with irony. "The wine has turned sour," he said then. "They're pouring it into another vessel, but it's still vinegar in another bottle."

It so happened that I was in St. Petersburg around the time of his death and burial, in January 1997. The service was in the funeral hall in Sverdlovskaya Hospital, which in its time had been built for the party elite. From talking to Zhenya, his son, I learned that David had not survived the trip to Spain. It had been too strenuous for him. Too much had been stirred up in his soul, too many memories and thoughts. And perhaps he saw the trip as a kind of stocktaking. What had he managed to do in those sixty years between his two Spains? I've already mentioned his wonderful book about the Spanish war. Yet even in this book he was not able to speak the truth, which he knew well, the truth of how Stalin betrayed the republicans, how he had weakened their front by punishing the Trotskyists and anarchists and then had arrested and punished the heroes of Spain—not only military heroes but even Mikhail Koltsov, the author of *The Spanish Diary*. The book should have been rewritten, but David could no longer find the strength. I still keep that book, with its poignant dedication, which begins with the words: "Among friends of my own age, I forget the number of years we have lived."

A Russian Writer and Two Jews

Some fifteen years after the memorable visit to Tauride Palace, A. I. Solzhenitsyn wrote a chapter called "Invisible" to add to his biographical book *The Oak and the Calf*, where the same episode is presented—quite accurately. Some details we recalled together when we met in Paris in 1975. However, here is how Solzhenitsyn comments on his story:

> I was categorically forbidden to go to the Tauride Palace to look at the hall where the Duma met and to visit the places of the February turmoil. And if I nevertheless got there in the spring of 1972—a Russian writer to a Russian memorial under "Russian rulers"!—it was at the risk and thanks to the resourcefulness of two Jews—Efim Etkind and David Petrovich Pritzker. (*Novy Mir*, no. 12 [1991], 37)

Reading these lines, I flinched (or shuddered?). For so many years, we had been close. We had confided so many things to each other that required the trust of friendship! It was not only I who felt this but he, too. Next to it were lines about our long-lasting friendship: "E. G. Etkind and I had already had an undeniable friendship of ten years by the time he was sent away [. . .] and of all the characters in this book [that is, *The Oak and the Calf*—E. E.], only he was openly attacked, publicly castigated, and thrown out of the country." However, the recognition of this ten year friendship had a footnote. I shall cite it in abbreviated form: "Our friendship initially continued abroad. But then, it changed. [. . .] Etkind turned into one of those who was ubiquitously spreading rumors about my being theocratic and antisemitic, which was never true" (footnote, 1986).

A. I. Solzhenitsyn wrote about our "undeniable friendship." In fact, we were very close to each other. Or were we really that close?

It turns out that I was always the other to him. He was a Russian writer, and David Pritzker and Efim Etkind were two Jews who helped him. We, the outsiders, the foreigners, the observers, assisted him, the native participant, Russian by blood, one of their own.

Can reasonable parents really be amazed by the fact that *Kids in a Cage* was written by the Jew Marshak for their Russian children? Can Solzhenitsyn really be surprised that the main book about WWII, the novel *Life and Fate*, was written by the Jew Vasily Grossman? Or that his, Solzhenitsyn's, prose was translated into German by Elisabeth Markstein, a Jew? Solzhenitsyn did not understand, and probably could not understand, that the very idea that a Jew was the other, an outsider, an observer, and not a participant by virtue of blood—that this concept was in itself a manifestation of antisemitism.

Needless to say, we have a limited vocabulary. We probably ought to have thought up another word, one that would reflect the difference between the attitude toward Jews of V. Shulgin and V. Rozanov and that of A. I. Solzhenitsyn. The latter did not call for pogroms, for liberation from Jewish domination. But he did not forget, while approving of his own, to push away the aliens. In the same chapter in *Calf*, delighting in the bravery of Igor Khokhlushkin, who had arranged for *Archipelago* to be printed underground, Solzhenitsyn exclaimed, "This is the way Russian boys cast their heads down so that *Archipelago* could march into the depths of Russia" (41). Further on, describing his future wife Natalya Svetlova, he wrote, "A spiritual closeness to her Russian roots, to the Russian essence, were seen within her as well as an extraordinary, loving mindfulness of the Russian language" (42). It is about this woman that he says (somewhat strangely, and particularly in terms of language and the "Russian essence"), "We are amazingly together, and as we go forward, we get even togetherer." But it was not possible to become "togetherer" with Lev Kopelev and a multitude of other similar assistants for they were not "Russian boys." . . .

Did I succeed in explaining the amazing phenomenon that followed me over the course of half a century, even if only superficially, briefly, and approximately? Did I succeed in showing when and how the alienation of the Jews from the "true population" of Russia reemerged during our century, and how the development of the concept of "otherness" turned into a conviction that they were the enemy?

There are simply two stages of antisemitism before us: the first is fraught with the second. To understand this, one has to know a lot about the history of culture. It does not hurt to remember how German patriots persecuted the "Jewish composer" Gustav Mahler, how the Nazis exposed the "Jewish physicist" Albert Einstein, how Felix Mendelssohn-Bartholdy suffered from racist persecution, and how (just recently) the journal *Molodaya Gvardiya* tried to remove the non-Russian Joseph Brodsky from Russian poetry and the Russian language.

David Pritzker and Efim Etkind did everything in their power so that A. I. Solzhenitsyn could see the location where his future novel was to take place. No, it was not two Jews who had helped the Russian writer. Strange that Solzhenitsyn did not see the solidarity of those who were a part of culture or appreciate the intelligentsia's need for mutual support, a need that was independent of the question of blood. Yet it was precisely this solidarity that made it possible for the author of *Ivan Denisovich* to be crowned with the Nobel Prize and helped him overcome exile and return to Russia triumphantly.

The Cowardice of a Brave Man

We met unexpectedly in some Italian airport after almost fifteen years. A symposium commemorating Mandelstam's one-hundred-year anniversary was opening in a day. I flew there from Paris, and he from Leningrad. I saw several acquaintances in the crowd. There were Leningraders and Muscovites heading for the next flight and, as always, Soviets walking in a solid group. Among them were people I was close to, including Sasha Kushner, his wife, Lena Nevzglyadova, and someone else. We embraced. In the back, there was someone who was standing straight, with military-like immobility (as if at attention). I looked at him and saw a startlingly aged and wrinkled Dudin. He held his arms at his sides and was averting his eyes. I understood: he was afraid that I would not shake his hand and didn't know how to deal with it. I brought him out of his discomfiture and spoke in a normal tone of voice, as if we had parted company just the day before. "Hello, Misha."

"Hello," he said, in a high-pitched and loud voice.

He squeezed my palm with both hands and from that moment on, he would not leave my side.

In Bari, we met in the hotel in the evening for dinner and in the morning before the meeting. Dudin was deliberately friendly and kept telling me about events from the past years at the Union of Soviet Writers in Leningrad and about marriages and deaths. I listened without saying anything, with only occasional interjections. Finally, there was a pause, and I said, "Misha, before we get to love each other that much, let us first clarify what happened fifteen years ago."

"Fifteen years ago?" he asked with strained ease, "And what was that?"

I glanced at this worn face of a youthful old man. I felt a bit sorry for him, but I continued. "You don't remember your speech at the secretariat, when they were expelling me from the union?"

"I don't remember," he said and repeated, "I don't remember. What did I say at the time?"

What was this, a silly boyish lie or a sincerely forgotten truth he so much wanted to forget? I don't know. To this day, I don't know.

"Misha," I said, embarrassed by my own forthrightness, "You were a brave soldier and an honorable man. You seldom committed base acts. That time at the secretariat, what you did was vile. Can it really be that you don't remember?"

"Honest to God, I don't remember," said Dudin. And so, I had to tell him, although I really didn't want to. I couldn't believe that he'd forgotten.

We were not close, but had gotten to know each other in the fifties. Starting in the postwar years, when we both wore military shirts and coats, we addressed each other in the familiar form of "you." I liked his poems. (I use this weak verb deliberately.) They contained a distant reflection of Gumilyov and Nikolai Tikhonov. There was a certain impulsiveness in them, a neat and dynamic rhythm, and a masculine firmness. But I understood all too well that compared to his predecessors Dudin was forgettably small, and next to contemporaries such as Gleb Semyonov, David Samoylov, Yevgeny Vinokurov, and Boris Slutsky he was uninteresting. Still, he had his own timbre, something resembling individuality (but not personality), and that evoked sympathy in me. What is more, he seemed to be talented in many areas. He drew many cartoons of his friends and himself and composed funny epigrams. Their main features were often absurdity and dumb but charming plays on words. It was he who created the quatrain that made you laugh each time you heard it:

> The hag of steel, Marietta Shaginian,
> Is deaf, alas, and cannot hear,
> But to a peasant and a proletarian
> She serves as a prosthetic ear.

The epigram was, of course, stupid, but there was a certain daring in it, even recklessness, and there was a mischievous play on words using clichés. Dudin was always brave to the point of recklessness, superficially charming, and frivolously mischievous. That put him in a special position, outside the orbit of the poets of the war years: the darkly stern Slutsky, the wise and elegant Samoylov, the ironic tzaddik Svetlov, the pathetic yet brave Simonov, and Tikhonov, who sang of military discipline.

But I digress. I'm not writing an essay about Dudin's poetry but a story about a person. It was not often that we met, but when we did, we always did so with a sense of warmth and wartime comradeship and a feeling of closeness through our poetic tastes. I remember that once he saw me in the Writer's House. He rushed up to me. He had just read "Moonlight Sonata" by Yiannis Ritsos, which I had translated. He gustily expressed his approval, loudly reciting some lines that had touched his soul.

A curious episode took place sometime in the mid-sixties, when Dudin was authorized by the housing commission of the Union of Soviet Writers to examine the living accommodations of the writers who had requested an "improvement of their living conditions." At the time, we were living in a huge communal apartment at fifty-nine Kirovsky Avenue, with nine rooms and the same number of families allocated to one kitchen. One of our neighbors was Pavlik, who collected lovebirds. He had more than one hundred of them, which he kept in a small room behind the kitchen. Promising Pavlik a half-liter bottle of vodka, I persuaded him to set the little green birds free when the commission arrived: let them fly around in the communal hallway. When the writers' commission headed by Dudin arrived, the little parrots began flying above their heads. They chirped happily and made a mess on Misha's felt hat. Giggling self-consciously, the commission left. Only Dudin appreciated my tactic and laughed loudly. After agreeing that a writer could not work under such conditions, Litfond let me have an apartment on Alexander Nevsky Street (previously called Red Square Street!). That was our last home in Leningrad. It was confiscated in 1974. We did not forget that we owed the apartment to Misha Dudin directly and only indirectly to Pavlik and his lovebirds.

Dudin was a soldier. That defined his merits and his deficiencies. His soldierly merits were the simplicity of his male comradery, the certainty that he would rush to your rescue, and his love for sharing meals. And his deficiencies were his unquestioning obedience to his superiors and his readiness to bow to an order. He could cheat or even betray someone, not from spite or deviousness or a desire for power, but from his thoughtless obedience. This weakness of his was known. He, by the way, was aware of it and excused himself with his own slightly vulgar humor. Once, V. Zavodchikov, a poet and translator, entered the restaurant of the Writer's House, and Dudin, who was sitting at the table slightly drunk, loudly shouted, "Zavodchikov has arrived, the king of translation."

Zavodchikov said, "Misha, all the rhymes that there are for your last name have already been used up. [. . .]. But I know one more, just wait a minute.

Zavodchikov probably remembered an epigram that was used a lot in spite of its absurdity (or possibly because of it):

> Mikhail Aleksandrovich Sholokhov
> was hard for the reader. Who stood in
> to write for the full-blown idiots?—
> Mikhail Alexandrovich Dudin!

[. . .] Dudin was mischievous, and it was quite natural that he liked Bezymensky's epigram about himself:

> All that is left of me, between us,
> Are a big belly and a small penis!

Let us return, however, to Zavodchikov. Several minutes later, he approached Dudin and, impromptu, read him an epigram where there was in fact a new (and merciless!) rhyme:

> The Union of Soviet Writers had
> That Dudin, spawn of Judin, as its head.
> The names in Russian rhyme, nothing's amiss:
> For both betray you with a friendly kiss.

Did Dudin laugh this time? That is unlikely. This epigram is one of those that remains stuck to you like a brand on your forehead.

The secretariat of the Writers' Union met on April 25, 1974, at three o'clock in the afternoon. They considered just one question: the expulsion of E. G. Etkind from the union. An official from the GB was present at the meeting. He read an official note declaring Etkind to be a systematic enemy of the Soviet regime. Then, one after the other, the secretaries spoke: Kholopov, V. N. Orlov, S. Botvinnik, Chepurov, and Dudin. According to the minutes, Dudin said that in Etkind's letter to young Jews "the most disgusting thing is the nationalism. From there, it is just half a step to fascism. This Zionism seeps from every line." An obvious absurdity. In the letter, I had urged young Jews not to leave for Israel and not to yearn for the freedom of others but to fight for their own freedom at home. You could call such a stance anti-Soviet, but in no way was it Zionist. It was, after all, openly polemical in regard to Zionism. A few days later, I learned what exactly Dudin had said, and I thought he'd deliberately chosen such a move so that it would be easier for me to defend myself. Alas, Dudin had simply obeyed an order. He was obedient like a soldier, and I could not stop repeating to myself with bitterness and misery: *That Dudin, spawn of Judin* . . .

I later remembered this episode several times. It's in the book *Notes of a Nonconspirator* and certainly deserves being analyzed psychologically. The thing is that Dudin had given a short but deadly speech denouncing an old comrade. A Zionism that borders on fascism: such a monstrous accusation could lead to my arrest and a term in a camp, even in 1974. Camp terms were given for much smaller sins. How could he let himself do it? Here, various factors had come together. First of all, he had assumed that no one would hear about this speech of his, as they were not taking down minutes. Second, the official from the GB was sitting close by. Third, Dudin was expecting the publication of a two- or three-volume collection of his poems. Fourth, he was not the first to speak. Everyone before him had spoken in the same way. Fifth, mention was made of Solzhenitsyn, who had recently been expelled from the country, with whom Etkind was closely associated. Sixth, Dudin had consumed a half-bottle of cognac before the meeting. Well, was it really possible for him not to say exactly what the authorities expected? The need to submit to the order and exhibit a soldier's obedience—this was the seventh and probably the most important reason.

I am, of course, interested in Dudin's psychology as a poet and a soldier. But I would like to understand why during Soviet times so many decent, brave, honorable people behaved like cowardly slaves.

We were standing in the foyer of the hotel in the city of Bari, and I was telling Dudin in brief what I have just explained above. Dudin said, "This isn't true. This can't be true. Where did you get this from?"

"From the minutes."

"No one took down minutes!" Dudin said.

"Officially, they didn't keep them, but I immediately received a recording, a very detailed recording of the meeting."

Dudin was silent for a long time. Then, he said, "What year was it?"

"You seldom behaved villainously," I repeated, "can it be that you forgot that it was in '74?"

He again fell silent and finally choked out a strange sentence, "I was still drinking at the time." I was surprised.

"Are you not going to say anything else?" But he said nothing more. Only, the next day, he gave me a gift of a miniature publication of his poems, with the inscription:

To Efim Etkind. After many long, mutually unaccountable years.
  The soul is spent,
  The body worn out,
  The limit is reached for words one has wrought,

Joy came and went,
Dreams burned out,
And an entire life has come to naught.

28 June 1988

Mikhail Dudin, Bari

The symposium ended, and we went our separate ways. After some time, I received a long letter—in essence an expression of remorse—from Dudin. I again felt sorry for him, especially when I saw that the famous poet and Hero of Socialist Labor had had misspelled the word "helpless." A year went by. I was in Boston, and he called from New York. "Come, you must come. I brought you a present." I could not come, as I was lecturing. He mailed his present, a very heavy hardbound volume of an anthology of twentieth-century Russian poetry edited by I. S. Yezhov and E. I. Shamurin, a first edition, put out in 1925. On the title page of this rarest of books, there was a carefully written dedication:

To Efim Grigorievich Etkind
In memory of Leningrad and Russian Poetry
M. D. 1989

M. Dudin was correcting his biography. He understood that he was standing on the precipice of death and that a poet must clean himself of blemishes.

On January 2, 1994, I called St. Petersburg from Bretagne to send my best wishes to my longtime comrade Daniil Granin on his seventy-fifth birthday. Thanking me, he said, "Misha Dudin died." They'd been neighbors for many years and had loved each other. Dudin's death was a difficult experience for him, and it turned out to be a blow for me, too. Dudin was a man of his country and of his generation: a hero and coward, a devoted friend and a base traitor at the same time. To understand Dudin is to understand the atrocious and wonderful era in which he and I lived.

Postscript

An obituary signed by the poet Igor Shklyarevsky was placed in *Literaturnaya Gazeta* on January 12, 1994. It stated very effectively, "Cheerful, tall, honorable, knew how to do good without being obliging, an Olympian who was above envy and squabbling, one of the last poets who was a fighter on the front, a resounding master of verse..." All of this was accurate, but all of this was also the start of a myth. An obituary has its own rules, and a myth has its own rules, too. But that does not mean that one should forget that there is also fairness.

Two Jewish Fates:
Reading the Diaries of Victor Klemperer*

Victor Klemperer (1881–1960) was one of my teachers. His book *The History of French Literature from Napoleon to Contemporary Times*, which was published in the middle of the twenties, became a go-to reference book for me when I was studying this subject at Leningrad University under the guidance of A. A. Smirnov, S. S. Mokulsky, V. M. Zhirmunsky, and B. G. Reizov. After the war, I became fascinated by his research in *LTI* (*Lingua Tertii Imperii*, or *Language of the Third Reich*), in which he had collected and analyzed the linguistic and stylistic peculiarities of the Nazi era. The book, which was published in Berlin in 1947–49, has the subtitle *Notebook of a Philologist*. It opens with the author's introduction, titled "Heroism."

The word "heroism" was extremely important in the Nazi press, alongside the word "militant" (*kämpferisch*). Both terms were used in a distorted and false way. True heroism is a rare phenomenon. "The more reserved, the less showy and decorative, the less advantageous to the hero, the purer and more significant heroism is." Yes, there was heroism in Hitler's time, too, but on the other side, among the anti-fascists. "Not a notorious death on the 'field of honor' but, in the best-case scenario, a public death by guillotine." Klemperer spoke with admiration about the

---

*   Victor Klemperer, *Ich will Zeugnis ablegen bis zum Letzten. Tägebücher, 1933–1945*, 2 vols. (Berlin: Aufbau Verlag, 1995). Further references to the volume and page number are in the text (only Russian translations are given throughout). [E. E.]

few "Aryan" wives who remained dedicated to their Jewish husbands. They were subjected to humiliation and beatings, people spat in their faces, the Gestapo insulted them with foul language, but they did not renounce their husbands, and in supporting them they shared the terrible fate of the Jewish people. I would add here that Professor Klemperer was similarly heroic. He kept a diary throughout; he wrote entries daily. He only skipped a day or two on rare occasions but never went more than a week without writing. Searches among the Jews became more and more frequent, and the danger persistently grew, but, realizing the danger that he was facing, he fulfilled the duty he believed he owed to himself and to history. Here is an entry for February 8, 1942: "Always the same fluctuation in feelings—up and down. Fear that my writing will doom me to a concentration camp. The sense of duty to write—this is my life's task, my calling. The feeling of *vanitas vanitatum* (vanity of vanities), the uselessness of my writing. Nonetheless, I keep writing my diary and *Curriculum* (autobiography)." In an entry from the same day, there were details of the previous day's search at a neighbor's home. A group of gestapo members had come to their home, eight thugs: "insulting, kicking, and hitting; Mrs. Neumann received five blows to the head. [. . .] They took whatever happened to be there: candles, soap, a suitcase, books, half a pound of jam (bought legally using ration cards), writing paper, tobacco, military medals ('You'll no longer need them!'). . . . 'Why do you all live so long? . . . You could hang yourselves . . . or you could turn on the gas in the kitchen!'" (2, 19–20).

In May, they came to the Klemperers' and ransacked everything. However, the Klemperers were lucky: they didn't take the Greek dictionary from the bookshelf in which the diary pages were kept. "If a page had fallen out from the dictionary and raised their suspicions, that would certainly have been the end of me. After all, they kill for much smaller offenses. [. . .] But I keep writing. That is *my* heroism. I want to preserve a testimony, a clear testimony" (2:99). "I will try to keep the diary going. I want to bear witness to everything, until the very end" (2:124). However, such records are rare. Professor Klemperer fulfilled his duty without reasoning, without hesitating, in solitude, with clenched teeth, and in silence. Only Eva, his "Aryan wife," knew about the diary. She understood perfectly well that they would both face death if the manuscript were found. She knew and tried to help her husband as much as she could.

The diary for 1933–45 came out in 1995, on the fiftieth anniversary of the end of the war. It comprised two huge volumes, about sixteen hundred pages in total. Why were Klemperer's notes not published earlier? Reading them was of course not easy, with the small, indistinct typed print and the deliberately hard-to-read handwriting. There were other, more serious reasons. Klemperer constantly pointed out the deep similarity between Hitler's Nazism and Stalin's Communism. "They both disgust me. I see their close relationship [. . .] but the racist idea of National Socialism appears most brutal to me (in the literal sense of the word)" (1:299). This is what Klemperer wrote in August 1936, when few understood how similar to each other these totalitarian regimes were. Five years later, in May 1941, he noted, "We now have the purest kind of Communism. But Communism kills in a more honest way" (1:594). There were many such statements in the diary. Was it possible to publish them under the conditions of the GDR? And Klemperer himself probably did not want to. After twelve years of Nazi humiliation, he also had to experience grief in "socialist" Germany. Here is a brief description of what happened to him after the war.

> On February 13, 1945, the Royal Air Force bombed and burned down Dresden, where the Klemperers were living in a "Jewish house," a dormitory, a building with many apartments to where the Jews who had escaped death were herded. The building burned down. Klemperer, wounded by the fragment of an incendiary bomb, managed to get through the fire to the Elbe, where he unexpectedly found his lost wife. She had been looking for him among the corpses. . . . After walking for a long time, the Klemperers got to Bavaria. In the village of Unterbernbach, they waited until the American troops arrived, and in June they finally returned to Dresden. The professor was full of hope and planned to build a new Germany. By the law of those years, people first had to prove to the occupying powers that they were not agents but victims of fascism. Was it possible to convince the vigilantly fierce

Soviet agents? Why was Klemperer not in a concentration camp, and why had he survived? The people in charge in the university were those who in the past had aided in chasing out the Jewish professor. One could fight them only by drawing on the support of the new master: the Communist Party. In November 1945, Klemperer decided to join its ranks. "The party is the only one that is truly persistent in the radical purging of Nazis. However, in place of the previous absence of freedom is the promise of a new absence of freedom!" (November 20, 1945).

Klemperer was gravely ill, his heart was failing, and his old age was taking a greater and greater toll on his strength. In 1951, Eva died. But he was unstoppable in his work: He was a professor in the universities of Dresden (1945–47), Greifswald (1947–48), Halle (1948–60), and Berlin (1951–54) and became a full member of the Berlin Academy of Sciences. Volumes of his works were published, among them *LTI* (1947 and 1949), *History of Eighteenth-Century French Literature*, and a collection of articles titled *Before 33/After 45*. He died in Dresden, living until he was almost eighty. In the last fifteen years of his life, he returned to his role as an educator of new generations of students, a teacher, a literary scholar, and an organizer in this area of studies. Given everything that we know about the suffering that befell him during the Nazi era, especially in the last years, such activity seems improbable. Victor Klemperer was animated by his dedication to literature, French and German, his love for his native culture, which had to be brought back to life after twelve years of barbaric tyranny, and his sense of duty to postwar Germany. He did as much as he could and what he could, aware that the old constraints on freedom were being replaced by new ones and that it was time to write a new book, *LQI* (*Lingua Quarti Imperii*, or *Language of the Fourth Empire*). He knew that it would be no more indulgent than the preceding one.

However, Klemperer considered overcoming fascism's monstrous consequences as his first task. "If one is to imagine a blackout as a symbol," he said as early as 1946, when he opened the Dresden Volkshochschule, "the blackout was not of windows but of minds, which gave us not just six years of darkness but twelve. There is hardly anyone more important in our country than a schoolteacher, and for each of us, whatever department we might belong to, there cannot be anything more important than overcoming this blackout, letting in the clear daylight, and promoting Enlightenment."* Victor Klemperer, a literary and cultural historian, came to the conclusion that the ideology of National Socialism represented a distorted development of the ideas of the German romantics: "The love for nature and the dream of merging with nature turned into teachings about the lack of spiritual freedom: man is tied to his blood and soil like an animal. [. . .] Love for one's native land turns into arrogant nationalism. The call of 'return to nature' turns into a call to 'return to the predatory beast,' and the idolizing of instinct, into a disdain for reasoning." All these romantic concepts, which for a long time had been the stuff of intellectual games, suddenly became a frightening reality. "And the feeling of disdain for thought, its suppression, and the systematic dumbing down of people became the goal of propaganda, which constantly operates with extremely vulgarized ideas of German romanticism. There was no doubt that the underlying basis of National Socialism is a distorted romanticism and romantic teachings about the domination of feelings."

Klemperer's analysis was accurate: distorted romanticism led—it is frightening to think and frightening to say—to Auschwitz. In Russia, the totalitarian structure turned out to be similar to the German one, but its underlying basis was different; it was, instead, a distorted rationalism. V. Klemperer chose as his model the "Encyclopedia, the Bible of the Enlightenment, the dictionary of dry rationalists evoking the aversion of Jean Jacques. [. . .] Over the course of twelve years, access to thought was shut off for the German people. Thought was distorted, disfigured, obscured, and banished. People were kept in an addled state for twelve years. There were no schools, no universities, not one book, not a newspaper

---

* "Über die Aufgaben der Volkshochschule. Rede zur Eröffnung der Dresdner Volkshochschule am 28. April 1946," in Victor Klemperer, *Vor 33 / nach 45: Gesammelte Aufsätze* (Berlin: Aufbau Verlag, 1956), 244. [E. E.]

that was not part of this key task of the Third Reich: to stupefy the people."*
For this very reason, V. Klemperer gladly agreed to head the Dresden
Volkshochschule. Only in this way would he be able to fight against what
he called the "blacking out" of people's minds.

In Russia during the 1990s, the ideal of the great Diderot and D'Alembert *Encyclopedia* was unthinkable. After all, many people believe that it was the ideas of "pure rationalism" originating from the encyclopedists' godless and ironic materialism taken to their extreme that had led to the transgressions of the Stalin era. It was not the *Encyclopedia*, as Klemperer had hoped, but the Bible that became the bible of the new era.

I read the diary of Victor Klemperer—his notes over the course of twelve years of Nazism—without stopping, experiencing feelings that were hard to define. I shall try to make sense of them.

For many years, I was tied to the German language and to German literature and culture. During the war, when I was working on "propaganda among the enemy troops," composing leaflets and publishing a newspaper for German military forces, I spoke with hundreds of captured soldiers, officers, and at times generals. I always tried to understand how it had happened, how this unthinking obedience to authority, this mindless, fanatic nationalism, this adoration of a hysterical führer, brutal hatred of foreigners, and unimaginable cruelty could come from the very same people who had created the poetry of Goethe, Schiller, Eichendorff, and Rilke, the music of Beethoven, Bach, and Schubert, the philosophy of Schelling and Hegel. ("Hermine Braunsteiner was the worst. She took part in the 'children's operation' of 1943. Many witnesses spoke of frightening details: how the senior supervisor, Elsa Erich, enticed children with candy to get into trucks that were heading to gas chambers, how other children were thrown into trucks that were already full, like bags of linen" [Minutes

---

*   Ibid., 243–44. [E. E.]

of the Trial of Majdanek, 212th day, December 8, 1977]).* To ask such a question of oneself or others half a century later is unwise; it's even banal. But how am I to get away from it? While translating poems by Hölderlin or Brecht, I thought about those "bags of linen" and about the German woman in Majdanek who had thrown them into the back of a truck. For fifty years, I wanted to understand but could not. Now, reading the brief notes of Victor Klemperer, I began to comprehend, for the first time in my life.

Victor Klemperer saw early (although he expressed it much later) the connection between the "blue flower" and the philosophy of "blood and soil," the mysticism of German romanticism and the "myth of the twentieth century." Theoretically, he understood the romantic genesis of Nazism later, in 1946. His diary allowed me to trace the development of his thoughts and capture the genesis of his conceptions. A diary is not literature—that is, not fine art—but the process of life itself, unadorned, not distorted, and usually not even subject to evaluation, judgement, or approval. It simply informs. In the weeks when I was reading Klemperer's diaries, I lived through twelve years of Nazism, hour after hour, next to him, together with him, next to his wife Eva and his friends. Together with him, I reconstructed the little home in Dölzchen near Dresden, then lost this house, moved to the communal "Jewish House," walked, panting because of a heart ailment, to buy food with ration cards between 3:00 and 4:00 pm, when a Jew with a yellow star on his lapel was allowed to walk in the streets and buy something. Together, we listened for steps on the staircase and hid small pages of the diary in the Greek dictionary. Together, we caught a compassionate look from a passing "Aryan" or shuddered when another became filled with contempt and hatred: "You haven't died yet, you damned Jew? Why don't you hang yourself there, on that branch?"

---

*   Günther Schwarzberg, *Der Juwelier von Majdanek: Tagebuch eines Prozesses* (Hamburg: Stern, 1981), 151. [E. E.]

It was frighteningly easy for me to be with him and next to him because he, belonging to a different generation (he was forty years older), seemed to be me, only from an earlier time and in a place further west. I did what he did: I taught French literature at a university. When the bad times began for him, when the National Socialists expelled him from the department, he was teaching a seminar on Corneille's dramaturgy. Forty years later, when I was driven out of the Herzen Pedagogical Institute, I was teaching a seminar on Victor Hugo's dramaturgy. Klemperer was a professor not in Berlin but in Dresden, the intellectual and artistic center of Germany, the city of the famous Zwinger art gallery. I was also a professor of French literature not in Moscow but in the Russian Dresden: Leningrad, a "provincial capital," a city celebrated throughout the world for the Hermitage, the Zwinger's rival. We were also similar in many other ways. He was persecuted, tormented, and forced out for being Jewish in Germany, as I was in Soviet Russia. The difference was that they called him a Jew, a Yid, and made him wear a yellow star on his sleeve and hang the same Star of David above his doorbell. I never heard the word "Jew" from anybody. It was substituted by various synonyms such as "cosmopolitan," "Zionist," "undocumented tramp," and "antipatriot."

Klemperer was a Protestant in his official papers but an atheist by conviction. I was an agnostic, very far from any Zionism. No one was interested in this: for the Nazis and the Communists, we were both Jews—by blood, by last name, by congenital alienness.

I would add to what has already been said: Victor Klemperer was a participant in the First World War. He joined as a volunteer in 1915. I, his student and colleague, also joined the army as a volunteer during the Second World War, in 1942. We both received military awards, which later prompted the powers that be to mock us derisively as they trampled us and chased us out as intellectuals and Jews.

There were, of course, differences, considerable ones. Klemperer, who had never been to Russia, guessed what they were. In his entry for August 14, 1942, he spoke about the cruelty with which the Germans transfer

Jews to Theresienstadt Concentration Camp. "They do not pay the least amount of attention to age, complete paralysis, and pain, and what seems much more disgusting to me compared to the Russians: there's nothing spontaneous in this. Everything is methodically organized and proper. This is a 'cultured' cruelty. Everything takes place hypocritically, in the name of culture, falsely; people don't just get killed for nothing here" (2:206). Three days later, on August 17, he developed this thought further:

> It seems more and more clear to me that at its core National Socialism is a German plant (*ein deutsches Gewächs*), no matter how much foreign matter it absorbs . . . National Socialism absorbs fascism, Bolshevism, and Americanism, processing all of it in German romanticism. '*Les extremes se touchent*' (extremes meet). A nation of dreamers and pedants; of silent obedience taken to absurdity (*der verschwiegene Überkonsequenz*), vagueness, and extreme order. We have organized everything, both cruelty and killings. Instead of spontaneous antisemitism, here we create the "Institute of Jewish Problematics." At the same time, all intellectualism is rejected as Jewish and shallow. A German has feelings and depth. (2:209–10)

We both experienced something similar—he in Germany, and I in Soviet Russia—with an interval of forty years. They forced us out of universities and took away our students. Our books were removed from libraries and banned by a special government order. Even the destroyed books are similar: his four-volume *The History of French Literature* (1925–32), and my two-volume *Seminar on French Stylistics* (1960–61). In both cases, it's obvious how absurd, even comical, it is to have a "political prohibition" on books on classical French literature and stylistics. Although in Russia they went in some ways further in this vein of comic absurdity. During several scandalously solemn meetings, the academic board of the institute publicly stripped me of all academic degrees and ranks (candidate and doctor of science, docent and full professor). Later, after twenty years had passed, the same board returned them to me (in 1994). With V. Klemperer, they did not do this. Perhaps in a German university they understood the evil comedy of doing so? On the other hand, to strip someone of a university degree in

Germany, even in Hitler's Germany, required proof of plagiarism. In our country, they considered this matter more simply. A scholarly degree, that of academic, was preserved only for A. D. Sakharov, and even then, it was against the will of party authorities. However, there was most likely another reason. The Nazis had just formulated a law (it was bloody and idiotic, but still a law) forbidding Jews to teach. In Soviet Russia, such a law could not exist. It would have contradicted the officially accepted Communist ideology of internationalism. This meant that one had to replace the law with a system of political paraphrases that expressed the same thing: "Jews have no place at universities." Professor Anatoly Domashnev, a Germanist, gave a talk at one of the meetings mentioned, in which he maintained that Etkind was an "anti-Soviet renegade and a double-dealer. . . . He did not leave for Israel but engaged in more subtle politics . . . There is no place for the likes of Etkind in the Soviet collective of teachers. He must be thrown out of the institute and stripped of the academic titles and degrees he also received at our institute" (Minutes of the Meeting of the Academic Board of the Herzen Institute on April 25, 1974). The other professors who spoke said the same thing: anti-Soviet, double dealer, renegade, and sometimes a Zionist. All this instead of saying "Jew." Fifteen years earlier, in 1949, they were expelling me, calling me a cosmopolitan. That also meant "Jew."

It was clear that the reason for our persecutions, for both of our "civil executions," was our Jewishness. At the same time, I would note that during difficult times, "Aryan wives" supported and even saved my German predecessor and me from disaster. For him, it was Eva Schlemmer (Klemperer's wife of forty-five years, from 1906 to 1951), and for me, it was Ekaterina Fyodorovna Zvorykina (my wife of forty-six years, from 1940 to 1986). He became a moral victor of the regime after twelve years, and I, his Soviet student, successor, and colleague, did so after fifteen years. Both he and I needed one-and-a-half decades for the ridiculous prohibition on our names and our books—in both cases on the culture and literature of France—to be removed.

This is why I read Victor Klemperer's diary with special feelings. I seemed to be re-living my own life. Soviet Communism was for me what German Nazism was for Klemperer. I repeat: we experienced something similar, although events developed differently. I was expelled from academia and literature three times: in 1949 for being a cosmopolitan; in 1964 for being a literary specialist who dared to step forward as a witness for the defense in the trial against the poet Joseph Brodsky (accused falsely of parasitism); and in 1974 for being in close contact with A. Solzhenitsyn, an enemy of the regime, as well as for being the author of an open letter calling on young Jews not to leave but to struggle for their freedom at home, in Russia—twenty-five years of uninterrupted persecution that took on various forms and that seldom weakened.

The life of Victor Klemperer turned out differently. The Nazi regime did not have any objections against him personally. He shared the fate of the people to which he belonged by blood, because Klemperer was, as stated earlier, a Protestant by faith, an atheist in terms of his worldview, and a German in terms of how he perceived himself. "Where am I to be classified? With the 'Jewish people,' such is Hitler's decree. . . . But I am nothing other than a German or a German European" (from an entry on October 5, 1935; 1:220). Klemperer returned constantly to this theme. From his point of view, what was often called the "Jewish question" did not exist. One of his comprehensive contemplations about this is in an entry on January 10, 1939 (after the monstrous pogroms of 1938, which shocked Europe, when the shop windows of "Jewish stores" were broken, many synagogues were burned, and "Jewish hospitals" were destroyed). I cite it in abbreviated form:

> No German or West European question exists. Anyone who acknowledges it by doing so only strengthens the false thesis of the NSDAP (Nationalsozialistische Deutsche Arbeiterpartei) and becomes this party's helper. Until 1933, and for at least a whole century, German Jews were undoubtedly Germans, nothing else. The proof is that many thousands of "half" and "quarter Jews" have a completely conflict-free existence and collaboration in many areas of German life. The constant

simmering of antisemitism is not at all proof of the opposing point of view, that there is alienation between Jews and "Aryans." The friction between them is incomparably weaker than the otherness separating Protestants and Catholics, or employers and employees, or, say, residents of East Prussia and Southern Bavaria, or the Rhineland and Berlin. German Jews were a part of the German people, just as the French were a part of the French, and so on. They occupied a specific place in German life and were in no way a burden to the entirety of that life. Their place was least of all that of urban and even less so agricultural workers. They were and remain for the most part (even if they themselves don't want to admit it today) German intellectuals, the representatives of the educated stratum of society. . . . "Nationhood," in the sense of the purity of blood, is a zoological concept that has not corresponded to any reality for a long time and that is already much less fundamental than the ancient, strict demarcation between the spheres of men and women. (1:457)

Klemperer went further still. He maintains that Jews who succumb to ideological manipulation and who as a result come to believe in having special "Jewish blood" "allow the Nazis to throw them back thousands of years" (1:458). He also says that it's impossible to turn the intelligentsia into peasants, that trying to do so is unnatural, and therefore the idea of a Jewish state is absurdly reactionary. But let us not forget that Klemperer's anti-Zionism came about in the twenties and thirties. Since then, a lot of water and a lot of Jewish blood has been spilt. However, the idea that historical progress and genuine democracy were incompatible with the "zoological idea" of "clean blood" has proven correct more than once. It is enough to refer to the recent "ethnic cleansings" in Yugoslavia.

Still, how did it happen that the Germans who had read Goethe and Theodor Fontane became the Germans who believed Goebbels and Strasser? I will pause to speak about only one aspect of their lives in the thirties.

Victor Klemperer was a professor at Dresden University from 1920 on. In 1933, when Hitler came to power, he was fifty-three. In academic circles, he was known for several books: the already cited *The History of French Literature of the Nineteenth and Twentieth Centuries* (1925–32); *Contemporary French Prose* (1923); *Roman Originality (Romanische*

Sonderart, 1926), a collection of fresh and thought-provoking articles; a piece of research titled *The Newest French Poetry* (1929); and a monograph *Pierre Corneille* (1931). Apart from books, there were many academic articles and reviews on the literature of France, Italy ("The Last Peaceful Months in Italy," 1915), Spain ("Does a Spanish Renaissance Exist?" 1927), Germany ("Christian Morgenstern and Symbolism," 1928), and other countries (World Literature and the Literature of Europe," 1929). In the *Brockhaus Encyclopedia*, Victor Klemperer appeared along with his famous brother Georg, a professor of medicine, and his cousin Otto Klemperer, a conductor who was even more famous.

Soon after the Nazis came to power in 1933, the head of the university invited Professor Klemperer over to let him know that for now, while he still could teach seminars, it was forbidden for him to ask questions or to give examinations to students. (Is it even conceivable that a Jew would give examinations to Aryans?)

Fewer and fewer students came (they were "advised not to study with a Jew"). By the end, there were only one or two of them. And so, in May 1935, no one was surprised when Klemperer was dismissed into early retirement (at the age of fifty-five). "Today, I handed the keys to the seminar room and to the whole building to Wengler. I stood before the door to the seminar room with the key in my pocket. I did not want to open it myself. The attendant approached—I knew him only by sight. He was in a stormtrooper's uniform. He shook my hand in an exaggerated, cordial manner, and then called Wengler over from the next room" (entry for May 31, 1935; 1:204).

And so, V. Klemperer was out of work. At the time, public executions had not yet been adopted as a practice. In April 1974, his Soviet colleague was dismissed with much more noise and deliberate drama. I've already spoken about several meetings of the academic board at the Herzen Institute in Leningrad, where my recent colleagues gave speeches one after the other and branded me an anti-Soviet and Zionist, and loudly exclaimed, trying to outshout each other, "He has no place here! He cannot be allowed to have contact with students! . . . Get him out of here!" However, that was forty years later and not in Dresden but in Leningrad.

The Dresden dismissal was arranged in just two years of Nazism. Here are several diary entries, beginning with March 1933: "The atmosphere is like the atmosphere before a pogrom (*wie vor einem Pogrom*) in the darkest period of the Middle Ages or in the depths of tsarist Russia. . . . We are hostages. . . . Basically, I am experiencing shame rather than fear. Shame for Germany. I have in fact always felt that I am German. I always imagined that the twentieth century and Central Europe would be different from the fourteenth century and Romania. How wrong I was!" (entry for March 30, 1933; 1:15). I, too, experienced shame for Russia—"shame, rather than fear." My shame may even have been sharper because in my "case" colleagues from the institute and the Writers' Union had stepped forward to speak and had given the order "out!" as did my brothers in literature, such as Vladimir Orlov, the poet Mikhail Dudin, and the prose writer Gleb Goryshin . . .

A day later, on March 31, Klemperer wrote:

> Today, the Dresden Student Society announced that . . . contact with Jews was inimical to the honor of German students. Jews are forbidden to enter a student dormitory. . . . In Munich, Jewish instructors were not let into the university building. The call and order of the Boycott Committee says, "Religion is immaterial. Only race is important. If the store owner is Jewish and his wife is Christian or the other way around, the store is considered Jewish." Consequently, it is subject to a boycott. (1:16)

A boycott was put into effect thus:

> On Saturday, there will be red slips of paper at stores saying, "Acknowledged as a German-Christian enterprise." Among them were closed stores, and before them were stormtroopers with triangular shields: "Anyone who buys from a Jew promotes foreign domination and destroys the German economy." People streamed along Prague Street and looked. And that was the boycott! For now, it was just on Saturday, then a break until Wednesday, except for banks. But it included lawyers and doctors. . . . Today, they arrested the presidents of Frankfurt University

and Braunschweig Technical School; Kantorovich, the head of the University of Bonn Clinic; and the editor of the stock exchange section of *Frankfurter Zeitung*, a Christian . . . There will be an explosion, but we will probably pay for it with our lives, we the Jews. The resolution of the Dresden Student Society was dreadful: To be in contact with Jews is inimical to the honor of German students . . . (1:18)

"An announcement on the wall of the House of Students (there are similar ones at all universities) said, 'If a Jew writes in German, he is lying.' He has the right to write only in Yiddish. Jewish books in German must be considered translations. This must be specified on the title page. I am drawing attention only to the most horrible things, only the shreds of madness in which we are immersed" (entry for April 25, 1933; 1:24).

Bans and resolutions came, one after another. Klemperer recorded each one of them:November 1933:

Jewish students were issued yellow certificates (and brown ones for Germans) (1:66);

March 1934: a ban forbidding Jews from defending their dissertations (1:98);

June 1934: a ban forbidding Germans from buying items from Jews. "You are not allowed to make purchases from Jews in Falkenstein? Falkenstein residents travel to the Jew in Auerbach, and Auerbach residents buy items from the Falkenstein Jew. For more substantial items, people from smaller towns travel to places where there is a large Jewish store. If people meet there, they don't acknowledge each other. There's a silent agreement" (1:110);

September 1935: "Nuremberg laws—in the name of blood and honor." Under the threat of imprisonment, Aryans are forbidden from marrying Jews or having extramarital contact with them. Jews are forbidden from hiring domestic servants younger than 45 years old (!);

April 1936: a ban forbidding all government officials from dealing with any Jews, no matter the reason;

October 1936: a ban forbidding all Jews from using the reading rooms of all public libraries;

October 9, V. Klemperer wrote, "This morning, I was told in the library carefully—in an attempt to spare me—that non-Aryans had no right to use the reading room. They would give me everything to take home or to take to the catalogue room, but an official ban was issued regarding the reading room" (1:34);

August 1938: a law on names. Jewish men are obligated to add one more—Israel—to their names. Klemperer would henceforth be called Victor Israel Klemperer. Jewish women must add the name Sarah;

October 1938: a ban forbidding Jews from renting rooms in hotels;

November 1938: In accordance with the order of the Berlin police chief of November 28, Jews are forbidden from entering theaters, cinemas, concert halls, museums, exhibits, open talks and lectures, sports competitions, skating rinks, and pools, public and private (1:747);

December 1938: Jews are forbidden from borrowing books from the library. Jews are forbidden from having driver's licenses and, consequently, driving a car;

September 1939: a ban on leaving the house after 8 pm;

August 1940: a ban (in Dresden) on entering city parks and gardens; a ban on using the telephone;

May 8, 1942, V. Klemperer wrote, "What wishes do I start to have? To not be afraid of every ring! To keep a typewriter. To be able to keep manuscripts and diaries at home. To be able to use the library . . . Food . . . The cinema . . . A car."

When Professor Klemperer was dismissed from the university in 1935, he began intensively to write the book that he had started earlier: *The History of French Literature of the Eighteenth Century*. His pension was not high. He could not hire a secretary-typist, and so, he had to put quite a lot of effort into learning how to use a typewriter and began typing up himself what he had written for the day. The ban on using the reading room in the city's public library was painful, but the professor was still able to take books home. The general ban on using libraries turned out to be a bigger blow. He had to cut short his work on eighteenth-century France and turn to a book that did not require academic literature. Klemperer began writing his autobiography *Curriculum Vitae*. In October 1940, they took away his typewriter. For his wife, who was sick and not young, it was difficult to shop for groceries. V. Klemperer began learning to drive in 1936. He passed the test after overcoming quite a number of difficulties. He received his license and bought a secondhand car. However, in December 1938, he was subject to a new ban: Jews may not own a car or drive one. The Klemperers had one last consolation: their cat, Mushel. But then it was forbidden to keep a cat. They had to put their beloved cat to sleep, in doing so breaking a law that required they deliver the animal to the city authorities. "The Markwalds were also obligated to give up their little bird. They found out that we had put down our cat and thought our actions had been terribly risky. What if the Gestapo found out about it!" (entry for May 22, 1942).

The last blow—or one of the last—turned out to be eviction. The Klemperers had to move into the "Jewish House," where the authorities, in trying to show them special consideration, had assigned them two rooms. The building emptied out before their very eyes. The residents were "evacuated" somewhere. The people who remained gradually began to realize what awaited them. "Since the beginning of the evacuation last fall in Berlin, 2,000 Jewish suicides have been recorded" (entry for May 22, 1943).

It seemed that the Nazi authorities tried with all their might to think of other bans. What other ways can you use to demean Jews morally and strangle them physically? Has everything already been forbidden? No, not yet. V. Klemperer noted down more and more new orders:

March 1941: a prohibition against milkmaids crossing the threshold of buildings where Jews live and selling them milk.

August 1941: a ban forbidding Jews from smoking. From that day on, if a Gestapo officer found a Jew with a cigarette or pipe, he would be obligated to arrest him. Such an arrest ordinarily ended with that person being sent to a concentration camp and getting killed: "killed in an attempt to escape" (1:658);

September 19, 1941: a terrible day. Jews are obligated (under the threat of arrest and death in a camp) to wear yellow, six-pointed stars on the lapels of their jackets or coats. Anyone who covers up the star with his hand, a newspaper, a book, etc., was subject to immediate arrest;

November 1941: an order forcing Jews to hand over their binoculars and cameras;

December 1941: a ban on the use of payphones, and a ban on riding buses (allowed only on trams, in the area at the front of the trailing car).

In the entry for March 1942, we read, "Today they announced a ban on using trams, after 'considering numerous disciplinary violations by Jews on trams.' A ban on buying illustrated magazines and weeklies or subscribing to them. A ban on the use of food tickets without the capital letter *J* (*Jude*)" (1:40). A few days later, a ban on Jews buying flowers (March 16) and a ban on buying food supplies were noted ("Jews are forbidden to store food; they have the right to buy only as much as the can eat in a day" [2:57]); a ban on appearing at train stations; a ban on using services provided by Aryan craftsmen (April 2, 1942; 2:59); a ban on standing in line, a ban on keeping pets, including dogs, cats, and birds (May 14; 2:85); a ban on using Aryan hairdressers: "Jews are obligated to take care of their own cleanliness and the presentable look of their hair (May 23; 2:96).

Not long after, he noted the requirement that Jews hand over all electrical appliances, vacuum cleaners, record players, and along with them records (2:132). Starting from June 30, 1942, Jewish schools were to be closed. Children were also forbidden from receiving education at home ("A spiritual death sentence, forced illiteracy. They will not succeed in that" [2:142]). In the middle of June, a ban on Jews reading newspapers and, of course, subscribing to them (that also applied to "Aryan wives"; 2, 174). In the entry of June 2, 1942, all the limitations, orders, and requirements were enumerated, including a ban on listening to the radio; on going to theaters, cinemas, concerts, and museums; on using transportation—Jews were only allowed to take transportation to work if it was further away than seven kilometers; on buying scarce products (*Mangelwaren*); on walking on streets along a city park, etc. After listing these thirty-one prohibitions, Klemperer concludes, "But all of them taken together are nothing compared to the constant anticipation of searches, mockery, prisons, concentration camps, and violent death" (2:108).

In October 1941, V. Klemperer noted the "evacuation of Jews to Poland." At first, he did not understand where to and why. Then they heard stories of annihilation and gas chambers, and the names Buchenwald, Majdanek, Auschwitz, and Treblinka were heard for the first time. Klemperer wrote more and more often about his fear. Searches and arrests became more and more frequent phenomena and were conducted with a previously unheard-of cruelty. "Searches are a nightmare for all Jews. Now, new instances of beatings, insults, all kinds of theft (lately also the theft of money), arrests, and summonses to the Gestapo (this was particularly feared). Every day, I wait for my turn to come" (March 22, 1942; 2:54). More and more often, there were suicides after the searches. Klemperer didn't have to wait long. At the end of May, they came to him (but he wasn't home), they insulted and beat his wife ("You're Aryan? You Jewish slut, why did you marry a Jew?" [2:93]), they dumped out the contents of all the cabinets and drawers and stole a lot. "The manuscript of the diary would undoubtedly have cost me my life . . . This time, we got off with fear and swore to each other to get our nerves under control. But what an incredible disgrace for Germany!" Two weeks later, they came again. Klemperer was reading a book by Alfred Rosenberg, *The Myth of the Twentieth Century*, an ideological textbook on Nazism. "They considered reading this a terrible transgression. They beat me over the head with this book, slapped me several times, and put a Käthchen straw hat on me for laughs. 'You look fine!' When I answered their questions and said that I had worked in a government job until 1935, two of them (I knew them from before) spat in my eyes. At that moment, Eva came back with the shopping. They took her bag right away. They insulted her because of my book. I wanted to stand up for her. They boxed my ears several times and pushed me into the kitchen with kicks" (2:126). In the book *LTI*, this episode is told with humor and terror:

> Never, never in all my life, has my head spun as much from a book as it did with Rosenberg's *Myth*. Not because his writings were exceptionally profound and difficult for the reader to comprehend, nor because reading it was emotionally overwhelming, but because Clemens kept hammering my head with this volume for several minutes. (Clemens and Weser were particularly cruel torturers of the Jews in Dresden, and they were generally called "the Hitter" and "the Spitter.") "How dare a Jewish pig like you presume to read a book of this kind?" Clemens yelled. To him it seemed like desecration. "How dare you have a book here from the lending library?" Only the fact that the volume had demonstrably been borrowed in the name of my Aryan wife and, moreover, that the sheet of notes about Rosenberg accompanying it had been torn up without being read saved me at the time from the concentration camp.*

That's how searches were conducted in Dresden in 1942.

In Soviet Russia, everything seemed different. At any rate, the agents who came with search orders conducted themselves in a matter that was more controlled. But in essence it was the same, exactly the same. In 1936–39 and in 1949–53, we, the intelligentsia of Leningrad and Moscow, primarily Jews, just like our brothers in Germany, we listened for cars driving up, steps on the stairs, and voices in our neighbors' homes. We were also convinced that a search would end with an arrest and an arrest with a disappearance (at the time, we did not yet know that it would be forever). After the arrest of Professor G. A. Gukovsky in 1948 and then of his students and colleagues A. G. Levinton and I. Z. Serman, I anticipated a search and arrest every night, just as V. Klemperer had. True, I acted differently from Klemperer. I destroyed my diary entries and burned many

---

* V. Klemperer, *III. Notizbuch eines Philologen* (Berlin: Aufbau Verlag, 1949), 18. [E. E.]

letters. It's strange now, almost funny, to recall how we burned the books that I kept, including the transcripts of the fourteenth and fifteenth party congresses. These official Soviet publications could have cost us our lives at the time. There were speeches by Trotsky, Zinoviev, and Radek in them. Only a suicide would keep such texts. Yes, the NKVD officers did not spit in the face of the people whose homes they searched or call our wives "Jewish sluts." They took people away to Bolshoy Dom. and there . . . It's amazing how similar the terrorizing measures of both tyrannies were, with some difference in outward form. Now, when people compare Germany and the Soviet Union, they try to guess which was worse and which better. I don't know which was worse. The Nazis shouted as loudly as they could about their hatred for the Jews and their intention to exterminate them. The Communists spoke aloud about the crime of antisemitism, but they acted in the same way that the Nazis had acted before them: they were preparing for the total annihilation of Russian Jews, their own variation of the "Final Solution" (*Endlösung*). Victor Klemperer did not know this. And we, too, were not aware of everything.

When the war ended, V. Klemperer found himself in the eastern zone of Germany, later in the GDR, which was created in 1949. This sharp, clever, conscientious person believed Soviet propaganda. It was the militant antifascism of the Communists that pushed him into their embrace. Could he not understand that the Soviet campaigns against cosmopolitans in 1948–52 were a direct, often unscrupulous continuation of Nazi antisemitism, of which he himself was a victim in the thirties and forties? Could he have failed to notice that the Communist Party of Stalin's last years was enacting a monstrous Jewish pogrom and camouflaging it with beautiful language? In his book *LTI*, Klemperer showed how knowingly the Nazis used language to hide the truth: "defeats" were called "crises," whereby they always spoke not of a German crisis but a worldwide crisis or a "crisis of Western humanity"; the "crisis" was averted because the "German Army had voluntarily separated itself from the enemy and consciously allowed it to go further into the country, so that it could destroy them with greater certainty"—all this instead of admitting defeat.* How is it that Klemperer, a philologist and an experienced anti-fascist, did not realize the cunning of the deceptive language of Soviet phraseology? How was it that he, a specialist of the Third Reich's language, did not figure out the language of the Communist Empire? His book *LTI*, after all, was published by the pro-Soviet publishing house Aufbau in 1949, just as Soviet newspapers, which were trying to compete against each other in ruthlessness, hit out against "cosmopolitans," that is, Jews. Of course, the German professor could not have known that on February 8, 1949, Stalin signed the decision of the Politburo to disband the organizations of Jewish writers in Moscow, Kiev, and Minsk and to close almanacs and newspapers published in Yiddish. That was the end of Jewish literature and culture in the USSR. That was when Jewish writers and workers of the Jewish Anti-Fascist Committee were arrested. In 1949, Jewish theaters were closed, including the Moscow, Belorussian, Ukrainian, and even the Birobidzhan theaters (the L. M. Kaganovich Theater). On January 28, 1949, *Pravda* published an ominous editorial titled "On an Antipatriotic Group of Theater Critics," which started an open (although under a transparent pseudonym) crusade against Jews, who would henceforth be called "rootless cosmopolitans." Some Jews were chastised for "bourgeois nationalism," adhering to Judaism, its traditions and language; others were blamed for rejecting their national culture, providing reasons to accuse them of "rootlessness." The playwright Surov declared loudly, "The roots of cosmopolitism are to be found in bourgeois nationalism" (who would not understand this?), ". . . despicable degenerates should not have a place among our people" (*Vechernyaya Moskva*, February 19, 1949). One of the leaders of the Union of Soviet Writers at that time, K. Simonov, declared in a report on February 18, 1949, in Moscow, "Cosmopolitanism in art is a desire to undermine national roots and national pride because it is easier to move people without roots from

---

*   Ibid., 226. [E. E.]

their place and sell them to American imperialism" (*Pravda*, February 28, 1949). Let us translate the euphemistic language of Simonov's assertions: "The dominance of Jews in art is undermining Russian national roots . . . Jews are agents of imperialism."

The period from 1949 to 1953 were years of militant antisemitism in the USSR, slightly disguised by the small fig leaf of "Marxist-Leninist internationalism." Was it possible not to notice this, even while living in Germany? I am far from blaming Victor Klemperer for collaborating with the Bolsheviks. He failed to see a lot of what was happening around him because he was absorbed with German problems: the degree of responsibility of each German had to be recognized; effective means to educate new generations had to be found so that fathers and sons could coexist. V. Klemperer racked his brains over this instead of reading the front-page articles in *Neues Deutschland*, which obediently followed *Pravda*. And maybe he did in fact think it was more important to fight the remnants of fascism leaning on the new masters.

One way or another, the second "Jewish fate," mine—which repeated a lot of what had happened to V. Klemperer—began when his misadventures were already behind him. In December 1949 (or, more precisely, December 21, on the seventieth anniversary of our leader and luminary), I was expelled from the Institute of Foreign Languages, where I was a docent. Before being dismissed, I was worked over at the Department of West European Literature at Leningrad University. V. M. Zhirmunsky was no longer in charge there; as a Jew, he had been expelled and replaced by one of his "Aryan" students, Tatyana Viktorovna Vanovskaya (who, by the way, was the wife of G. P. Berdnikov). Professor Aleksey Lvovich Grigoryev gave a speech devoted to tearing apart my candidate's dissertation. He was terribly pale and kept stammering, but he fulfilled his obligation to the party: he had found cosmopolitan distortions in my work about Emile Zola. Just think, the author dared to argue that Zola had influenced Gorky—their French, bourgeois Zola influencing our Russian, proletarian Gorky! This was inexcusable. It was suggested that the defense of the

1947 dissertation was invalid and that the candidate's degree should be taken away from Etkind. However, some professors, people of dignity and honor, still remained in the department: A. A. Smirnov, K. N. Derzhavin, and their students N. Ya. Diakonova and N. A. Sigal-Zhirmunskaya. It was impossible to force them to accept the party committee's decision. I remained a candidate of philological sciences until April 1974, and after some time, I found a position at the Tula Pedagogical Institute, where several Jews already worked, cosmopolites who had been dismissed from universities in the capital.

The hounding that had started with this episode in the era of the "fight against cosmopolitans" died down at times, only to flare up again, and that lasted a quarter of a century. In 1974, I was fired from the Herzen Institute on accusations, among other things, of writing an open letter to young Jews, where I had urged them not to leave but to fight for equal rights and freedom at home, within the bounds of their own language and culture. I fought for another few months, from April to October, for the right to remain in Russia. I was ready to take any work. During a "chat" with the party's regional committee in Leningrad, I even suggested that I could become a taxi driver. Kruglova, the secretary of the regional committee at the time, derided me: "You will drive foreigners, then the Western papers will begin to slander us, saying a professor works as a chauffeur!" In October, I had to emigrate, formally to Israel but in fact to France, where I have lived for more than twenty years.

When they chased me out of the Leningrad institute, I was fifty-six. When Victor Klemperer was dismissed from Dresden University, he was almost the same age, fifty-five. Each of us, in our own way, insisted on belonging to the culture around us. From the first day of Nazism, V. Klemperer maintained in his diary that he—he specifically—was a German. In November 1933, Klemperer, still a professor at the university, describes an argument with Kaufman, a Jew, who had condoned Hitler: "I stopped trying to control myself, hit the table with my fist, and shouted my question at him several times: Did he or did he not consider those leaders whose politics he defended criminals? With a sense of calmness worthy of Nathan the Wise, he avoided answering my question . . . He, for his part, asked me mockingly why I remained in my position. I answered that it was not this government that had appointed me and not this government that I was serving; that I represented the interests of Germany with a clear conscience; and that I was a German, I specifically!" (1:67).

This conviction repeated itself each year, although at times, other feelings come through: "Contempt, disgust, a deep distrust. That is what I feel regarding Germany, and I cannot escape it. Until 1933, I was so convinced of my Germanness (*Deutschtum*)" (October 27, 1937). And yet, in spite of everything, five years later: "I think in German. I remain a German. It was not I who acquired this for myself, and I cannot tear it out of myself" (2:56). "I cannot leave my Germanness" (Aus dem Deutschtum kann ich nicht heraus; 2:88). An entry for June 25, 1942, about Theodor Herzl, the founder of Zionism: "And still, he is not right . . . I am just a German. For me, anything else would be playing a comedy" (2:144). Three days later, on June 28, an entry about an argument with someone by the name of Zelikson: "He carried on the discussion with passion, and I with uncertainty: 'You must be a Jew. You must teach Jews. They would accept you in Jerusalem. You would find your own place there.' 'No, I am German and nothing else. I cannot be otherwise. The National Socialists are not the German people. The German people of today do not comprise all of Germany.' He hates all of Germany. All that is German has long been cruel and barbaric. It's better to live outside Germany in complete poverty than in tolerable conditions in Germany, etc. And for me, even if I hated Germany, I would not become a non-German from that. I could not tear my Germanness from within me. And I would like to help with the new construction here. In addition, in Jerusalem, I would be a renegade, an opportunist, a traitor . . ." (2:148).

Forty years later, I maintained the same thing regarding my devotion to Russian culture. In the book *Notes of a Non-Conspirator*, this is repeated more than once, but I will not quote myself. I would add a reminder that Anna Akhmatova's lines serve as the epigraph to the whole book:

> No, not under a foreign sky,
> No, not cradled by foreign wings—
> Then I was with my people, I,
> With my people, there, sorrowing.
> (Trans. A. S. Kline)

The author's introduction ends with words about the country: "It is mine, and I have no other."

The reader, after learning about these two Jewish fates, which were divided by an interval of forty years and are incredibly similar to one another, might come to the conclusion that I identify the two totalitarian regimes, the German and the Soviet, with one another. But that would be incorrect. I see a clear difference between them with regard to the Jewish question.

Recently, a book by Daniel Goldhagen was published in the United States: *Hitler's Willing Executioners*. The Harvard researcher proves that the "Holocaust," during which over six million Jews were exterminated, was carried out by hundreds of thousands of the most ordinary Germans, who were killing by conviction and not by compulsion. Goldhagen wrote, "My explanation—and that is new to the scholarly literature on the perpetrators—is that the perpetrators, 'most ordinary Germans,' were animated by antisemitism, by a particular type of antisemitism that led them to conclude that the Jews deserved death. . . . They judged the mass annihilation of Jews to be justified."* Goldhagen reminds us that the Germans bragged about their executioners' "accomplishments." Not only were they not ashamed to tell their wives and their loved ones about them; they were proud of themselves and willingly shared—even with their children—photographs that to us are monstrous. Goldhagen is probably essentially right. Nazi

---

* Daniel Jonah Goldhagen, *Hitler's Willing Executioners: Ordinary Germans and the Holocaust* (New York: Knopf, 1996), 14. [E. E.]

propaganda turned out to be effective. It was aimed at showing that Jews were to blame for all disasters: Jews had ignited the war, had purposely made Germany starve, were poisoning the Germans, and killing them; Jews were pushing the Americans and the British to bomb German cities to annihilation; Jews were organizing partisan groups in the East; Jews were commissars in the Red Army and the founders and leaders of the Bolshevik Party. Most of Goebbels's articles in *Das Reich* are dedicated to proving this thesis. For twenty years, the newspapers blamed the Jews for everything. Here are two entries by V. Klemperer. For September 12, 1933: "Now, during the Fifth Party Congress, they are again provoking hatred against the Jews. Jews are destroying Spain, Jews are a nation of criminals, all crimes can be traced to Jews (Goebbels, the official "*Sturmer*" and minister). And the people are so stupid that they believe everything" (1:378). For June 24, 1943: "The endless hounding of the Jews continues. It is so endless, so stupid, repeated so monotonously and ridiculously that it can't possibly work anymore. St. Laurentius Cathedral has been damaged by bombing. Those were Jewish pilots. It was the Jews who declared war on Christianity. The suggestion in some Chicago paper that England should become an American state: a Jewish plan for the ultimate takeover of power. Then, the Jews will settle in the White House and rule the world" (2:409–10). Nazi propaganda was built on the fact that Jews were not people but filth, insects to be exterminated, like cockroaches, bedbugs, and lice. The gradual prohibitions we analyzed above through Klemperer's diary were one facet of this propaganda. Bit by bit, Germans developed a stronger conviction that the country could reestablish normality and build a secure future for German children by cleansing itself of Jews. The satanic propaganda was accomplishing its task. Antisemitism became ubiquitous and transformed itself from an ideology into real action, into the practice of annihilation.

This did not exist in the Soviet Union. Even the campaign against cosmopolites did not transform into Jewish pogroms. After all, who in Russia aside from highly educated people could understand that the bizarre word "cosmopolite" meant "Yid"? In order to awaken the masses, they thought up "doctor poisoners." An understandable hatred by the Russian man in the street for "killers in white coats" was to grow into mass antisemitism. In the journal *Komunist* (1953, no. 2), D. I. Chesnokov attacked "professor doctors, the hirelings of imperialist espionage agencies hiding their despicable faces of murderers and spies behind the high calling of a doctor." He was apparently the author of a theoretical work that laid the foundation for the future plan of deporting Jews to the Far East. An official report in *Pravda* on January 13, 1953, "Arrest of a group of doctors-saboteurs," accused terrorist doctors of collaborating with Joint, a Jewish nationalist organization, which had sent a directive about the extermination of the leading personnel of the USSR through the Moscow doctor Shimeliovitch and the well-known Jewish bourgeois nationalist Mikhoels." However, the delusional "doctors' plot" fell apart immediately after Stalin's death. Already on April 4, 1953, the press reported that everyone who had been arrested in the case had been released. It had been about to incite the national masses against Jews—but it had only begun to do so.

The basic difference between Nazi Germany and Soviet Russia in relation to Jews lay in the mass terrorist antisemitism in Germany and in the government and party one in Russia, fortunately not too actively supported from below. This difference also appeared in the story of the two Jewish fates I recounted.

"Youth in a Military Blouse" of My Contemporary

> *What frenzied hordes of thunderstorms*
> *I weathered—beyond measure,*
> *As clouds assembled in tenebrous swarms*
> *And gobbled up a short-lived azure . . .*

Igor Mikhailovich Diakonov wrote these lines in 1960. At forty-five, he was already summing up his tumultuous life. The poems were published as an appendix to his *Book of Memoires*, which covered his life up to 1945. He was barely thirty at the time. His thirty books about ancient history and Afro-Asian languages that earned this author a world reputation did not yet exist. Also not yet in existence were his excellent poetic translations of the Assyrian epics of Gilgamesh nor the biblical poems Song of Songs of King Solomon and the Ecclesiastes, which allowed us Russians to read the cuneiform writing and the Bible anew and recognize the previously unknown value of Russian free verse. The book *The Ways of History* did not yet exist; it would be published half a century later, in 1994, and it would show in a new light the path of humankind, from Pithecanthropus to the approaches to the twentieth century (". . . here, I suggested a new periodization of the historical process that is based not only on changes in the character of production and social relations but also on changes in motivation for social activity, in the area of social psychology"). Remembering his military youth many years later, the author would say, "We were boys still, / badges intrigued us, / didn't yet smoke shag, / were still proud of . . . . . ." And in the last lines, there was this variation: "Still didn't die like moths." Everything lay in the future. Today, in 1995, saw the publication of *The Book of Memoires*, a book about the childhood and youth of the generation born during the First World War, and readers could, together with the author, see these "frenzied hordes of thunderstorms" and be amazed at how many challenges arose for the generation. The year 1915, the year that I. M. Diakonov was born, was an amazing one in our culture. That was the year when the Silver Age most probably came to an end and when simultaneously came "Nightingale Garden" by Blok, "A Cloud in Trousers" and "Backbone Flute" by Mayakovsky, "Marburg" by Pasternak, "I Don't Pity, Don't Call, Don't Cry" by Esenin; and "Insomnia. Homer. The Row of Stretched Sails" by Mandelstam...

Igor Diakonov spent his childhood in Norway (where his father, Mikhail Alexeyevich, served in the Soviet Trade Comission) and later lived and studied in Leningrad, where one disaster came after another: hunger and terror in the twenties, the murder of Kirov and terror, terror again at the end of the thirties, war, and three years of blockade in his home town. Again, and again, and again: the death of people close to him, fellow colleagues, and teachers; the arrest and murder of his father; the death of his younger brother at the front. Not only poems, a lyrical diary over a period of half a century (1935–87), were appended to *Memories* but also "Synodic," a stunning work even for highly experienced readers. As the author writes, "In memory of those identified in my book whom I knew personally or through friends, who did not die their own deaths." This list included scholars specializing in Eastern studies, writers, poets, translators (his father had been a great translator, above all from Norwegian; we are indebted to him for Sigrid Undset's novel *Kristin Lavransdatter*, for example). There were also students, graduate students, professors, teachers, and lawyers. Of them, eighty-six died in camps or were executed ("died from genocide"), thirty "were repressed but survived," twenty-eight "died of hunger during the blockade," and twelve "died at the front." More than 150 tragic deaths in the life of a thirty-year-old young man who was just beginning his creative and scholarly life.

I. M. Diakonov constantly reminded himself and us that he—he personally!—was very lucky: shells and bombs landed around him, bullets flew past him, he was interrogated by the NKVD and KGB but not arrested. I'll note parenthetically that I, the author of these lines, was also incredibly lucky: by some amazing luck I did not end up in the Synodic," although I could have fallen into any of its four divisions. I was one of those people about whom one of the poems cited above would say, "So many standing shoulder to shoulder!" Here are the lines:

> The ground would shake and shudder
> as shells exploded far and near . . .
> So many standing shoulder to shoulder!
> All gone now! And I'm still here . . .

I indeed stood nearby. When Mikhail Alexeyevich Diakonov was arrested in 1938 (he was executed in the same year for being a spy for . . . Venezuela; the formula was, of course, that there would be "ten years with no right to correspondence"; his wife waited for all ten years). And during the war, we were together on the Karelian front. ("Meager north, land of gloom, / Like a sickness in my brain; / Only the red barracks / I cannot leave behind . . .").

And after the war, in the years of Stalin's new—how many had there been?—annihilation of the intelligentsia, and in the years full of hope during the short thaw . . . We were separated for twenty years, when I was forced out of the country in 1974, yet I returned, and we were together again, and now we remembered Robert Burns, which (perhaps not without special intent) was translated by Marshak:

> John Anderson my jo, John,
> We clamb the hill thegither,
> And monie a cantie day, John,
> We've had wi' ane anither;
> Now we maun totter down, John,
> And hand in hand we'll go,
> And sleep thegither at the foot,
> John Anderson, my jo!

I couldn't not write about this book, which is all about our shared life. But do I have the right? Am I not too close to the author, not too biased?

After all, not only did we go up and down the same hills together "hand in hand," but our lives were similar. (Was it only our two lives that were similar?) His father was executed in 1938; mine was arrested a little earlier, exiled, and died of hunger in the blockade in 1942. His two brothers perished: the younger one at war, and the older one soon after the war. My two brothers died in the seventies, both as a consequence of harassment directed at me and on the rebound at both of them as well. Another (secondary) similarity: he and I were both members of a few Western academies, while our native land preferred to ignore us. I am very far from comparing myself to I. M. Diakonov as a scholar, but the similarities in our biographies are a fact. And here is something else that is important. We must talk about it here and now.

Many still think that our political emigration had been united, almost monolithic. But it was torn apart by contradictions. One of them had to do with the role of the intelligentsia in the USSR. Our opponents thought (and think to this day—you can read about this in the newspaper *Russkaya mysl*, for example) that in Soviet Russia there were hangmen and victims, and a "middle class" could not exist: the intelligentsia either sold themselves to the Communists or died in jails and camps. We, the people who held a different point of view, knew that this was either a mistake or a lie: the Russian intelligentsia continued to fulfill their duty, even without entering into a political conflict with the regime by using legal means. The regime, which was cracking down on many people, had been obligated to tolerate it. For me (and not only for me!), I. M. Diakonov was the ultimate model of this kind of Russian intelligentsia, the kind that cleverly managed to preserve its human dignity and independence (yes, yes, independence) of thought. The almighty propaganda could not shake its sense of justice, tolerance, and deeply rooted sense of democracy, even its inherited devotion to internationalism and socialist ideas.

In *Book of Memories*, there's a chapter titled "About Time," which opens the second part: "Youth in a Military Shirt." That chapter was an attempt "to say what exactly we thought and knew before the beginning of the war" (482). I would like for all people—everyone, without exception—of succeeding generations to read this honest confession in which he is merciless to himself and his contemporaries, this testimony of a scholar, war veteran, thinker, and knight of culture—this victim of a regime who remained a patriot of his country, no matter what political system it had. At the center of the era was the idea of a world revolution: "Nobody wanted to stand in the way of the victorious world revolution; and since it was assumed that this revolution was bringing light to the people, the intelligentsia believed that in spite of all reservations, its place was with the revolution and not against it" (486). "The global character of the revolution that was taking place removed all national questions for us" (487). Diakonov examines the attitude of his contemporaries toward NEP, collectivization, and the absurd mass terror of the twenties and thirties, and amid the whole nightmare of these years, he maintains, "The strength of the belief in the necessity and inevitability of socialism was such that even the terrible years of 1937 and 1938 could not destroy it. Of course, I—and my friends, I believe—felt socialism should not be built with such methods, yet that it still had to be built—there was no doubt" (490). The reasoning regarding fear was interesting: "It was not fear but a lack of understanding about what was taking place that kept us from condemning what they told us was socialism. [. . .] It never occurred to any of us, of course, that you could side with the enemy in this war. While the rethinking of our own terror occurred silently and gradually, we had no doubts that German fascism was evil. And the fact that we would have to defend our own country, whatever was happening in it, was also self-evident" (492).

Whatever was happening in it . . . Igor Diakonov did defend his country, without sparing himself but not forgetting the death of his father, the "spy for Venezuela," and that of many others, such as my father-in-law, F. A. Zvorykin, a similar "spy." The idea of ethics was for him always central. He formulated it frequently in different ways in different places in the book. It was for this very reason that the young film director Alexei

Yankovsky dedicated a documentary film to his father and called it *Kirkenes Ethics*.

Kirkenes is a small port city in Norway near the Russian border. Captain Diakonov wound up there at the end of war with the advancing Soviet forces. He speaks about this episode rather comprehensively; this is a "novel within the novel" *Book of Memories*. In his usual ironic style, he tells about how he, a young civilian scholar, was forced to play the role of a military commander of a newly liberated city. "They put me in the hull of an airplane, into the bomb hatch. The plane was flying without bombs for some other mission. I joked with myself: What if the pilot became distracted and pushed a button, releasing the bomb hatch, and I would fly at the Germans instead of a bomb? I was flying for the first time in my life" (648). In Kirkenes, the whole population went into hiding underground. It helped that he knew the Norwegian language and the customs of the country in which he had spent his childhood. His knowledge of the Soviet Army also helped, including how its soldiers and generals, commissars and special agents worked. This knowledge allowed I. M. Diakonov to become the conciliator in Kirkenes, the savior of its population, which had miraculously avoided first German dynamite and then Soviet rapists. Captain Diakonov became a legend in Norway. Recently, he was a guest in Kirkenes—on the fiftieth anniversary of the city's liberation. I know that the former Captain Diakonov was received as a hero of the war not from his memoirs but from conversations with Norwegian philologists and from the Norwegian press. Why did the Russian newspapers stay silent about this? After all, this was our pride, our national honor.

There's no point in being surprised. I. M. Diakonov, a great contemporary historian and linguist, was not elected to the Russian Academy of Sciences (like another brilliant philologist, V. V. Ivanov). And for a long time, he could not find a publisher for his book of memoirs, which was so important for our era. Thank God he did. Evropeyskiy Dom started a series, Diaries and Memoirs of Leningrad Scholars. Thank you, Evropeyskiy Dom. We would have been even more grateful if the editorial board had edited the manuscript and deleted the annoying repetitions (an author often does not see such faults) and mistakes in the quotes (for example, on Griboyedov's tombstone it does not say "Your name . . ." but rather "Your mind and your deeds are immortal . . ."). The book was published with a tiny print run: seven hundred copies in all. Let us hope that for the next edition Evropeyskiy Dom will not try to economize on an editor.

I. M. Diakonov's *Book of Memories* is especially important today. It was written by a scholar who was searching for patterns in the historical process and was able to understand his own life in view of those patterns. It was written by a poet who was assessing those very same events in a different way, applying the principles of art. It was written by a novelist who was able to take a step back and observe himself from the outside. He was able to see himself as a young, naïve person who was gradually maturing, and to see changes, development, and the process as he and many of his contemporaries became better individuals. I want to end with a saying by Diakonov that describes his worldview of today: "Instead of God," he wrote, "I place the conscience, inherent to all. This is also biology. The species that has a conscience will survive. The species in which all are enemies and hate each other is sure to perish" (743). I'm not sure what the natural sciences would say; it's possibly a fantastical idea. But from the point of view of humanity, it's true. Or we would wish it to be so.

Afterword: A Knight of Culture

For those of us fortunate enough to have known Efim Grigorievich Etkind as mind and person, there is much to be grateful for. He was awesomely erudite, his precise knowledge of major and minor texts of European literature second to none. Through his teachings and writings his special brand of stylistically attuned "poetic" translation became its own school. In a kind of fatidic parallax, Etkind's name is closely associated with two of the five Russian writers awarded the Nobel Prize in literature, Aleksandr Solzhenitsyn and Joseph Brodsky. Similarly, his academic training led back to foundational figures like Viktor Zhirmunsky and Grigory Gukovsky, scholars whose works established parameters for the study of modern Russian literature. And his massive list of publications responded to that training with its own forward momentum, eventuating over the decades in a formal and prosodic precision coupled with an awareness of historical context and a poem's underlying experiential arc he called "structuralism with a human face."

His public lectures were Efim Grigorievich at his lively best, however. Of all the words one might marshal to try to capture the essence of this complex and fascinating man, "vigor"—intellectual, physical, performative—is the first to leap to mind. His energy, never seeming to wane even as others his age were visibly slowing down, informed his every activity, from his morning calisthenics to the way he put out his cigarette before proceeding, erect and ready for battle, to the lectern. One must assume that those of us witnessing Efim Grigorievich deliver a lecture at the Middlebury and Norwich Russian Schools in the 1980s and 90s were seeing a rather pale reflection of 1960s and 1970s Leningrad. Yes, the hall was full with a hundred or more students and faculty, and yes, the lecturer kept the audience on the edge of their seats with each conspiratorial tilt of his head and with each clue to the drama he was so artfully constructing: how Nicholas used the noblemen's own code of honor to break down the Decembrists after their failed coup; what it would feel and look like to be a grandee in the time of Pushkin's Yusupov ("K vel'mozhe" / To a Grandee, 1830); how the autobiographical anxieties and existential dilemmas of a great poet, such as the revolutionary Blok of *Dvenadtsat'* (The Twelve, 1918) or the suffering mother Akhmatova of *Rekviem* (Requiem, 1934–63), are suddenly brought to life by the hidden musculature of a work's compositional symmetries. As part of the drama there was always the experience of the poems being recited by heart, with long sections declaimed in one breath and key words or phrases stressed after a strategic pause. But the atmosphere of these wonderful presentations was, indeed, had to be, considering the context, more "staged" and thus less "real" than it must have been in the earlier years in Leningrad, when there was so much hanging in the balance for both the messenger and his audience. For let it be said that although Efim Grigorievich was a world-renowned scholar and author, there was in each and every of his public appearances the spark of a performing artist—the *improvisatore* (however much one suspected the master left little to chance) to the scholar's closeted Charsky. What he wrote about A. A. Smirnov could be said with equal force about Efim Grigorievich himself and about our smallness compared to his largeness,

> All that he [Smirnov] wrote about Shakespeare and Molière, Mérimée and artistic translation pales in comparison to the brilliance of those improvisations. In each of his analyses, one sensed the presence of an experienced master, a "weigher" of words and sounds, and at the same time a highly erudite literary historian, an expert on France, England, Ireland, and Spain, and a connoisseur of the Renaissance and the Romantic era. Many years later, I had to lead a similar studio for translations of German prose. *I was always aware that it was ridiculous for us to compare ourselves to the older generation. We did not even have one-tenth of the cultural knowledge that A. A. Smirnov retained with amazing*

natural grace. I am not thinking of erudition or talent but culture [my emphasis].

It was this spark of personality (*lichnost'*) that was the real Efim Grigorievich and that was evident in the inherent drama of a work such as *Stikhi i liudi* (People and Verse, 1988).*

But, with its roving focus on family, personal relations, and private matters, *Barcelona Prose* is a much different collection of writings than Etkind's essays and books on the sound and sense of poetry, and it is on that difference that I would like to pause in this brief afterword. More than anything else, the memoiristic pieces in *Barcelona Prose* recount the scholar's various encounters with the challenge of making moral choices (both his and others) in a heavily politicized environment. They also tell the story of his own journey as secular Jew and prominent member of the intelligentsia through the trials (literal and figurative) of Soviet history: how his ethnicity played a role in his assignments in World War II, how it caused him to be sacked in the years after the war (the campaign against cosmopolitanism), how it played a role in the difficulties associated with his decision to be a witness for the defense in Brodsky's trial for parasitism (*tuneiadstvo*), and how ultimately it led to his being stripped of his academic titles and position, his books banned, and he and his family forced to emigrate because he had helped Solzhenitsyn conceal the manuscript of *The GULag Archipelago* and also because he had written a letter to young Soviet Jews advising them to remain at home—that is, not leave for Israel—and in doing so fight for the culture they loved. But perhaps most compelling about these essays, aside from the sharpness of remembered detail and the vividness of the different portraits, is that Etkind does not so much speak about his own moral choices, for the impression is consistently given that the

---

* See David M. Bethea, "Efim Grigorievich Etkind (1918–1999), Form as Content: The Life and Work of Efim Grigorievich Etkind," *Slavonica* 7, no. 1 (2001): 91–97, esp. 94.

choices were mostly second nature and not particularly agonized over, but about his witnessing of the moral choices of others, and how those choices either belonged to the "knights of culture"* or to those who, like the editor A. L. Dymshits, chose a career ladder that ultimately led down and not up, and, whether they acknowledged it or not, to their own moral ruination.

These thoughts about serving culture's higher purposes bring me back to Efim Grigorievich and an official occasion we once attended. The reader will forgive me for speaking *pro domo sua*. It was June 1995 and the Russian School at Middlebury College was celebrating its fiftieth anniversary. By now Efim Grigorievich had been giving graduate seminars at the summer school for many years and I, as a previous director during the 1980s, had been invited to share the podium with him. In typical fashion, Efim Grigorievich began by congratulating the Russian School as well as colleague and friend Sergei Davydov on their half-century birthdays and then proceeded to give a brilliant talk on Pushkin's premarital frame of mind as he composed "Besy" (The Devils). For my part I spoke about the notion of freedom and natural rights (John Locke) as understood by Thomas Jefferson and the notion of freedom and natural rights (Kunitsyn at the lyceum) as understood by Pushkin—how Jefferson, the author of the Declaration of Independence and a renaissance man who realized, literally and figuratively, so much in his lifetime, and how Pushkin, the ultimate poet who was Russia's renaissance man of the word—how these two individuals represent watershed moments for the expression of outer (practical, political) and inner (spiritual, poetic) freedoms for their respective cultures, and also how the idea of school (Jefferson's university, Pushkin's lyceum) occupied a mythical space at the center of their worldviews. I bring this up because freedom, which is never absolute and always contextualized, is again under

---

* "A. A. Smirnov was a model Russian intellectual. In our circle, we defined this concept, that of the Russian intellectual, in this way: a person able (and inclined) to engage in selfless intellectual work—in other words, a knight of culture" ("Conquistador").

threat closer to home and again requires moral choices to protect it and because Etkind's response to my talk is a tiny piece of our correspondence that I treasure to this day: "Дорогой Давид, еще и еще раз выражаю вам восхищение по поводу вашего доклада" (Dear David, over and over again I want to express to you my delight at your talk) (June 25, 1995).* Despite the obvious cultural differences and despite Efim Grigorievich's effortless erudition and nonpareil charm, I felt that at some level we spoke the same language.

In any event, to repeat, I paint this general picture, on the one hand, because it has nothing to do with Efim Etkind's trials and tribulations as a Russian-Jewish intellectual during Soviet times and, on the other, because it has everything to do with them. Materialist, reductionist thinking— thinking that stipulates something happens in history once and then is never repeated the same way again—insists that what the Nazis did to the Jews as "Final Solution" and what the Soviets did to the Jews in terms of the campaign against cosmopolitanism or Doctors' Plot are not comparable. Even to "go there," as is said today, is considered bad taste. After all, as Etkind himself explains, the Nazis used terms like "kike" and sent millions to the gas chambers, while Stalin's minions called people "anti-patriots" and "double-dealers" and fired them from their jobs (or sometimes worse). But the larger point of *Barcelona Prose,* as Etkind himself comes to understand in his essay on the German-Jewish scholar Victor Klemperer ("Two Jewish Fates"), is that morally speaking the comparison is *absolutely legitimate*: as ethnic Jews who felt a powerful kindred bond to the literary cultures of the lands of their births, their fates were eerily parallel. Looking back at their schooling, Etkind and his wife Katya (Yekaterina Fyodorovna Zvorykina)

---

*   Private correspondence. The lecture was subsequently published as "Pushkin i Dzhefferson: mysli po povodu piatidesiatiletiia Russkoi shkoly v Midlberi" (Jefferson and Pushkin: Thoughts on the Occasion of the Fiftieth Anniversary of the Middlebury College Russian School), in the volume entitled "*Ot zapadnykh morei do samykh vrat vostochnykh*": *A. S. Pushkin za rubezhom*, ed. V. M. Piskunov (Moscow: Gos. IRIa im. A.S. Pushkina, 1999), 358-366.

realized only later that their circle was comprised mostly of Jewish boys, but that Jewishness was not yet a marked category:

> Erik Naidich, Misha Gabe, Lenya Salyamon, and Yasha Shokhor during our school years; and in university, Vladimir Shor, Eleazar Krever, Dav Frankfurt, Akhill Levinton, Grisha Bergelson, Yury Lotman, Ilya Serman and David Pritzker . . . They were all Jewish, but did Jewishness worry anyone or even interest them? In our group of Jews, there were also Russians: Alyosha Diakonov, then his older brother, Igor, Alexei Almazov, Anatoly Kukulevich. But they didn't feel the difference either. Jews were not *others* to them. [. . .] A person's national background was not important to any of them or to any of us. In the thirties, Soviet people did not divide themselves into national groups. The party authorities required that a ratio be met on admission to university, but what they required was not in relation to nationality but class—which was barbaric nonsense of a different kind.
>
> During our student years, the Jewish last names of Soviet Russian intellectuals were famous throughout the world: chess players Botvinnik and Bronstein, musicians Gilels and Oistrakh, writers Ehrenburg and Grossman, Marshak and Pasternak, philologists Zhirmunsky and Gukovsky, journalists Radek and Koltsov, physicists Ioffe and Landau, composers Katz and Dunayevsky, performers Reizen and Mikhoels, film directors Eisenstein and Romm. Could you imagine our culture without them? We saw them least of all as Jews. For us, they were the pride of the Soviet land and Russian culture. ("The Other")

And so, Etkind's understanding of moral choice, his and others', brings him, soberly and without pathos, to each remembered story and its plot. The special attraction of the essays is their focus on the moment when word becomes deed, especially the misstep that leads down the proverbial "slippery slope." Yes, he is revisiting his own roads taken and not taken, like when his family, already strapped for space in their apartment on Kirovsky, takes in the long-suffering but selflessly dedicated translator of Byron's *Don Juan* (1819–24), Tatiana Gnedich, great-great grand-niece of Pushkin's contemporary and legendary (Pushkin called the feat worthy of Achilles) translator of *The Iliad*, who has recently returned from prison and has no place to stay. Gnedich, herself clearly a "knight of culture," has lived under a cloud for decades because of her aristocratic origins, another case of an immutable characteristic over which a person has no control, and Etkind, understanding implicitly the unfairness, and deeply respecting her for her translating gifts and her love of her métier (she knows huge swaths of Byron by heart), does not hesitate to step in to help. They are serving the culture, its highest aspirations and subtlest beauties, and that is who they are more than anything else. There is an essentialism, but it is not an essentialism of blood. Indeed, one of Etkind's proudest moments is when Gnedich's translation of *Don Juan* finally sees the light of day and is published in a huge print run of 100,000. Not forgetting their shared "knighthood," Gnedich goes so far as to write on the title page of a subsequent edition "a poem in octaves [that is, like *Don Juan*], ending with words of gratitude for the help I'd offered her during some difficult days" ("Triumph of Spirit").

Although he doesn't say so, Etkind would have conferred knighthood status on a number of unsung heroes of the Soviet age, including Professor A. A. Chemodanov, who lectured brilliantly in backwater Tula in 1951 to audiences of rapt students on the dangerous topic of linguistics, Stalin's recently acquired bailiwick. The added fillip in Chemodanov's case was that he lectured totally without notes and while drunk:

> He was a genius of a lecturer; I've never met anyone like him. Perhaps, if at some point his students' notes are found, a book on what he said can be written. He built his lectures like an architectural construction. He added turns and transitions, asides and silences. A lecture was for him an end in itself, not something intermediate, as it was for many of us. If lecturing were an art form, he was a classic of this art. He understood that he was like an ice sculptor. The statue would melt, only a puddle would remain. What about it? He did not aspire to anything else. At times, he spoke about theater: the performance, too, would disappear forever, only the audience's enthusiastic exclamations and the critics' vain attempts to make a concrete written record of the mise-en-scènes would remain.
>
> We often spoke about these "statues of ice." I urged him to write down his findings, to record them more concretely—even just for himself, so that he wouldn't have to begin the following year from scratch. He would get angry. I won't become an ordinary craftsman, he'd

say. I'd rather stitch shoes together than repeat myself every year! The meaning of creation was to create something anew each time! Otherwise, it would be better to drop it all and throw it all away.

Unstable by nature and not able to withstand the constant imposition of collectivist ideas, Chemodanov soon thereafter committed suicide. But the very fact that he had been able to lecture in the first place, without compromising, without taking steps down slippery slopes, attested to his otherwise unacknowledged knighthood status (without Etkind's notes he would presumably have been lost to history). Likewise, his appointment at the Tula State Pedagogical Institute would not have been possible save for the institute's director A. M. Bogdanov, who allowed Chemodanov to lecture and then went so far as to attend his performances because they were so compelling and he couldn't help himself, even though he risked denunciation by others for his reckless leadership. Of course Bogdanov also hired a "disgraced Jew" like Etkind during the campaign against "cosmopolitans" when other institutes and universities would have nothing to do with them. One of the things Etkind wants to underscore is that when the history of the Soviet intelligentsia is written it will be important to document how the many small steps down slippery slopes were also countered by many steps upward.

What this also means, according to Etkind, is that the ethnic Jews in the Soviet Union who choose personal safety over friendship and loyalty are not simply victims of endemic antisemitism. David Pritzker is the telling counterexample here: a highly regarded historian with diplomatic talent and an expert on the Spanish Civil War, he tells the authorities that Etkind did not inform him that the guest he (Etkind) was bringing to the history faculty at the Higher Party School (the former Tauride Palace) was Solzhenitsyn, who was working on *The Red Wheel* and needed to see the building's interior to complete a passage. When confronted with a moral dilemma—either admit that he knew Solzhenitsyn was the person in question (those in the know had referred to him ironically as VPRZ, the initials signifying "Great Writer of the Russian Land") or suggest that Etkind had not alerted him to this fact, and in that way place the blame on his friend—he did the latter. There are numerous other instances of these false moves, some beginning as minor and others evidence of stark betrayal from the start, scattered throughout these mini-narratives: the story of F. M. Levin, who was denounced by three colleagues in Murmansk during the war because they had had conversations with him that were critical of leadership and would have gotten them in trouble, so they turned on him instead, and then, when he was released from custody for lack of a crime and returned to his unit, the total embarrassment and humiliation of the malefactors; or the poet Mikhail Dudin, who had been a brave soldier during the war but was willing to follow orders and participate in the formal removal of Etkind from his professorship at the Herzen Institute, up to and including reading a statement at the proceedings testifying to his former friend's "Zionist" leanings (again, an absurdity, given Etkind was urging the young Russian Jews to remain in the Soviet Union).

Patriotism does not mean belonging to the land. It is about an idea. The knights of culture serve the best in the country's spiritual patrimony. It is true Solzhenitsyn's Matryona is a creature of authentic (*kondovaia*) Russia. But her sturdy human substrate does not derive primarily from her linguistic quirkiness (an aesthetic authenticity) or risible lack of culinary talent (the heartburn produced by unimaginative dishes translating into a kind of folksy charm), but from her willingness to live according to a still shared moral code. What was good in Matryona was what was good in Russia and this was a goodness that Etkind also appreciated and lived by, even though he wouldn't connect it to the Russian land per se. This also led to the misunderstanding between Solzhenitsyn and Etkind when the former mentioned in his diary that he had been helped by two Jews (as opposed to Russians) when he visited the Higher Party School. Etkind is developing the idea that the class animus that defined Marxist economic and social policy before World War II morphed into ethnic animus (antisemitism) both as a result of what was happening in Nazi Germany prior to the war but also as a result of Stalin's need to tap into notions of "sacred Russia" (*sviataia Rus'*), the church, and patriotism tied to nation and soil. This is also the time when

Soviet Jews first experienced rejection: "The 'process of rejection' began, it seemed, when Stalin's Soviet Union drew nearer to Hitler's Germany, in 1939. It was then that the first prohibitions (in full reality) and limitations for people with Jewish last names appeared: diplomacy (that's what it began with), physics, military technology, upper-level army appointments, and on and on, in breadth and depth, until it led to the mass hysteria of 1948–53" ("The Other"). Thus, what happened between Solzhenitsyn and Etkind as they both looked back at the situation in 1974 is a classic case of "semantic overload": Solzhenitsyn was chastising the lack of basic decency in the current corrupt version of the Russian nation where it took outsiders ("two Jews") to demonstrate the courage of a helping hand. In other words, it's possible that the "VPRZ," who like his prototype Tolstoy was not known for moral nuance, meant that in this context those on the outside were acting in a more "patriotic," more "Russian" way than those protecting their status on the inside. However, for the one being labeled as age-old outsider "by blood" after all that had transpired this logic and its ethical voice zone (the semantics) seemed improbable at best. Etkind had every right not to consider himself an outsider. In short, that Solzhenitsyn and Etkind, and the "Russias" they represented, drew apart in emigration was not then surprising.

Etkind ends *Barcelona Prose* with an essay on the words and deeds of one of his oldest and dearest friends, the distinguished Sumerologist/Assyriologist and war veteran Igor Diakonov (1915–1999). The piece is also self-revealing since it brings us close to Etkind's own worldview and system of values (otherwise, being the expert of composition, he wouldn't have given these ruminations ultimate placement). Despite all the hardships that had befallen him, despite all that had been destroyed by Stalinist savagery and the war that followed,

> Diakonov did defend his country, without sparing himself but not forgetting the death of his father, the "spy for Venezuela," and that of many others, such as my father-in-law, F. A. Zvorykin, a similar "spy." The idea of ethics was for him always central. [. . .]

> Kirkenes is a small port city in Norway near the Russian border. Captain Diakonov wound up there at the end of war with the advancing Soviet forces. He speaks about this episode rather comprehensively; this is a "novel within the novel" *Book of Memories* [Diakonov's *Kniga vospominanii* (1995)]. In his usual ironic style, he tells about how he, a young civilian scholar, was forced to play the role of a military commander of a newly liberated city. [. . .] In Kirkenes, the whole population went into hiding underground. It helped that he knew the Norwegian language and the customs of the country in which he had spent his childhood. His knowledge of the Soviet Army also helped, including how its soldiers and generals, commissars and special agents worked. This knowledge allowed I. M. Diakonov to become the conciliator in Kirkenes, the savior of its population, which had miraculously avoided first German dynamite and then Soviet rapists. Captain Diakonov became a legend in Norway. Recently, he was a guest in Kirkenes—on the fiftieth anniversary of the city's liberation. I know that the former Captain Diakonov was received as a hero of the war not from his memoirs but from conversations with Norwegian philologists and from the Norwegian press. Why did the Russian newspapers stay silent about this? After all, this was our pride, our national honor. ("Youth in a Military Blouse")

Igor Diakonov represented the *real* Russian intelligentsia, the intelligentsia that continued to exist against all odds. It was, we might say, the substrate of high culture that Solzhenitsyn would associate with the land (*"kondovaia"* Russia) and the common folk in Matryona—"Soviet" in terms of its historical time-space, "Russian" in terms of its ideals. And this was the intelligentsia to which Efim Grigorievich belonged and whose ethical standards, drawn from the best in the culture, prevented the missteps that lead down slippery slopes.

> Our opponents thought (and think to this day—you can read about this in the newspaper *Russkaya mysl* [Russian Thought], for example) that in Soviet Russia there were hangmen and victims, and a "middle class" could not exist: the intelligentsia either sold themselves to the communists or died in jails and camps. We, the people who held a different point of view, knew that this was either a mistake or a lie: the Russian intelligentsia continued to fulfill their duty, even without entering into a political conflict with the regime by using legal means. The regime, which was cracking down on many people, had been

obliged to tolerate it. For me (and not only for me!), I. M. Diakonov was the ultimate model of this kind of Russian intelligentsia, the kind that cleverly managed to preserve its human dignity and independence (yes, yes, independence) of thought. ("Youth in a Military Blouse")

Perhaps fitting then to stop here with the words, belonging to Igor Diakonov but also characteristic of the "knightly" Efim Grigorievich himself, that conclude *Barcelona Prose,*

> I want to end with a saying by Diakonov that describes his worldview of today: "Instead of God," he wrote, "I place the conscience, inherent to all. This is also biology. The species that has a conscience will survive. The species in which all are enemies and hate each other is sure to perish." I'm not sure what the natural sciences would say; it's possibly a fantastical idea. But from the point of view of humanity, it's true. Or we would wish it to be so. ("Youth in a Military Blouse")

Madison, Wisconsin
September 2021

Index of Names

A
Adenauer, K., 67
Admoni, V. G., 121
Admoni, Johann, 170
Afanasyev, Y. N., 126
Akhmatova, A. A., 6-7, 124, 159, 224, 235
Akimov, N. P., 105, 114
Alexander, VI of Borgia, 159
Alexeyev, V. P., 31
Almazov, A., 181, 239
Alterman, S. A., 181
Altausen, D. M., 159
Andreyev, L. N., 123
Andropov, Y. V., 185
Antokolsky, M. M., 164
Antokolsky, P. G., 9, 158-61, 164-68
Antsiferov, N. P., 34-35
Aragón, L., 38
Augustus, 6
Avranov, 54-55
Axer, E., 127, 133

B
Babel, I. E., 85, 89, 126
Babushkin, Y., 181
Bach, J. S., 204
Baklanov, G. Y., 125-26
Balukhaty, S. D., 35
Barbier, A., 9, 159, 162-64, 166-67
Barta, D., 75
Barto, A. L., 11
Basilashvili, O. V., 127

Batthyány-Esterházy, M., 65, 69
Batthyány, L., 60
Batthyány, F., 59-69
Bazhanova, Z. K., 167
Baudelaire, C., 7-9, 159, 167
Beethoven, L. van, 204
Belinsky, V. G., 5
Benediktov, V. G., 162
Ben, G. E., 116
Berdnikov, G. P., 221
Bergelson, G. Y., 50-52, 156, 181, 187, 239
Betaki, V. P., 116
Bezymensky, A. I., 194
Blagoi, D. D., 12
Blok, A., 33, 52, 159, 170, 184, 228, 235
Bogatyrev, K. P., 8
Bogdanov, A. M., 97-102, 241
Bogdanov, G. P., 115
Boileau-Despréaux, N., 9
Bonaparte. *See* Napoleon I
Bondi, S. M., 12
Botvinnik, M. M., 181, 239
Botvinnik, M. N., 1
Botvinnik, S. V., 195
Brahms, J., 47
Braunsteiner, H., 204
Brauchitsch, W. von, 186
Brecht, B., 119-20, 122, 127-28, 130, 205
Brezhnev, L. I., 5, 158, 186
Brik, L. Y., 167

Brodsky, J. A., 7, 116, 147, 168, 189, 209, 234, 236
Bronstein, D. I., 181, 239
Bronstein, L. D. *See* Trotsky, L. D.
Bryusov, V. Y., 8, 33
Budenny, S. M., 185
Bukharin, N. I., 131
Burns, R., 7, 229
Busch, E., 120
Byron, G. G., 8, 105, 107-8, 110-111, 113, 116, 239-40

C
Calderón de la Barca, P., 38
Cervantes, M., de, 30
Char, R., 8
Charady, J., 69
Chemodanov, A. A., 97, 99-101, 103-4, 240-41
Chepurov, A. N., 195
Cherkasov, N. K., 181
Chernyakhovsky, I. D., 186
Chesnokov, D. I., 226
Chicherin, G. B., 3, 186
Chkalov, V. P., 125
Chukovskaya, E., 151
Chukovsky, K. I., 31, 114
Clemens, 218
Corneille, P., 38, 206

D
d'Alembert, J., 204
Derzhavin, G. R., 135-36, 159
Derzhavin, K. N., 222
Desnitsky, V. A., 106
Diakonov, A., 4
Diakonov, I. M., 51-52, 84-86, 143, 169, 227-28, 230-32, 243-45
Diakonov, M. A., 229
Diakonov, M. M., 8
Diakonova, N. Y., 101, 146, 222
Diderot, D., 204
Dikman, M. I., 6

Domashnev, A. I., 208
Donskoy, M. A., 8-9
Druzhinin, A. V., 33
Dudin, M. A., 116, 191-97, 212, 242
Dudintsev, V. D., 124-26
Dumas, A., 27
Dunayevsky, I. O., 45, 181, 239
Dymshits, A. L., 118-26, 129, 237

E
Edison, T., 97
Efron, A. S., 9
Ehrenburg, I. G., 7, 181, 239
Erich, E. 204
Eidelman, N. Y., 12
Eichendorff, J., 204
Einstein, A., 189
Eisenstein, S. M., 181, 239
Elke. *See* Liebs-Etkind, E.
Éluard, P., 8, 122
Emmanuel, P., 8
Engelke, A. A., 8
Engels, F., 122
Esenin, S. A., 228
Esterházy, M. *See* Batthyány-Esterházy
Esterházy, P., 66
Etkind, E. G., 28, 50, 71, 102-4, 143-57, 172-73, 188, 190, 195-97, 208, 222, 234, 236, 238-43
Etkind, G. I, 15, 142
Etkind, M. G., 144
Etkind, M. I., 142
Eventov, I. S., 99
Etkind-Shafrir, M. E., 95, 144, 148

F
Fadeyev, A. A., 160
Fedin, K. A., 160
Feldman, E. L. *See* Linetskaya, E. L.
Fish, G. S., 185
Fontane, T., 210
Fradkin, I. M., 121
Franco, F., 138

Frankfurt, D., 4, 181, 239
Freiligrath, F., 119-22
Frenkel, R. V., 41

G
Gabe, M., 180, 239
Ganz, A., 71-74
García Lorca, F., 8
Geller, M. Y., 1-2
Georgy Pavlovich. See Bogdanov, G. P.
Gerasimov, A. M., 128
Gilels, E. G., 10, 181, 239
Gillelson, M. I., 5
Ginzburg, L. V., 8-9, 121
Gnedich, N. I., 111, 114
Gnedich, T. G., 8, 105-117, 152, 239-40
Gnediches, 106
Goebbels, J., 120, 132, 210, 225
Goethe, J. W., 7, 204, 210
Gogol, N. V., 5, 23, 184
Goldenberg, S. I., 51
Goldhagen, D. J., 224
Goldstein, B. E., 10
Goltsev, V. A., 87
Gorky, M. A., 11, 31, 128, 221
Goryshin, G. A., 212
Göring, H., 132
Granin, D. A., 197
Griboyedov, A. C., 233
Grillparzer, F., 116
Grisha. See Etkind, G. I.
Gromyko, A. A., 186
Grossman, V. S., 181, 188, 239
Guderian, H. W., 186
Gukovsky, G. A., 5, 12, 24, 26, 94, 181, 218, 234, 239
Gumilev, N. S., 33

H
Hegel, G. F. W., 204
Heine, H., 7, 9, 121
Hemingway, E., 6

Herzl, T., 223
Herzen, A. I., 5,
Himmler, H., 60
Hitler, A., 4, 12, 60, 62, 66, 72, 131, 133, 182-83, 199, 201, 208-9, 222, 224, 243
Hoche, L., 9
Homer, 111, 228
Hölderlin, J., 205
Hughes, L., 116
Hugo, V., 7, 81, 159, 166, 206

I
Inber, V. M., 109
Ioffe, A. F., 181, 239
Ivan. See Sokolov, V. S.
Ivanov, V. V., 8, 232
Ivanova, N., 55-56

J
Jasieński, B., 85

K
Kasatkin, A. A., 52
Katya. See Zvorykina, E. F.
Katz, S. N., 181, 239
Katzes, 19
Kazhdan, A. P., 95, 99
Kenuville, R., 81-82
Kerensky, A. F., 48
Kharms, D. I., 11
Khlebnikov, V. V., 135
Khmelnitskaya, T. Y., 29, 41
Kholodkovsky, N. A., 8
Kholopov, G. K., 195
Khokhlushkin, I., 189
Khrennikov, T. N., 128
Khrushchev, N. S., 90, 128-29, 171, 186
Kipling, R., 9
Kirov, S. M., 228
Kleist, F. von, 7
Klemperer, G., 211
Klemperer, O., 211-22, 224, 238

Klemperer, V., 199
Klemperers, 200
Koch, H., 81
Koltsov, M. E., 181, 187, 239
Komarova, I. B., 116, 150
Kopelian, E., 127
Kopelev, L. Z., 152, 189
Korchagina-Alexandrovskaya, E. P., 181
Korneyev, Y. B., 8, 36-39
Kotlyar, M., 61
Kovalenkov, A. A., 87-88
Krever, E., 4, 24-28, 181, 239
Krivosheina, N. A., 174
Krivosheins, 174
Kroneberg, A. I., 33
Kruglova, Z. M., 222
Kuzmin, M. A., 33
Kukulevich, A. M., 181, 239
Kuprin, A. I., 184
Kurochkin, V. S., 8, 87
Kushner, A. S., 191

L
Labé, L., 7
La Bruyère, J., 26
La Fontaine, J., de, 26
Lafayette, M. J., 26
Landau, L. D., 181, 239
La Rochefoucauld, F., de, 26
Lafitte, J., 81
Lavrikov, 130
Lavrov, K. Y., 127
Lavrov, P. 35
Lebedev, E. A., 127, 133
Lebedev-Kumach, V. I., 45-46
Leconte de Lisle, C., 36
Lena. *See* Levina, E. F.
Lenin, V. I., 9
Leontiev, 56
Leopardi, G., 7
Lermontov, M. Y., 7, 159
Leśmian, B., 7
Levenfish G. Y., 7

Levenfish, E. G., 1
Levick, W. V., 8
Levin, F. M., 85-90, 92, 144, 242
Levina, V., 144
Levinton, A. G., 26, 94, 181, 218, 239
Levinton, G. A., 25
Liebs-Etkind, E., 66
Linetskaya, E. L., 8-9, 29, 112
Lipkin, S. I., 8-9
Litvinov, M. M., 3, 186
Likhachev, I. A., 8
Livshits, B. K., 8
Livshits, M. A., 181
Longfellow, H. W., 120, 122
Lokhovits, A. B., 51
London, J., 98
Lope de Vega, F., 38
Lotman, Y. M., 5, 12, 181, 239
Lozinsky, M. L., 8-9, 31, 33-35, 38, 106-8, 111
Lysenko, T. D., 128

M
Magaziner, N. Y. *See* Diakonova, N. Y.
Mahler, G., 189
Makanović, H., 73-74
Makarenko, A. S., 89
Malama, A. M., 175
Malama, T., 169, 171-74
Malamas, 171, 174
Mallarmé, S., 7
Mandelstam, O. E., 45, 122-24, 159, 191, 228
Manevich, L. E. *See* Starostin, Y. N.
Marconi, G., 97
Markstein, E., 199
Marlowe, C., 30, 38
Marr, N. Y., 11, 102-3
Marshak, S. Y., 7, 10-11, 121, 160, 181, 188, 229, 239
Martynov, L. N., 7
Marx, K., 121-22
Masha. *See* Etkind-Shafrir, M. E.

Maupassant, G., de, 29-30
Maximov, V. E., 3
Mayakovsky, V. V., 11, 45, 118-19, 128, 135, 161, 228
Mekhlis, L., 182
Melluppi, G. Y., 79
Mendelssohn-Bartholdy, F., 189
Meretskov, K. A., 186
Mérimée, P., 29-30, 235
Michaux, H., 8
Michurin, I. V., 128
Michurina-Samoilova, V. A., 181
Mikhalkov, S. V., 11
Mikhoels, S. V., 181, 226, 239
Mokulsky, S. S., 24, 26-28, 199
Molière, J. B., 26, 29-30, 235
Molotov, V. M., 3, 18, 186
Morgenstern, C., 211
Moreau, K. V., 9
Mravinsky, E. A., 181

N

N. K. *See* Khruschev, N. S.
Naidich, E. E., 180, 239
Napoleon I, 9, 62, 163-64
Nekrasov, V. P., 155
Nekrich, A. M., 2
Nevzglyadova, E. V., 191
Nikiforovich, 77-80
Nina. *See* Ivanova, N.

O

Oistrakh, D. F., 10, 181, 239
Oksman, Y. G., 5, 12
Oleynikov, N. M., 11
Orlov, V. N., 195, 212
Orlova, R. D., 152

P

Paperny, Z. S., 124
Parayeva, O., 54-56, 58
Pasternak, B. L., 6-7, 25, 38, 47-48, 159, 181, 228, 239

Pavlov, I. P., 11, 128
Penkovsky, L. M., 8
Perse, Saint-John, 8
Petőfi, S., 7
Petrarca, F., 30
Petrov, S. V., 8
Petrovykh, M. S., 7
Pilnyak, B. A., 85
Pius XII, 159
Platonov, A. P., 2
Platonov, S. F., 106
Pletnev, D. D., 44
Polevoy, B. N., 98
Polonskaya, E. G., 8-9, 112
Popov, A. S., 97
Potapov, 59, 61, 63-65
Prévert, J., 8
Pritzker, D. P., 1, 3-4, 52, 176-81, 184-86, 188, 190, 239, 241
Propp, V. Y., 4
Pushkin, A. S., 6, 11-12, 33-34, 45, 106, 108, 111, 114-16, 124, 130, 135, 166, 170, 235, 237-39

R

Rabelais, F., 38
Rabinovich, M. B., 1-2
Racine, J., 9
Radek, K. B., 181, 219, 239
Rakov, A. I., 139-40
Rannit, A., 138-39
Rannit, T. O., 137
Reizen, M. O., 181, 239
Reizov, B. G., 199
Renan, J., 15
Repin, I. E., 11
Reshetovskaya, N. A., 129, 134
Rilke, R. M., 7, 204
Rimbaud, A., 122
Rimsky-Korsakov, V. N., 181
Rit, M. P., 180, 185
Ritsos, Y., 193
Rivin, A., 40-45, 47-48

Robespierre, M., 164
Robinet, J., 53
Rozanov, V. V., 184, 189
Rokossovsky, K. K., 186
Roma, E., 131, 133
Romm, M. I., 181, 239
Ronsard, P., de, 37
Rosenberg, A., 217-18
Rostand, E., 166
Ruzov, L. V., 185
Rumyantsev, A. G., 50, 57, 185
Rustaveli, S., 7, 9
Ryazansky, A. *See* Solzhenitsyn, A. I.

S

Saint-Just, L., 166
Sakharov, A. D., 208
Salyamon, L. S., 139-40, 180, 239
Samoilov, D. S., 7, 40, 48, 121
Sapgir, N. P., 17
Savich, O. G., 8
Schelling, F., 204
Schiller, J. C., 7, 121, 204
Schubert, F., 204
Schwarzberg, G., 205
Semyonov, G. S., 88, 192
Severyanin, I., 135
Serman, I. Z., 5, 94, 153, 181, 218, 239
Shadrin, A. M., 8
Shaginian, M. S., 192
Shakespeare, W., 7, 27, 29-30, 32-33, 35, 38, 116, 235
Shamurin, E. I., 197
Shapirova-Lozinskaya, T. B., 35
Sharko, Z. N., 127
Shchepkina-Kupernik, T. L., 33
Shengeli, G. A., 8
Shevyrov, S. P., 135
Shimeliovitch, B. A., 226
Shklyarevsky, I. I., 198
Shokhor, Y. N., 180, 239
Sholokhov, M. A., 194
Shor, V. E., 8, 112, 121, 181, 239

Shulgin, V. V., 189
Shusterman, 99
Sigal-Zhirmunskaya, N. A., 222
Silman, T. I., 8
Simonov, K. M., 159-60, 182-84, 193, 220-21
Sinyavsky, A. D., 155
Smirnov, A. A., 29-39, 199, 222, 235, 237
Slutsky, B. A., 7, 192-93
Sokolov, V. S., 80
Solzhenitsyn, A. I., 90, 128-32, 134, 136-40, 148-49, 168, 176-79, 187-90, 196, 209, 234, 236, 241-44
Spevskaya-Etkind (born Spivak,) P. M., 142
Spivak, A. M. *See* Malama, A. M.
Spivak, M., 169
Stalin, J., 1, 3, 5, 7, 9-11, 35, 56, 67, 71, 81, 100-101, 110, 127, 131, 158, 166, 182, 185-87, 201, 204, 219-20, 226, 229, 238-40, 242-43
Stanislavsky, K. S., 11, 127-28, 181
Starostin, Y. N., 81
Shteinberg, A. A., 8
Stendhal, 30
Strasser, G., 210
Suomalainen, M., 54-58
Surov, A. A., 220
Suvorin, A. S., 178-79
Svetlov, M. A., 47, 159, 193
Svetlova, N. D., 189
Svirsky, L. S., 57-58

T

Talleyrand-Périgord, C. M., de, 4
Tarkovsky, A. A., 8
Tarle, Y. V., 4
Tatyana Borisovna. *See* Shapirova-Lozinskaya, T. B.
Tikhonov, N. S., 159-60, 181, 192-93
Tolstikov, V. S., 130, 132-33
Tolstoy, A. K., 108, 130

Tolstoy, L. N., 98, 177, 243
Tolubeyev, Y. V., 181
Tomashevsky, B. V., 12
Tovstonogov, G. A., 127, 130, 132-33
Trotsky, L. D., 219
Tukhachevsky, M. H., 186
Tvardovsky, A. T., 90, 134, 159
Tvardovsky, K. T., 134-35
Tsvetaeva, M. I., 7, 10, 159, 166
Tynyanov, Y. N., 9, 12

U
Uborevich, I. P., 186
Undset, S., 228
Usova, G. S., 116

V
Vavilov, N. I., 181
Vavilov, S. I., 181
Vanovskaya, T. V., 221
Vasiliev, S. D., 165, 181
Vasiliev, V. E., 116, 181
Vasilievs, 181
Verlaine, P., 7, 122
Verno, V., 82
Villiers de l'Isle-Adam, F. de, 29
Villon, F., 38-39
Vigny, A., de, 36, 38-39
Vinokurov, E. M., 192
Vinogradov, V. V., 12
Volovich, 19
Volynsky, A. L., 31
Voropayev, G. I., 105
Voroshilov, K. E., 44
Vuchetich, E. V., 128
Vyshinsky, A. Y., 186

W
Wachsmacher, M. N., 8
Weerth, G., 121-22
Weigel, H., 119-20
Weinberg, P. I., 33
Wengler, 211

Wertzman, I. E., 181
Weser, 218

Y
Yablochkov, P. N., 97
Yakir, I. E., 86
Yankovsky, A. I., 232
Yezhov, I. S., 197
Yezhov, N. I., 43-44
Yursky, S. Y., 127

Z
Zabolotsky, N. A., 6-7, 9, 160, 181
Zavodchikov, V. P., 194
Zenkevich, M. A., 121
Zerov, M., 116
Zharov, A. A., 159
Zhdanov, A. A., 82, 186
Zhirmunsky, V. M., 12, 31, 121, 181, 199, 221, 234, 239
Zhukov, G., 186
Zhukovsky, V. A., 8
Zinoviev, A. A., 219
Zola, E., 221
Żuk, W., 71-72, 74, 76-77, 82
Zvorykin, F. A., 231, 243
Zvorykina, E. F., 52, 144, 146-48, 151, 180, 185, 208, 238

www.ingramcontent.com/pod-product-compliance
Lightning Source LLC
Chambersburg PA
CBHW021853230426
43671CB00006B/379